Jung, Jungians, and Homosexuality

Jung, Jungians, and Homosexuality

Robert H. Hopcke

SHAMBHALA
BOSTON & LONDON
1991

SHAMBHALA PUBLICATIONS, INC.
Horticultural Hall
300 Massachusetts Avenue
Boston, Massachusetts 02115

SHAMBHALA PUBLICATIONS, INC.
Random Century House
20 Vauxhall Bridge Road
London SW1V 2SA

9   8   7   6   5   4   3   2   1

First Paperback Edition

Printed in the United States of America on acid-free paper
Distributed in the United States by Random House, Inc.,
in Canada by Random House of Canada, Ltd, and in the
United Kingdom by the Random Century Group

The Library of Congress catalogues the hardcover edition of this work as
follows:

Hopcke, Robert, 1958–
    Jung, Jungians, and homosexuality / Robert Hopcke.—1st ed.
    p.   cm.
    Bibliography: p.
    Includes index.
    ISBN 0-87773-472-0 (alk. paper)
    ISBN 0-87773-585-7 (pbk.)
    1. Homosexuality—Psychological aspects.   2. Psychoanalysis.
I. Jung, C. G. (Carl Gustav), 1875–1961.   II. Title.
RC558.H66   1989   89-10051
306.76'6—dc20   CIP

To Paul, with love
and to gay men and lesbians everywhere

Contents

Acknowledgments

ON THE LONG ROAD from conception to publication of this work, a number of people have been indispensable. First, my two advisors at California State University, Hayward, Dorlesa Barmettler-Ewing and Don McKillop, witnessed and aided the birth of this book in its first form as my master's thesis. David Stockford and J. Michael Steele are also due thanks for reading the thesis at this stage and lending me their knowledge of Jung and analytical psychology to ensure the accuracy of my work.

As this work grew and attained adolescence, making the rounds in search of a home, Kimn Nielsen of Shambhala Booksellers in Berkeley recognized the value and importance of this book, for which she has my eternal gratitude. Jonathan Green, Emily Hillburn Sell, and Kendra Crossen of Shambhala in Boston should be acknowledged for all their hard work and for their help in guiding me through to publication. Kenneth Hale's meticulous editing of the manuscript should also be recognized on this score; his care and appreciation of my work is due much thanks. It is a joy not only to have one's work published but to do so with a group of people such as those at Shambhala.

At the C. G. Jung Institute of San Francisco, librarian Joan Alpert and her volunteer assistants aided me in my research and helped me locate at times even the most obscure bits of Jungian writing on homosexuality. The members of our monthly group, which met to discuss issues concerning homosexuality and Jungian psychology, deserve to be named. Without the moral support, intelligence, and sensitivity of Scott Wirth, Karin Carrington, and Rita Cahn, I would have been racking my brains alone with some of this material. With their support, I found a like-minded and sympathetic community. Finally, my analyst, Raymond Kilduff, has earned my many thanks for his dedication to my individuation as a gay man, as a writer, and as a therapist over the past five years. His personal interest and his analytic presence have helped me to bring forward what I know in my heart and head to be true, and without his help, I surely could not have finished this project.

Acknowledgments

I extend heartfelt gratitude to my friends, who have lived with me and this project for over a year: Mark Castillo, Jennifer Diaz, Gery Short, Rosanne Alexander, Nora and Megan, Larry DiRocco, Jill Johnson, Dan Fee, and Ray Campton. Finally, I would like to express my profound appreciation to all my clients and supervisees, who have taught me at least as much as they have learned from their work with me, and especially to all the gay men and lesbians whose lives I have been privileged to share for a little while as a therapist. If this book serves to have stories such as theirs heard with greater clarity and compassion, then the purpose of my writing will have been served.

Jung, Jungians, and Homosexuality

Pain, Analgesia, and Anesthesia[?]

1. Why Jung, Jungians, and Homosexuality?: A Brief Introduction

A HOST OF IMPULSES lie beneath the conception and execution of a book, and this book is no exception. The title of this volume presents quite succinctly the purpose of this book, that is, to examine what Jung and Jungian writers have had to say about homosexuality. However, the reasons for this examination are numerous and the impulses behind my writing this book are important to elucidate before beginning.

Among these many impulses is, as one might expect, an impulse with a deeply personal intention. For this reason, perhaps it is best right off to confess that much of what has given rise to this book has been my wish to understand myself more fully as a gay man. Though my homosexuality certainly is not all there is to my personality, it is definitely one aspect of who I am that has given my life a certain shape and has often required me to walk a certain, very individual path through life. However, because I am also a psychotherapist who sees both homosexual and heterosexual clients, individually and as couples, my personal impulse toward self-understanding has a potentially larger use. Whatever self-understanding I gain of my own sexual orientation, I intend to use therapeutically; for, in unlocking one of the many mysteries of that mighty god Eros—the passionate puzzle of why we love whom we do—I might be able to better help my clients grow, change, or celebrate their individuality and their own sexuality, whatever its form.

The realization that one is gay, that one's primary erotic attraction is to another man or another woman, is usually a momentous point in the development of one's personality. Enshrined for gay people in an experience that is now the popular catchphrase for any revelation of radical self-acceptance, coming out of the closet often means the first step on a long road to what Jung and Jungians have called individuation, the establishment of a unique and individual personality of true depth and substance. Yet gay people, because of the long period of unconsciousness about their sexual orientation that typically occurs in our society, often experience themselves as a riddle to be solved. Whence come these longings that should not exist, longings for a soul mate in a form so different from what one has been told to expect? What does this mean, to love another like myself, fully, physically? How can I live such a life and be whole, fruitful, happy, successful, fulfilled? How I do balance inner imperatives toward self-realization with the outward requirements of form and propriety? How can I be faithful to my own nature?

In the course of this twin search for understanding myself and others, a search that took the form of my analysis, education, and training as a psychotherapist, I was fortunate enough to be able to structure a year-long independent study of *The Collected Works of C. G. Jung* late in my graduate studies, reading all eighteen of those formidable volumes cover to cover, over the period of one academic year. The effect of reading Jung in this way, at my own pace and with all the thoroughness I could bring to the task, was transformative, igniting a dream life within me that I never knew existed, permitting me to bring into my practice as a therapist aspects of the human personality conspicuously absent from my largely psychoanalytic training: myths, stories, religion, spirituality, art, and beauty. Thus Jung and his followers, whether I have met them in person or simply through their work, have exercised an indelible influence on my personal and professional life. But what do these people, Jung and Jungians, have to say to me as a gay man and to the clients I see? What piece of the riddle do they illuminate? How do their attitudes and theories help me and my clients resolve our struggles and enjoy our lives as embodied sexual beings? This book exists as an initial answer to these questions, an answer that gave the lie to my initial impression of analytical psychology's treatment of homosexuality. Despite the seeming paucity of attention and desultory focus on homosexuality among Jung and his followers, Jung and Jungians have had a great deal to say about homosexuality over the years and much of it is of great help in deepening and broadening our perspective on homosexuality *and* heterosexuality.

One of the slogans of the feminist movement is that the personal is political, and perhaps no issue more than homosexuality demonstrates the truth of this maxim. To search for a greater understanding of homosexuality, to look hard and long at the contribution Jung and Jungians have made to such understanding, cannot fail to have a political and historical meaning. Thus another impulse comes into play in the conception and birth of this work—a political and historical motive for examining Jung and Jungians on homosexuality.

There are several explanations for the fact that no monograph in English to date exists on homosexuality from a Jungian perspective. The lack of concerted attention paid to homosexuality by Jung and Jungians might, of course, mean that analytical psychologists do not have much of consequence to say and that, since a theory of homosexuality in Jungian psychology has never been developed, perhaps there never should be one. However, I have chosen to read and examine what has been written only to find that the lack of more extended treatment is precisely that: a lack, something missing. This book, therefore, is an attempt at repairing a hole in a literature so rich in certain areas, a way of giving back to those who have found their individuality in analytical psychology a certain piece of their intellectual history. This book is a starting point for a more extended examination of a form of love that is universally present between man and man, woman and woman.

In addition, we are at an unusual moment in the history of homosexuality and, though it might be interesting to recapitulate the political history of the last twenty years of gay liberation here, more to our point is the history of homosexuality in psychology. The present moment in this history of homosexuality is largely the result of two occurrences whose impact forever changed the position of homosexuality and homosexual individuals in psychological thinking and in clinical practice.

The first of these occurrences was the appearance of the Kinsey report in 1948.[1] For the first time on record, an impeccably executed, empirically based study of American sexual behavior was made public, and the data gathered by Alfred Kinsey and his researchers revealed, among many other surprising things, that 37 percent of the American male population had engaged in homosexual behavior to ejaculation after the age of puberty.[2] In an era in which society at large considered homosexuality blasphemous, sick, or illegal, the evidence that over a third of American men had had homosexual experiences as adults came as a shock from which American society has not yet recovered, and perhaps never will. The significance of this piece of data can hardly be exaggerated. It challenged all the current prejudices about homosexuality as a strange abnormality, a peculiar immoral aberration indulged in by a small percentage of lonely, maladjusted perverts, and the fact that all of Kinsey's subsequent studies support and continue that challenge to American thinking on sexual orientation has made the 1948 study a watershed in current thinking on homosexuality.

The so-called Kinsey scale is perhaps the best symbol of the revolution in thought on sexual orientation that Kinsey's research has wrought. Participants in his study on human sexual behavior rate themselves from 0 to 6 on a range of sexual orientation that goes from exclusively heterosexual (0) to bisexual in the center (3) to exclusively homosexual (6). The idea that sexual orientation is actually a *range* of behaviors and identities rather than a *condition*, that homosexuality is one of a number of normal variations in human sexual behavior, is one that Kinsey's numerous research studies have subsequently found to be both true and theoretically helpful in understanding human sexual behavior. Clearly, if over a third of the American male population has engaged in homosexual behavior as adults, one is hardly justified in seeing such prevalent behavior as abnormal—sexually, statistically, or psychologically.

The second moment of note in the history of American psychological thought on homosexuality came twenty-five years later, in 1973, when the American Psychiatric Association (APA), after a long and bitterly contested internal debate, removed homosexuality from the List of Mental Disorders. This decision came as a direct result of political action on the part of gay liberation activists, political action that had its beginnings in the late 1960s and early 1970s. This movement of gay men and women had reconceptualized the social and individual meaning of homosexuality, challenged the dominant negative social attitudes toward homosexuality, and exposed false stereotypes and erroneous assumptions regarding the lives, feelings, and actions of individual gay men and women.

Though gay liberation activists attacked the psychiatric establishment's view of homosexuality as a mental disease on political grounds, the success they enjoyed in their struggle with the APA owed less to the political intimidation of psychiatrists than to the pertinent data of such researchers in previous decades as Havelock Ellis, Magnus Hirschfeld, Alfred Kinsey, Cleland Ford, Frank Beach, Evelyn Hooker, Thomas Szasz, and Judd Marmor.[3] These researchers had uncovered that many psychological commonplaces concerning homosexuality did not correspond to reality. These researchers had begun, therefore, to formulate for themselves what gay liberation's political analysis eventually consolidated into its most significant insight: the realization that certainly more harmful than homosexuality was the overwhelming social stigma, dubbed homophobia, attached to being gay or having same-sex feelings of attraction.

The story of how and why the APA took this revolutionary step is a fascinating study in psychiatry's role as a handmaiden to and agent for the creation of sociocultural values. The step begun in 1973 by this decision, however, has only recently reached completion with the newest edition of the APA's *Diagnostic and Statistical Manual of Mental Disorders*, in which "ego-dystonic homosexuality," that is, homosexuality considered unwanted by and disturbing to an individual, has also been removed as a mental disorder.[4]

The net effect of both Kinsey's studies and the APA's removal of any form of homosexuality as a mental disorder is to depathologize homosexuality once and for all and thereby irrevocably change psychological thinking on the nature of this form of human sexual behavior. Current attitudes toward homosexuality, therefore, are at a critical juncture historically and psychologically, a state of radical transformation. The older line of thought, still held in many quarters, that homosexuality is a sickness, a deviation from heterosexuality, which is seen as the only mature expression of sexual behavior, has thus been challenged, and successfully so, by a newer line of thought that views homosexuality as a normal variation in human sexual expression and sees gay people as normal individuals who, if they suffer at all, suffer from unwarranted bigotry and social prejudice.

In this regard, we find ourselves in the midst of a shift, caught between old and new, for clearly American public opinion and social values have not caught up to the momentous change in attitude already accomplished in the realm of psychology. Though there are large, vocal, and politically active gay communities in every major American city, the Supreme Court nevertheless recently upheld the state of Georgia's right to declare sodomy illegal and deserving of criminal punishment. Though there are huge communities of people who are responding with compassion and practical care to the overwhelming number of gay men who are presently dying horrible deaths from AIDS, there are still those voices on the television and in the newspaper who declare this deadly disease a scourge and a punishment, a plague visited by God upon gay people for their sin of homosexuality. Though gay men and lesbians in the United States and around the world are visible in a way unprecedented in human history, Californians were asked in 1988 to consider for the *second* time a state proposition that would set up provisions for mass quarantines of people determined to be infected with human immunodeficiency virus, which plays a role in the development of AIDS. Social change has clearly lagged far behind psychology's depathologization of homosexuality.

This book emerges from an impulse to see how one of the twentieth century's greatest psychological theorists, C. G. Jung, dealt with homosexuality in his writings and in his practice, in the hope of being able to chart a course between the old and the new in this time of social and psychological transformation. Curiosity about Jung and homosexuality is especially keen since Jung is known very little for his attention to sexuality, and even less so for his writings on homosexuality. As this book will demonstrate, Jung indeed never put forth a coherent theory of homosexuality, but he nevertheless wrote about homosexuality clinically and theoretically on a number of occasions, in the *Collected Works*, in numerous letters and interviews, in the recently published but long unavailable *Dream Seminars*, and finally in his autobiography, *Memories, Dreams, Reflections*.

Whereas the historical impulse behind this book leads me to ask how Jung and his followers fit into this larger shift of psychological thinking on homosexuality, the academic impulse behind this book, if one might call it that, leads me to attempt to correct, through this closer study of Jung's writings on homosexuality, the misconceptions and erroneous characterizations often heard from analytical psychologists on this subject—for instance, that Jung had little to say on homosexuality, that what he did say was insignificant, or that he held only one particular theory or attitude. The thorough examination of Jung's statements on homosexuality that follows will reveal a number of attitudes as well as a number of theories concerning homosexuality that offer a fresh and profound perspective on the human soul, which is the hallmark of Jung's psychology. In the course of this examination, we will find that Jung's views of homosexuality, which seemed to be of rather narrow, parochial, even pedantic interest, in fact contain a whole range of issues from political, social, and intercultural to spiritual, theoretical, and archetypal. This study illuminates Jung's thought on homosexuality, therefore, almost as much as it illuminates Jung's thought as a whole, highlighting, through examination of one slice of his thinking, the invaluable contributions he made to the way we think, feel, experience, and respond to the promptings of our inner lives.

Alongside the historical and academic impulses that lie behind the conception of this work is another, perhaps even more powerful impulse, one that Jungians might call the impulse toward wholeness. One rarely is drawn to Jung's thought or to Jungian analysis by dry academic interest or clear-cut historical curiosity. Analytical psychology is perhaps unique in the field of psychology in the way that Jung's followers have taken his insights on the nature and dynamics of the psyche and developed from them a body of work that, like a mandala, encompasses thinking, feeling, intuition, and sensation, the whole of human experience rather than a single, isolated piece. This book examines in detail the writings of those who came after Jung, both the "first generation" of those who knew Jung personally and the "second wave" of Jungian analysts and writers, with the purpose of gaining a truly comprehensive sense of the depth and diversity of Jungian thought on homosexuality. If the impulse toward wholeness is to be honored fully, the comprehensive nature of this review of the Jungian literature may be said to be an expression of this book's individuation process, its striving toward a unique and coherent view of a phenomenon of great meaning and astonishing diversity.

A depth psychology in the truest sense of the term, analytical psychology consistently aims toward elucidating a level of human existence that is often forgotten in the modern world: the level of the collective unconscious, the symbolic life, the soul, that dark place in each individual where mythic, primordial human experiences flow and shape our conscious daytime personality, where passionate dreams and strange figures inhabit our thoughts and feelings, becoming sometimes unlikely companions on a road leading to realization, an end that lies still shrouded in a mist but toward which we are nevertheless inexorably drawn. Jungian psychology provides a very needed antidote to the hypertechnicality of the two major American schools of psychological thought, Freudian psychoanalysis and Skinnerian behaviorism, and it does so by returning again and again to the way in which each of us is a unique individual and at the same time shares a common and profoundly nourishing spring of life, the collective unconscious. My hope is that this book, by viewing homosexuality through a Jungian looking glass and in examining the wide range of issues that Jung and Jungians have illuminated through their thought on homosexuality and homoeroticism, will push us all toward a deeper and more individualized understanding of the place of homosexuality in everyone's sexuality. If successful, our examination will clarify the meaning of homosexuality on the level of archetypal reality and reveal something unique and significant about what I have come to call the life of Eros, the binder and loosener of human passion. Though Psyche herself may have been blind to him at first, we will tempt fate and try to catch a glimpse of this god in all his multiple incarnations.

To this end, the latter part of this book will be devoted to using the great wealth of the last sixty years of Jungian theories on homosexuality to examine contemporary American gay male culture from a perspective not often used but sorely needed, that is, an archetypal perspective. Just as American psychological thinking has long been dominated by Freud and B. F. Skinner, so, too, has homosexuality been treated primarily as an external issue, a sociocultural phenomenon, a political movement of an oppressed minority. Though the political activism of gay people in the United States must certainly not be discounted or diminished in any way, the fact remains that homosexuality as a form of human relationship and as an expression of sexual passion has existed since the beginning of the human race and in every culture on the face of the earth. It did not appear overnight at the Stonewall riot, that rebellion of drag queens in Greenwich Village taken to signal the beginning of the gay liberation movement in 1969. This study of Jung, Jungians, and homosexuality will raise questions that go beyond the basically external concerns of social and political activism:

• What archetypal themes are expressed in such a universal and passionately charged form of human relationship as homosexuality and homoeroticism?
• What draws man to man, woman to woman, and what individual meanings find their best possible expression through homoerotic longings and homosexual relationships?
• Do gay people differ from heterosexuals psychologically, clinically, or symbolically?
• Might there not be common archetypal themes that undergird the incarnation of Eros in homosexuality or, indeed, any expression of erotic involvement with another person, man or woman, same sex or different?

By examining contemporary gay male culture for archetypal themes, using the insights of analytical psychology, this book finally attempts to respond to perhaps the last important impulse that has given rise to it, namely, the theoretical impulse, the urge to provide what has heretofore been lacking in analytical psychology: a coherent theory of sexual orientation that is archetypally based, empirically supportable, psychologically profound, and spiritually evocative. Though this book can be only an initial contribution to such a theory, the vast and largely unorganized body of Jungian theory on homosexuality makes such an attempt at a more comprehensive, synthetic view of homosexuality long overdue and sorely needed. This attempt to provide an archetypal theory of sexual orientation is important for gay people in helping them toward that which is often missing in the rhetoric of the gay political movement but which is the hallmark of Jung's psychology, namely, a profound individual sense of self-understanding. Such inward understanding and significance is, of course, made doubly important in this age of AIDS, when gay communities everywhere face death and redemption in a real way day in and day out. However, an archetypal theory of sexual orientation is obviously just as important for heterosexuals, who may be surprised to find that a good look at homosexuality from an archetypal perspective illuminates facets of their own masculinity or femininity too long ignored, repressed, or unappreciated.

As is probably clear from this introduction, this book assumes familiarity with analytical psychology. Since Jung's discoveries and elaborations required that he develop new concepts to describe his findings, the reader unfamiliar with Jungian psychology may wish to consult one of the many general overviews of his work. Because my own experience of transformation came from reading Jung directly, rather than from reading *about* Jung, I am inclined to suggest that the uninitiated consult my book *A Guided Tour of the Collected Works of C. G. Jung*, which is a short introduction and study guide to reading Jung directly, rather than an overview of his theories.[5]

The structure of this book is dictated first and foremost by my fondness for using my thinking function when writing, since when dealing with a topic as diffuse and scattered as homosexuality in the writings of Jung and his followers, logical organization and chronological order make things easier for once. We will begin by looking at Jung and his various statements concerning homosexuality from the beginning of his career to the end, stopping after this review for a summary and a discussion of Jung's attitudes and theories concerning homosexuality. We will then go on to look at what has been written concerning homosexuality by those whom I call first-generation analysts, and only then will our examination expand further to include all other writers who have published important contributions concerning homosexuality from a Jungian perspective. With the whole countryside of Jungian thought then spread before us, we will tentatively consider a theory of sexual orientation that brings together all the many strands of Jungian thought. Then, turning our gaze toward contemporary gay male culture in the United States, we will attempt to discern archetypal themes in the collective and personal lives of these gay men. The aim in shifting our view here is to show that the archetypal theory of sexual orientation suggested earlier is not simply of academic or theoretical interest in analytical psychology but of great help in seeing and understanding the rich diversity of the real lives gay men lead today in America. Finally, by using both our familiarity with the theoretical lay of the land and our acquaintance with its many inhabitants, our final chapter will attempt to chart a course forward and propose, perhaps for the first time in analytical psychology, how a synthetic, coherent, and archetypally based theory of sexual orientation that is faithful at once to Jungian insights and to the empirical reality of contemporary gay people can be used to understand all sexuality more deeply.

Analytical psychology begins with Jung and so with Jung we begin our journey.

2. C. G. Jung and Homosexuality

THE TASK AT HAND is to read Jung, what he did and did not say on homosexuality, what he developed fully and what remained mere intimation. However, as many have found, reading Jung is not always so easy. A prolific writer, Jung produced a quantity of work that can be daunting to the nonspecialist. His peculiar terminology may block rather than aid one's understanding, and his wide range of knowledge generally means that, whatever the focus of his inquiry, he approaches it in a way that can be highly indirect and intuitive, at times even scattered. The word *circumambulatory* comes to mind when considering this characteristic of Jung's writings; Jung frequently walks around a topic rather than cleanly, logically, and rigorously walking right through.

Those familiar with Jung's writings know, however, that Jung never really set out to build a comprehensive and linear theory of the human psyche. Much more interested in describing and interpreting the facts he saw around him than in promulgating theoretical positions, Jung never left very many definitive statements on much of anything, especially homosexuality. In the eighteen volumes of his *Collected Works*, homosexuality is mentioned little more than a dozen times; one of those references merely duplicates a case discussion, and all of the references occur in articles whose major focus is in elucidating subjects other than homosexuality itself.

There is no doubt that the scarce mention of homosexuality in Jung's writings reflects the relative lack of importance homosexuality occupied in his thought, a fact that must be emphasized before we go forward and look at what he did write on the subject. The lack of any extended discussion on homosexuality certainly has to do with the distinctively inward character of Jung's psychological focus. As the body of his work demonstrates, Jung examined almost exclusively the inner workings of the human mind, its images, its symbols, its process. Human behavior of any sort, whether homosexuality, social rituals, or the two world wars, was always viewed from his position as a psychologist wondering what the inner meaning of this behavior could be for individuals. This does not mean, of course, that Jung never made evaluative statements on human behavior, but rather that evaluative statements on behavior always came second to Jung's primary purpose: an understanding of the whole human being, inwardly and outwardly, based on the principles of scientific investigation.

Another reason for the small emphasis homosexuality has in Jung's published thought is the relative lack of importance sexuality in general held for Jung following his movement away from Freud. Jung, though connected with Freud in his early career, apparently did not see himself as one of Freud's disciples. Writing a correction to an inaccurate prefatory note for one of his articles in 1934, Jung states:

> I did not start from Freud, but from Eugen Bleuler and Pierre Janet, who were my immediate teachers. When I took up the cudgels for Freud in public, I already had a scientific position that was widely known on account of my association experiments, conducted independently of Freud, and the theory of complexes based upon them. My collaboration was qualified by an objection in principle to the sexual theory, and it lasted up to the time when Freud identified in principle his sexual theory with his method.[1]

Such an observation does not imply that Jung did not consider sexuality important at all or that he never dealt with sexual issues (the following examination of his view on homosexuality is sufficient to indicate that Jung addressed himself at considerable length to sexual issues). Rather, Jung typically eschewed a single-minded focus on sexuality as the basic element of the human personality or as the only key to understanding the psyche.

Along with this inward focus and Jung's relativization of sexuality, Jung's notorious distaste for what he called dogma plays a role in understanding why no definitive statements on homosexuality (or many other issues) are to be found in his writings:

> A dogma, that is to say, an undisputable confession of faith, is set up only when the aim is to suppress doubts once and for all. But that no longer has anything to do with scientific judgments; only with a personal power drive.[2]

The fact remains, however, that Jung had, over the course of his career, numerous occasions to bring homosexuality up in his writings, treated clients who were homosexuals, and was, of course, faced with the more general question of what place human sexuality, in all its variations, occupied in the larger sphere of the whole personality of an individual.

For the reader, the relatively little attention Jung seemed to pay to homosexuality in his writings is, so to speak, both good news and bad news. The good news is that our review will not require the herculean efforts of a professional scholar to follow. Indeed, as we will see, the brevity of his attention reveals a conciseness of thought some might call unusual for Jung. The bad news is that we will have to forsake the cherished Western value of quantity and choose instead an appreciation of the quality of what Jung said, judging Jung's references to homosexuality on their merit rather than by their length or breadth. This may be tricky at times; as always, one must remember that Jung never was and never intended to be a major theorist on homosexuality. We must at all times refrain from blowing any of his statements out of proportion, but, by the same token, neither are his discussions to be prematurely dismissed or discounted.

These relatively few references to homosexuality allow us to go carefully and chronologically through what he did write: fifteen references in the *Collected Works*, seven references in his published correspondence, two references in his autobiography, *Memories, Dreams, Reflections,* and a small number of references in his *Dream Seminars*[3] and the interviews reported in *C. G. Jung Speaking.*[4] Our review of these writings will be divided into three parts based on periods in Jung's career. First we will examine his early writings, that is, from 1908 to 1920, a period in which Jung was still much influenced by psychoanalytic theory, though he broke with Freud in 1912. In the second period of his career, 1920 to 1927, Jung began to develop his own insights into the workings of the human psyche; this was a period of theoretical complexity and consolidation. Third, we will look at what might be called Jung's mature thought, the period from 1936 to 1950, which expands his previous insights into areas that typically held his interest throughout his later years. Since our purpose here is not strictly academic, we will not always linger on minor or repetitious passages, focusing instead on those places where Jung puts forth characteristically Jungian ways of approaching homosexuality clinically and theoretically. In the interest of completeness, however, even minor passages will be indicated in the course of our discussion and a complete list of references is included in the notes to this chapter, so that readers with more scholarly intentions may pursue the subject to their own satisfaction.

THE EARLY "PSYCHOANALYTIC" WRITINGS: 1908–1920

The first references Jung makes to homosexuality occur in that period of his life when he was still closely identified with psychoanalysis, during his early association with Freud and after his break with the father of psychoanalysis in 1912. In a brief review of Lowenfeld's *Homosexualität und Strafgesetz* (*Homosexuality and Criminal Law*), a book concerned with giving a "concise history of the clinical concept of homosexuality," Jung quotes the "present state of opinion" from Lowenfeld: "'Though homosexuality is an anomaly that may appear . . . in association with disease and degeneration, in the majority of cases it is an isolated psychic deviation from the norm and cannot be regarded as pathological or degenerative and is not likely to reduce the value of the individual as a member of society.'" In this review Jung comments on Section 175, the article of the German penal code that made homosexuality a criminal offense, calling it "not only useless and inhuman, but directly harmful as it offers opportunities for professional blackmail with all its tragic and repulsive consequences."[5]

Despite the brevity of this review and its distinctly nonpsychological topic, this first statement of Jung's makes clear that he was of the opinion, shared by many psychiatrists of his time, that homosexuality ought not to be a concern of legal authorities. One must be aware, on this point, that in the history of scientific opinion on homosexuality, the notion of considering homosexuality an illness rather than a criminal act or a shocking perversion of Christian morality is comparatively recent. Early twentieth-century psychiatrists, joined by homophile activists of the time, often thought of themselves as the saviors and protectors of homosexuals through their declaration that homosexuality was a disease and not a matter for legal prosecution. That Jung shared this opinion of homosexuality, enlightened for its time, is highly likely on the basis of this reference. The fact that half of the U.S. states still have sodomy laws on the books that are used, even today, to prosecute and imprison gay men and women (with the support of the U.S. Supreme Court) makes this passage and this "enlightened" opinion more relevant than one might at first think.

A more substantial example of Jung's early thoughts on the subject, however, is his remarks in *The Theory of Psychoanalysis,* published in German in 1913. This extensive article was originally a series of lectures delivered at Fordham University in New York in September 1912, and, therefore, both chronologically and conceptually it dates to the time shortly after Jung's break with Freud. The purpose of these lectures was clearly to provide a critical exposition of the major ideas of psychoanalysis as propounded by Freud, and thus homosexuality is mentioned in the second lecture of the series, "The Theory of Infantile Sexuality."

After first qualifying what psychoanalytic theory means by sexuality, Jung goes on to explain that psychoanalysis had conceived of sexuality as a "plurality of separate drives" made up of several more or less fixed "components." However, he cites a case in which a young man's initial homosexual interests were eventually replaced by a "normal" interest in women, only to find that, following a disappointing rejection by a girlfriend, the young man began to experience "a dislike of all women, and one day . . . discovered that he had become homosexual again, for young men once more had a peculiarly irritating effect upon him."[6] Of this case, Jung says:

> If we regard sexuality as consisting of a fixed heterosexual and a fixed homosexual component, we shall never explain this case, since the assumption of fixed components precludes any kind of transformation. In order to do justice to it, we must assume a great mobility of the sexual components, which even goes so far that one component disappears almost completely while the other occupies the foreground. If nothing but a change of position took place, so that the homosexual component lapsed in full force into the unconscious, leaving the field of consciousness to the heterosexual component, modern scientific knowledge would lead us to

infer that equivalent effects would then arise from the unconscious sphere. These effects would have to be regarded as resis-
tances to the activity of the heterosexual component, that is re-
sistances against women. But in our case, there is no evidence
of this.[7]

The issue that Jung addresses here is how the psychoanalytic
concept of sexual energy, or libido, is a truer description of reality than the outmoded concept of fixed sexual components.

> It was, therefore, urgently necessary to give an adequate explana-
> tion of such a change of scene. For this we need a dynamic hy-
> pothesis, since these permutations of sex can only be thought of as
> dynamic or energic processes. Without an alteration in the dy-
> namic relationships, I cannot conceive how a mode of functioning
> can disappear like this. Freud's theory took account of this neces-
> sity. His conception of components . . . was eventually replaced
> by a conception of energy. The term chosen for this was libido.[8]

Agreeing here that libido is a more useful concept than fixed,
static components in explaining sexual functioning, Jung will
later go far beyond the psychoanalytic conception of libido as
strictly sexual and eventually use the term as a general label for
all psychic energy.

In grappling with various explanations of how a homosexual
component could disappear "without leaving any active traces
behind it," Jung goes on to note that, in fact, the homosexual
component of consciously heterosexual men shows itself

> most readily in a peculiar irritability, a special sensitiveness in re-
> gard to other men. According to my experience the apparent rea-
> son for this characteristic behavior, of which we find so many ex-
> amples in our society today, is an invariable disturbance in the
> relationship with women, a special form of dependence on
> them. . . . (Naturally this is not the real reason. The real reason is
> the infantile state of the man's character.)[9]

Jung may indeed mean "irritability" in the common sense of
being annoyed, since psychoanalysis might see such irritability
as a defense against the anxiety caused by unconscious homosexual impulses. Yet the previous use of the word *irritating* in the
case of the man whose homosexuality reemerged after a rejection

suggests that "excitability" might be a more accurate contemporary translation. However ambiguous his terms, Jung's thought is clear on one point in this passage: Homosexuality derives "invariably" from a disturbed, dependent relationship to women that arises from psychological immaturity.

At the time of this article's appearance, Jung still had close ties with the psychoanalytic movement and, in fact, identified himself with the movement in the foreword to the first edition of this paper. In his own words, this article represents an attempt to satisfy "the duty of applying a just criticism ourselves, based on a proper knowledge of the facts. To me, it seems that psychoanalysis stands in need of this weighing-up from inside."[10] Thus his view of homosexuality here is in line with a basic psychoanalytic understanding of adult homosexuality as a manifestation of psychological immaturity, a fixation or arrest in psychosexual development, and, for this reason, disturbed.

In contrast to this last, somewhat theoretically dense passage, Jung's next reference to homosexuality occurs in the presentation of a dream analysis from a case Jung had treated, reported in the essay "On the Psychology of the Unconscious." This paper, first published in 1912 as "Neue Bahnen der Psychologie" ("New Paths in Psychology"), was subsequently revised so extensively that Jung gave the article a new name when he published it again in 1917, making the original article an appendix to the newer version. Jung saw fit to revise the article with each new edition, in 1918, 1926, 1936, and 1943, as his thought developed, until "On the Psychology of the Unconscious" and its companion article, "The Relations between the Ego and the Unconscious," were published together as *Two Essays on Analytical Psychology.* In the words of Read, Adler, and Fordham, editors of the *Collected Works,* these two essays represent "a turning point in the history of analytical psychology, for they revealed the foundations upon which the greater part of Professor Jung's later work was built."[11]

As with many of Jung's references to homosexuality, the mention of homosexuality in "On the Psychology of the Unconscious" comes in a discussion on another topic entirely, in this case, Jung's method of dream interpretation, in the chapter entitled "The Synthetic or Constructive Method." To illustrate the difference between an analytical interpretation of a dream, which Jung sees as characteristically psychoanalytic, and his own method of dream interpretation, which he calls "synthetic" or "constructive," he gives the following example:

> A woman patient, who had just reached the critical borderline between the analysis of the personal unconscious and the emergence of contents from the collective unconscious, had the following dream: *She is about to cross a wide river. There is no bridge, but she finds a ford where she can cross. She is on the point of doing so, when a large crab that lay hidden in the water seizes her by the foot and will not let her go.* She wakes up in terror.[12]

That this dream is concerned with homosexuality is revealed by the woman's associations, which link her difficulties in crossing the stream to a fight she had had with a female friend. Of this friendship, Jung says:

> There is something peculiar about her relations with this friend. It is a sentimental attachment, bordering on the homosexual, that has lasted for years. The friend is like the patient in many ways, and equally nervy. They have marked artistic interests in common. The patient is the stronger personality of the two. Because their mutual relationship is too intimate and excludes too many of the other possibilities of life, both are nervy, and, despite their ideal friendship, have violent scenes due to mutual irritability. . . . *Faute de mieux,* this quarreling had long been for both of them a pleasure substitute which they were unwilling to relinquish. My patient in particular could not do without the sweet pain of being misunderstood by her best friend, although every scene "tired her to death." She had long since realized that this friendship had become moribund, and that only false ambition led her to believe that something ideal could still be made of it. She had formerly had an exaggerated, fantastic relation to her mother and after her mother's death had transferred her feelings to her friend.[13]

Jung's example of an analytical or causal-reductive interpretation explains why the patient maintains this difficult friendship: She is unwilling to give up this friendship because she is unwilling to sacrifice the "infantile wish" to play a masculine role with her friend, a wish accompanied by "corresponding sexual fantasies."[14] This wish is infantile because it arises from an inappropriate desire to re-create her relationship with her mother. The view of homosexuality implied by this causal-reductive interpretation again is in line with an orthodox psychoanalytic position: Homosexuality, more or less subconscious in this case, results from an unresolved wish to remain in an infantile relationship to a fantasy parent. Jung distances himself theoretically from this reductive approach to dream analysis. He calls such an interpretation of the dream "a severe depreciation of the patient's exalted ideal of friendship," even though the patient, already conscious of her homosexual tendencies, would probably have accepted the interpretation. Jung declares forthrightly in his discussion that "the interpretation, in fact, tells the patient nothing new; it is therefore uninteresting and ineffective."[15]

Does Jung's negative evaluation of this psychoanalytic method mean that he also takes issue with the psychoanalytic judgment that the woman's homosexual attachment is psychologically immature? Unfortunately, to answer this question, one must forgo a discussion of the exceedingly rich dream analysis Jung presents. Though Jung's method of dream interpretation is considerably less simplistic and much more evocative than the analytical interpretation, Jung's view of the homosexuality involved remains essentially the same. Through the woman's association of the crab with cancer and then with a woman she knew who died of cancer following "a series of adventures with men," Jung sees the woman as clinging to the problematic friendship as a defense against a "frivolous streak" that "might betray her into leading an amoral life." "Accordingly," Jung states, "she remains at the infantile, homosexual level, because it serves her as a defense. (Experience shows that this is one of the most potent motives for clinging to unsuitable infantile relationships.)"[16]

Jung repeats his view of homosexuality as infantile yet a third time, again in the context of a case discussion, in the same article. In a chapter entitled "The Archetypes of the Collective Unconscious," Jung uses the case of a young man he has treated as an illustration of how he came upon the idea of archetypes in the level of consciousness below the personal, which he called the collective unconscious. Important for our purposes, however, is that, with this reference, we have a case report by Jung himself in which the patient's homosexuality is the focus of the treatment.

First I must acquaint the reader in some measure with the personality of the dreamer, for without this acquaintance he will hardly be able to transport himself into the peculiar atmosphere of the dreams. . . . The dreamer is a youth of a little over twenty, still entirely boyish in appearance. There is even a touch of girlishness in his looks and manner of expression. The latter betrays a very good education and upbringing. He is intelligent, with pronounced intellectual and aesthetic interests. His aestheticism is very much in evidence: we are made instantly aware of his good taste and his fine appreciation of all forms of art. His feelings are tender and soft, given to the enthusiasm typical of puberty, but somewhat effeminate. There is no trace of adolescent callowness. Undoubtedly he is too young for his age, a clear case of retarded development. It is quite in keeping with this that he should have come to me on account of his homosexuality. The night preceding his first visit he had the following dream: *"I am in a lofty cathedral filled with mysterious twilight. They tell me that it is the cathedral at Lourdes. In the centre there is a deep dark well into which I have to descend."* [17]

The description of the young homosexual man here gives one a sense of the balance and openness with which Jung tended to approach people, regardless of his theoretical stance. Although he certainly makes note of the boy's immaturity, he also notes the boy's well-developed intelligence, his aesthetic sensibilities, and his air of experience, uncommon for an adolescent.

The patient's associations to this initial dream in analysis lead Jung to see the dream as compensatory, with the patient relinquishing his personal parents in the dream for an initiation into a higher form of masculinity, represented in the dream by the priesthood. Jung therefore concludes, "According to the dream then, what the initiation of the treatment signifies for the patient is the fulfillment of the true meaning of his homosexuality, i.e., his entry into the world of the adult man." [18] Jung sees the boy's desire for masculine initiation awakened first by the patient's mother, but

> there was no priestly instructor to develop it further, so the child remained in the mother's hands. Yet the longing for a man's leadership continued to grow in the boy, taking the form of homosexual leanings—a faulty development that might never have come about had a man been there to educate his childish fantasies. The deviation towards homosexuality has, to be sure, numerous his-

torical precedents. In ancient Greece, as also in certain primitive communities, homosexuality and education were practically synonymous. Viewed in this light, the homosexuality of adolescence is only a misunderstanding of the otherwise very appropriate need for masculine guidance.[19]

By no means does Jung seem to hold a positive view of his patient's homosexuality. Yet the language he uses to describe the condition as "faulty development" and a "misunderstanding" of an otherwise very appropriate need does not indicate severe condemnation either. Jung's attempt to see this "deviation" in a historical context wider than the post-Victorian morality of the early twentieth century similarly indicates a neutrality surprising for that time.

Most significant is Jung's attempt to find the meaning of this adolescent's homosexuality. Though Jung certainly thought that a discovery of the symptom's meaning would facilitate a cure and thereby resolve the patient's homosexuality, he nevertheless begins by assuming that there *is* an individual meaning to this patient's homosexuality, regardless of Jung's own analytic judgments. This search for individual meaning in a patient's pathology is characteristic of Jung's approach to psychological phenomena, and the present case report is an excellent example of this especially Jungian attitude toward health and sickness.

The patient's second dream continues the theme of initiation:

I am in a great Gothic cathedral. At the altar stands a priest. I stand before him with my friend, holding in my hand a little Japanese ivory figure, with the feeling that it is going to be baptized. Suddenly an elderly woman appears, takes the fraternity ring from my friend's finger, and puts it on her own. My friend is afraid that this may bind him in some way. But at the same moment there is a sound of wonderful organ music.[20]

Jung takes this second dream as confirmation of his previous interpretation, as a sign that the patient is making progress toward overcoming the homosexuality for which he sought treatment. The presence of the priest as a symbol of masculinity, the passing of the ring from the patient's homosexual boyfriend to the elderly woman, a mother replacement, and the wonderful music that accompanies the ceremony are all interpreted as "a step beyond the mother towards masculinity and hence a partial conquest of his adolescent homosexuality," referred to earlier in the passage as a "relatively childish condition."[21]

These four passages from Jung's early writings therefore seem to indicate that, at this time in his career, Jung viewed homosexuality as a form of immaturity caused, in part, by a disturbance of the relationship with the parents, particularly the mother. This view is psychoanalytic in its essence but there is at least one important difference. Jung appears to see the parent-child disturbance as more varied than the psychoanalytic theory of a universally present Oedipal complex would have one believe. Despite his readiness to cure this relatively "childish" condition, Jung shares with Freud the tolerant attitude toward homosexuality characteristic of early psychoanalysis (tolerant, again, in comparison with the social and religious values of that period), and Jung's attempt to put homosexuality in a historical perspective, as well as the open-minded approach he takes in searching for what the patient's homosexuality might mean, are both noteworthy. In this way, these passages presage what will become hallmarks of Jung's analytical psychology.

THEORETICAL COMPLEXITY AND CONSOLIDATION: 1920–1927

The publication of *Psychological Types* in 1921 marks the end of the long period of inner examination for Jung that began with his public "expulsion" from psychoanalytic circles at the end of 1913. Written largely between 1913 and 1917, this work was undertaken by Jung primarily out of his need to "define the ways in which my outlook differed from Freud's and Adler's"[22] and thus represents the first example of Jung's distinctive and mature thought.

The peculiarity of the concepts Jung used in *Psychological Types*, developed during a period of professional isolation, a "fallow period" of inner struggles, made necessary the inclusion of the rather long chapter "Definitions" at the end of the book. In this comprehensive glossary of Jungian terms, Jung mentions homosexuality in his definition of the "soul-image"—what will

later be called the anima/animus—and he provides an explanation for one way in which homosexuality comes about:

> For a man, a woman is best fitted to be the real bearer of his soul-
> image, because of the feminine quality of his soul; for a woman, it
> will be a man. Wherever an impassioned, almost magical relation-
> ship exists between the sexes, it is invariably a question of a
> projected soul-image. Since these relationships are very com-
> mon, the soul must be unconscious just as frequently—that is,
> vast numbers of people must be quite unaware of the way they are
> related to their inner psychic processes. Because this uncon-
> sciousness is always coupled with a complete identification with
> the persona, it follows that this identification must be very fre-
> quent, too. . . . Conversely, it may also happen that the soul-
> image is not projected but remains with the subject, and this re-
> sults in an identification with the soul because the subject is then
> convinced that the way he relates to his inner processes is his real
> character. In that event the persona, being unconscious, will be
> projected on a person of the same sex, thus providing a foundation
> for many cases of open or latent homosexuality, and of father-
> transferences in men or mother-transferences in women. In such
> cases there is always a defective adaptation to external reality and
> a lack of relatedness, because identification with the soul pro-
> duces an attitude predominantly oriented to the perception of
> inner processes, and the object is deprived of its determining
> power.[23]

This seemingly offhand discussion of the nature of the anima
presents for the first time one of the major ways Jung came to
understand many cases of homosexuality, namely, as a result of
identification with the contrasexual archetype of the anima or
animus ("soul" or "soul-image" in the definition just quoted). A
man's identification with his unconscious femininity thus leads to
a projection of his persona, that is, his "outer" masculinity, onto
another man. This projection of masculinity, as Jung says here,
creates the same-sex attraction of homosexuality, since the person projecting his masculinity will experience the carrier of this
masculine projection as possessing something essential and irre-
sistible, specifically, that part of an outward masculine identity
that has been "thrown away" because of an identification with his
inner feminine side. In this way, certain cases of homosexuality

are examples of a "defective adaptation to external reality and a lack of relatedness," insofar as the person projecting his masculine persona is not really relating to the other person but rather to a part of his own soul that has not yet been integrated, his masculinity.

This explanation is extremely interesting for a number of reasons. First, in terms of Jung's own theoretical development, the anima-identification theory does not modify the views that we saw in Jung's earlier writings, that is, the view of homosexuality as a form of psychological immaturity based on inappropriate parental transferences. In fact, Jung's concept of the anima/animus provides an explanation for both homosexuality *and* the previously observed father and mother transferences: For a man, the parental transferences and a man's homosexuality both grow out of his identification with an immature and unintegrated femininity, his anima.

Second, Jung states that both homosexual attraction and heterosexual passion are the result of the same psychological mechanisms, identification and projection. For homosexuality, the persona is projected because of anima identification; for heterosexuality, the anima/animus is projected because of persona identification. What Jung considers defective in these cases, therefore, is neither homosexuality nor heterosexuality per se but rather the unconscious nature of the psychic contents being projected, the archetype of the anima/animus, hence the often misguided nature of sexual passion, whether homosexual or heterosexual.

Third, Jung announces no universal principle here. Anima identification is merely a "foundation" for many cases of "open or latent" homosexuality. It is not a cause inexorably leading to all cases of homosexuality, nor is homosexuality understood in a purely genital sense. Homosexuality, as Jung uses the term in this passage, is as much a psychic state of same-sex attraction as the behavioral expression of this sexual attraction with another man or woman.

By now, it should be quite clear that Jung had given homosexuality a great deal of thought, even if it never occupied center stage in his writing or thinking. We see taking shape in these passages a certain approach, a particular attitude, a tentative theory about the phenomenon. We know that as early as 1918, Jung saw patients who either were homosexual or at least had homosexually tinged relationships with others. We see him using and revising psychoanalytic concepts to account for same-sex erotic attraction, and we see in his theory of the soul image or anima/animus a theory all his own.

Jung's lecture to students at the University of Zurich in late 1922, entitled "The Love Problem of a Student," was originally published in English in 1928. As one of Jung's most extensive expositions of his views on the interconnection between sexuality and love, this short article accordingly contains his most extensive discussion of homosexuality. Since the topic of the lecture is love, Jung begins by enumerating the various ways the term has been used, including

> "the love of boys," meaning homosexuality, which since classical times has lost its glamour as a social and educative institution, and now ekes out a miserable, terror-stricken existence as a so-called perversion and punishable offence, at least where men are concerned. In Anglo-Saxon countries it seems on the other hand that female homosexuality means rather more than Sapphic lyricism, since it somehow acts as a stimulus to the social and political organization of women, just as male homosexuality was an important factor in the rise of the Greek *polis*.[24]

Here again one encounters Jung's historical perspective and lack of judgmentalism in his acknowledgment of the important place occupied by the homosexual teacher-student relationship in ancient Greek civilization as well as the part it plays in the contemporary social and political equality of women. One also must remark on the slightly disapproving tone Jung takes toward the social and judicial treatment of homosexuality as a "so-called perversion," disapproval consonant with both his historical perspective and his psychiatric open-mindedness.

The rest of the lecture makes clear, however, that the forms of homosexuality Jung speaks of here are the classical models of either adolescent attraction or mentor-student relations. Still identifying homosexuality with psychic immaturity, Jung writes:

> The onrush of sexuality in a boy brings about a powerful change in his psychology. He now has the sexuality of a grown man with the

soul of a child. . . . The psychic assimilation of the sexual complex causes him the greatest difficulties even though he may not be conscious of its existence. . . . At this age, the young man is full of illusions, which are always a sign of psychic disequilibrium. They make stability and maturity of judgment impossible. . . . He is so riddled with illusions that he actually needs these mistakes to make him conscious of his own taste and individual judgment. He is still experimenting with life and *must* experiment with it in order to learn how to judge things correctly. Hence there are very few men who have not had sexual experiences before they are married. During puberty it is mostly homosexual experiences, and these are much more common than is generally admitted. Heterosexual experiences come later, not always of a very beautiful kind. [25]

However, the following passage is Jung's most extensive and powerful statement on homosexuality:

Homosexual relations between students of either sex are by no means uncommon. So far as I can judge of this phenomenon, I would say that these relationships are less common with us, and on the continent generally, than in certain other countries where boy and girl college students live in strict segregation. I am speaking here not of pathological homosexuals who are incapable of real friendship and meet with little sympathy among normal individuals, but of more or less normal youngsters who enjoy such rapturous friendship that they also express their feeling in sexual form. With them it is not just a matter of mutual masturbation, which in all school and college life is the order of the day among the younger age groups, but of a higher and more spiritual form which deserves the name "friendship" in the classical sense of the word. When such a friendship exists between an older man and a younger its educative significance is undeniable. A slightly homosexual teacher, for example, often owes his brilliant educational gifts to his homosexual disposition. The homosexual relation between an older and a younger man can thus be of advantage to both sides and have a lasting value. An indispensable condition for the value of such a relation is the steadfastness of the friendship and their loyalty to it. But only too often this condition is lacking. The more homosexual a man is, the more prone he is to disloyalty and to the seduction of boys. Even when loyalty and true friendship prevail the results may be undesirable for the development of personality. A friendship of this kind naturally involves a special cult of feeling, of the feminine element in a man. He becomes gushing, soulful, aesthetic, over-sensitive, etc.—in a word, effeminate, and this womanish behavior is detrimental to his character.[26]

Jung continues with observations on female relationships:

Similar advantages and disadvantages can be pointed out in friendships between women, only here the difference in age and the educative factor are not so important. The main value lies in the exchange of tender feelings on the one hand and of intimate thoughts on the other. Generally, they are high-spirited, intellectual, and rather masculine women who are seeking to maintain their superiority and to defend themselves against men. Their attitude to men is therefore one of disconcerting self-assurance, with a trace of defiance. Its effect on their character is to reinforce their masculine traits and to destroy their feminine charm. Often a man discovers their homosexuality only when he notices that these women leave him stone-cold.

Normally the practice of homosexuality is not prejudicial to later heterosexual activity. Indeed, the two can even exist side by side. I know a very intelligent woman who spent her whole life as a homosexual and then at fifty entered into a normal relationship with a man.[27]

These passages are evidence that Jung holds no authoritative or one-sided condemnation of the phenomenon, candidly acknowledging the wide variety of relationships that are encompassed by the word *homosexuality* and noting the "advantages and disadvantages" of each, from the "higher and more spiritual" friendships of boys, to the educative passion between teacher and student, to the relationships of "tender feelings" and "intimate thoughts" between "high-spirited" women. Merely to make the distinctions among these relationships as Jung does, not to mention his attitude that such "punishable offences" might have advantages and disadvantages, is a far more positive attitude than many psychologists since Jung have taken when writing about homosexuality. Jung states earlier in the article that he does not automatically include homosexuality in a concept of sexual perversion "because very often it is a problem of relationship,"[28] and the passage just quoted, with its distinctions among different kinds of homosexualities, bears out Jung's relational view of the issue.

Jung nevertheless does not indiscriminately approve of homosexuality in all its forms, and its negative side is frankly discussed. He ends his lecture with the comment that he passes "no sort of moral judgment on sexuality as a natural phenomenon but prefer[s] to make [his] moral evaluation dependent on the way it is expressed."[29] Jung's evaluation of homosexuality here is illustrated in his example of a relationship between an older man and a younger man, a relationship that can, in Jung's eyes, be valuable given mutual "steadfastness and loyalty." Yet even such conditions do not always make for the "development of the personality" because of the threat of anima identification and its resultant "womanish behaviour . . . detrimental to [a man's] character." The same cautious evaluation is made later of lesbian relationships, when Jung comments that lesbians' negative attitudes toward men reinforce "their masculine traits," thereby vitiating "their feminine charm."

Despite the undeniable negative evaluation here, one must note that homosexuality per se, as a natural phenomenon, is decidedly *not* condemned by Jung. Rather, Jung seems to evaluate each homosexual relationship on the basis of its helpful or harmful effect on the person's character, looking to see whether or not its expression integrates or hinders integration of the anima/animus.

Implicit in this method of moral evaluation is the idea that one's homosexuality may be separated from one's character. Jung clearly does not hold to the existence of a homosexual personality universally present in men and women with same-sex feelings. In Jung's view, the fact that one has homosexual feelings or relationships says nothing positive or negative a priori concerning someone as a person, since, in his words, homosexuality is simply a "natural phenomenon."

To step back a bit from the thick of theory here, one notices that Jung appears to follow a two-step process in working with homosexual patients, beginning with an open-minded and nonjudgmental examination of how the homosexuality is expressed in the patient's life, followed by a moral evaluation of the homosexuality on the basis of its effect on the patient's character or, to use the more contemporary term, personality. All the same, Jung doubts that certain values can be maintained in a homosexual relationship that would render it truly worthy of a positive moral judgment, values such as loyalty and steadfast friendship. Only infrequently does Jung actually judge a homosexual relationship as a positive factor in a patient's personality and development.

This pessimistic tone seems to come from what one might call his "quantitative" view of homosexuality. The "more" homosexual a man is, the less he seems to hold to such redeeming values as loyalty and steadfastness in friendship, whereas a man only "slightly" homosexual in fact might be able to achieve brilliance as an educator precisely because of his "homosexual disposition." Jung does not explain what he means by a man being more or less homosexual.

One possibility might be that Jung was referring to the frequency of sexual liaisons. The instinctive urgency in a man with a homosexual disposition could result in promiscuity and thereby make loyalty and steadfast friendship difficult to maintain as values. Another possibility is that Jung would characterize a man as more or less homosexual based on the observable extent of his identification with his anima. A man very much identified with his anima, hence more homosexual, would suffer from all the effects of expressing this unconscious and therefore inferior femininity, consequently finding himself "oversensitive" and "gushing," qualities at odds with steadfastness and loyalty in Jung's opinion. However, a man only slightly identified with his anima, hence less homosexual, would probably have a fairly good relationship with his feminine side and fare better in navigating the treacherous waters of male-male relationships. The first explanation is more probable than the latter, since anima identification and homosexuality are by no means synonymous, and Jung would not use the terms so interchangeably. This odd view of how homosexual one may be, however, appears important in aiding Jung's moral determination of the value of homosexual expression in an individual's life.

The last significant point is Jung's observation that normally homosexual practice does not preclude heterosexual practice and the two can coexist. He does not state whether he would hold the opposite statement to be true, namely, that heterosexual practice does not exclude homosexuality, though he probably would not object. Despite many rumors concerning the identity of the woman to whom Jung refers here (for example, that she might be one of the well-known female Jungian analysts analyzed by Jung; among them Marie-Louise von Franz, Barbara Hannah, and Esther Harding are sometimes mentioned in Jungian circles), Jung's use of the word *normal* seems to indicate qualitative rather than quantitative value, especially since Jung's point is that even confirmed homosexuals can eventually achieve a normal relationship. Given his consciousness of the extreme variety of homosexual relationships and in the absence of any other explanation, one has the sense that by a normal relationship Jung meant marriage. Jung's basic approach remains the same, however: The woman's homosexuality did not preclude her intelligence.

This rich passage provides a great deal of insight into Jung's views on homosexuality. Seeing the phenomenon of homosexuality not as a unitary phenomenon but rather as a variety of relationships, each with its advantages and disadvantages, Jung removes homosexuality from the realm of sexual perversion and makes moral judgments based on its function in the individuals' personality, which is seen as independent of the homosexual proclivities. Though he acknowledges that certain homosexual relationships may be positive and growthful, he doubts that most are helpful to the individual, because of the frequent underlying anima/animus identification. Likewise, though he acknowledges the fluidity of sexual orientation and practice, he gives a single example in which a lesbian fifty years of age enters into a normal relationship with a man. The rather simple view of his earlier years, in which homosexuality was a form of psychological immaturity, has undergone quite a development, and this more developed view is now based on concepts that are peculiar to Jung's thought.

For the less theoretically minded, it is refreshing to note how Jung's discussions of homosexuality often occur in the context of a case presentation. In the third of three lectures to the International Congress of Education in London in 1924, published as *Analytical Psychology and Education,* Jung mentions the case of a thirteen-year-old girl to show how the parents' psychological disturbances are often manifested through the child. Suffering "from a tremendous pressure of pent-up emotions which fed more upon

homosexual fantasies than upon real relationships . . . she con-
fessed that she sometimes longed to be caressed by a certain
teacher, and then suddenly she lost track of what was being said
to her; hence her absurd answers." As the daughter of an absent
father and a narcissistic mother,

> the child is not given a grain of real love. That is why she suffers
> from premature sexual symptoms, like so many other neglected
> and ill-treated children, while at the same time she is deluged
> with so-called maternal love. The homosexual fantasies clearly
> show that her need for real love is not satisfied; consequently she
> craves love from her teacher but the wrong sort. If tender feelings
> are thrown out at the door, then sex in violent form comes in
> through the window, for besides love and tenderness a child
> needs understanding.[30]

This case illustrates once more the two-step process that Jung
used to evaluate the expression of homosexuality. Rather than
condemn the homosexual fantasies as aberrant, he approaches
the whole person of the little girl and finds that her homosexual
fantasies serve as a fantasy substitute for the real love that she
lacks at home.

This case makes an interesting contrast to the possibility,
which Jung mentioned previously, of a homosexual relation between an older and younger man having a positive educative
value. Here the essentials of this social relationship are the same:
a potential homosexual relationship between an older woman
and a young girl. However, the intensity of the sexual charge behind this girl's fantasies is directly related to her "tender feelings" being "thrown out at the door" by her parents' lack of true
care. Jung sees this lack of care, not the girl's homosexuality, as
the primary focus of treatment: "The right thing in this case
would naturally be to treat the mother. . . ."[31]

This case discussion is valuable in illustrating why, for Jung,
definitive statements on homosexuality were rare. The homosexuality here is secondary to underlying emotional dynamics
within the family. To treat the child for her homosexuality on the
assumption, for instance, that she was suffering from unresolved
Oedipal feelings or even, in Jungian terms, an animus identification to compensate for the absence of her personal father would

be to miss Jung's point entirely. The homosexual fantasies that Jung observes here are evaluated according to other criteria, specifically the positive or negative effect such impulses have on the whole of the girl's personality. The girl's putative homosexuality, itself debatable, seems incidental to the real problem the girl suffers: a precocious sexuality owing to a keenly experienced lack of love.

In following year, 1925, Jung gave a lecture to the same organization, the International Congress of Education, this time in Heidelberg, in which he mentions once again the case of the adolescent who consulted him for cure of his homosexuality and anticipated the course of treatment with an initial dream of a well at Lourdes. Despite the obvious development in Jung's thought since the time of the first publication of the case in 1917, Jung repeats his analysis of the case with no modification, frequently verbatim. One must, therefore, assume that side by side with the more complex view of homosexuality expounded in "The Love Problem of a Student," Jung still conceived of some cases of homosexuality along the earlier lines of psychological immaturity and unresolved mother transference. Because of the pains Jung takes to describe the somewhat effeminate, aestheticizing character of this young man, one is rather surprised that Jung did not reinterpret this case in a deeper way using his concept of the soul image, that is, anima, to explain the boy's personality traits, his mother transference, his religious leanings, as well as his dreams. That he did not do so might be explained by the fact that the case is cited not within a discussion of sexuality or homosexuality but rather as an illustration for an assembly of educators of Jung's method of dream interpretation.

Yet Jung provides evidence that indeed, even at this time, his theory of homosexuality as being a result of an attachment to the personal mother remained in his thought. In the same year, 1925, he cites the following example in "Marriage As a Psychological Relationship:"

> The worst results flow from parents who have kept themselves artificially unconscious. Take the case of a mother who deliberately keeps herself unconscious so as not to disturb the pretence of a "satisfactory" marriage. Unconsciously she will bind her son to

her, more or less as a substitute for a husband. The son, if not forced directly into homosexuality, is compelled to modify his choice in a way that is contrary to his true nature. He may, for instance, marry a girl who is obviously inferior to his mother and therefore unable to compete with her; or he will fall for a woman of a tyrannical and overbearing disposition, who may perhaps succeed in tearing him away from his mother.[32]

However, in 1927, Jung published "Woman in Europe," an extended discussion of the changing place of women in European society from a psychological point of view. In this, one of Jung's more well-known articles and a perfect example of how Jung dealt with significant social issues as a "medical"—that is, clinical—psychologist, Jung discusses the psychological advantages and disadvantages for women when entering the previously male-dominated spheres of politics and work. Among the disadvantages is the danger of animus identification for women who find themselves in a new, masculine role:

> The mental masculinization of the woman has unwelcome results. She may perhaps be a good comrade to a man without having any access to his feelings. The reason is that her animus (that is, her masculine rationalism, assuredly not true reasonableness!) has stopped up the approaches to her own feeling. She may even become frigid, as a defence against the masculine type of sexuality that corresponds to her masculine type of mind. Or, if the defence-reaction is not successful, she develops, instead of the receptive sexuality of woman, an aggressive, urgent form of sexuality that is more characteristic of a man. This reaction is likewise a purposeful phenomenon, intended to throw a bridge across by main force to the slowly vanishing man. A third possibility, especially favoured in anglo-Saxon countries, is optional homosexuality in the masculine role.[33]

Here again homosexuality is identified with animus possession, though Jung makes clear that such animus possession can take many concrete forms and derives more from socioeconomic than from personal factors.

The astute reader will notice how Jung identifies feminine with women and masculine with men. In the discussion that precedes the passage just quoted, Jung states variously that "we can see that woman is in the process of breaking with the purely feminine sexual pattern of unconsciousness and passivity and has made a concession to masculine psychology by establishing herself as a visible member of society," and "by taking up a masculine profession, studying and working like a man, woman is doing something not wholly in accord with, if not directly injurious to, her feminine nature. She is doing something that would scarcely be possible for a man to do, unless he were a Chinese. Could he, for instance, be a nursemaid or run a kindergarten?" In another place in the same paper he states, "Since masculine and feminine elements are united in our human nature, a man can live in the feminine part of himself and a woman in her masculine part. . . . [But] a man should live as a man and a woman as a woman."[34]

This identification of sex role with gender is also reflected in Jung's distinction between a masculine role and the unstated alternative of a feminine role in the "optional homosexuality" just mentioned. To be sure, later developments in analytical psychology will turn these concepts of the feminine and the masculine into psychological principles unallied intrinsically with gender. Here, however, the sex-role and gender distinction is not made, and consequently Jung's understanding of female homosexuality at this point remains a cross between a purely archetypal view and a view that sees lesbians as wanting to be men and resolving their wish through optional homosexuality.

Just as Jung acknowledges a variety of homosexual relationships with a variety of possible advantages and disadvantages, he holds to a variety of explanations and interpretations of homosexual behavior in this period of his thought. Some explanations and interpretations of homosexuality are based on factors that Jung has termed archetypal, such as the anima/animus; other of his interpretations of homosexuality as a psychological phenomenon rest on factors he identifies with the personal unconscious, namely negative parental complexes and unresolved mother or father transferences.

This distinction between the personal mother and the archetypal figure of the anima in a man's soul is purely artificial, for, in Jung's view, the two are inextricably linked. In one of his most significant works, published first in 1912, *Wandlungen und Symbole der Libido* (*Symbols of Transformation*), Jung examines the myth of the hero, the hero's battle for freedom from the mother, and the process such a "battle for deliverance" entails. In the chapter entitled "The Dual Mother," Jung points out that myths as well as the dreams and fantasies of modern-day people confirm the "duality" of the mother symbol in a variety of ways, both in the character, or "valence," of the symbol as positive (constructive to individual growth) or negative (destructive to growth) and in the symbol's dual nature as both personal and archetypal. In regard to this duality, Jung puts forth the "psychological rule" that "the first carrier of the anima-image is the mother,"[35] and this idea makes a great deal of psychological and common sense.

To return to Jung and these passages on homosexuality from the middle period of his life, one sees that his view of homosexuality has become quite complex, to say the least. Jung puts homosexuality into a cultural and historical perspective and acknowledges openly the varied character of homosexual relationships. As a clinician, he applies a two-step process of moral evaluation, looking first at a patient's homosexuality in the context of the patient's whole life and only secondarily making a clinical judgment on the positive or negative function of the patient's homosexual thoughts, feelings, or actions. Without excluding the possibility of positive judgments, Jung undeniably passes negative judgments more frequently, at least in the works we have examined thus far. As we have seen, the only cases he mentioned were cases in which the manifestations of homosexuality appear to originate in disturbed relations with the anima/animus or the patient's personal parents or both, which makes the disturbance itself a complex mixture of archetypal and personal factors in an individual's soul.

Jung's Mature Thought: 1936–1950

Jung's view of homosexuality gets no less complex as he grows older, and his later writings examine still other factors involved in the psychological phenomenon of homosexuality. For those who would like to believe that Jung was predisposed to an exclusively negative attitude toward homosexuality, the following passage from "Concerning the Archetypes, with Special Reference to the Anima Concept," first published in 1936 and revised in 1954, should correct that erroneous impression.

> Younger people who have not yet reached the middle of life (around the age of 35), can bear even the total loss of the anima without injury. The important thing at this stage is for a man to be a man. The growing youth must be able to free himself from the anima fascination of his mother. There are exceptions, notably artists, where the problem often takes a different turn; also homosexuality, which is characterized by identity with the anima. In view of the recognized frequency of this phenomenon, its interpretation as a pathological perversion is very dubious. The psychological findings show that it is rather a matter of incomplete detachment from the hermaphroditic archetype, coupled with a distinct resistance to identify with the role of a one-sided sexual being. Such a disposition should not be adjudged negative in all circumstances, in so far as it preserves the archetype of the Original Man, which a one-sided sexual being has, up to a point, lost.[36]

Though he does say that "after the middle of life, however, permanent loss of the anima means a diminution of vitality, and of human kindness," Jung clearly indicates in the passage just quoted that he does not always consider an anima identification strictly pathological. In fact, he sees such an identification as the psychological explanation of the artistic stereotype often applied to homosexuals.

What is more noteworthy is that Jung links homosexuality with the archetype of the Hermaphrodite or the "Original Man," an archetype of psychological wholeness—indeed, the Self. If homosexuality results from resistance to a "one-sided" sexuality, if it is connected to the hermaphroditic wholeness of the Self, it can scarcely be condemned. The link Jung posits here between homosexuality and the archetype of the Hermaphrodite makes his view of homosexuality more complex, not less.

The hermaphroditic archetype and the union of opposites that it symbolizes is a good image to bear in mind at this point. The next passage in which Jung mentions homosexuality, from his 1938 lecture "Psychological Aspects of the Mother Archetype," revised in 1954, shows how Jung holds both a positive and a negative evaluation of homosexuality. Identifying homosexuality as one of the typical effects of a mother complex (along with Don

37

Juanism and "sometimes impotence"), Jung links homosexuality once again with the anima: "In every masculine mother-complex, side by side with the mother archetype, a significant role is played by the image of the man's sexual counterpart, the anima."[37] Here, however, his thinking becomes much more finely shaded:

> Since a "mother complex" is a concept borrowed from psychopathology, it is always associated with the idea of injury and illness. But if we take the concept out of its narrow psychopathological setting and give it a wider connotation, we can see that it has many positive effects as well. Thus a man with a mother-complex may have a finely differentiated Eros instead of, or in addition to, homosexuality. (Something of this sort is suggested by Plato in his *Symposium*.) This gives him a great capacity for friendship, which often creates ties of astonishing tenderness between men and may even rescue friendship between the sexes from the limbo of the impossible. He may have good taste and an aesthetic sense. . . . He may be supremely gifted as a teacher because of his almost feminine insight and tact. He is likely to have a feeling for history, and to be conservative in the best sense and cherish the values of the past. Often he is endowed with a wealth of religious feelings, which help to bring the *ecclesia spiritualis* into reality; and a spiritual receptivity which makes him responsive to evaluation.[38]

Given the context of these descriptions, one almost wonders whether Jung is describing the possible positive effects of a mother complex or the social stereotypes of gay men: artistically inclined and aesthetically attuned, deeply feeling and emotional, innately suited for service professions such as teaching, and attached to the past. With regard to such stereotypes, the modern-day identification of the gay liberation movement with politically liberal or progressive causes might leave one puzzled with Jung's characterization of homosexuals as conservative. Yet such is the content of at least one stereotype of gay men and gay culture: gay men are supposed to be enthralled with older movies, elevating such stars of the past as Judy Garland, Bette Davis, Joan Crawford, Gloria Swanson, and others to the cult status of goddess. Gay men are commonly seen as having an affinity with effusive decorating styles, again drawn largely from past eras, baroque ornamentation, art deco motifs, and so forth. Gay men's relationship to spiritual concerns is also a commonplace among church circles, especially those denominations in which celibacy or ostentatious ritual play a large part, and such a gay religious instinct, as it were, seems to have historical precedents, which I will examine later in this book.

These stereotypical images of gay men Jung seems to see as tied to what he terms the mother complex at the base of homosexuality, though this passage makes quite clear that Jung holds a positive, if not laudatory, opinion of such effects for the culture at large. The reason for his positive opinion may be found in his insistence that the notion of a complex be viewed in a genuinely complex way: not simply as a narrow, pathological element in one's soul but rather as a "feeling-toned group of representations"[39] potentially both positive and negative.

These nearly glowing evaluations of homosexuality complement the negative examples and formulations examined earlier, and in the next reference Jung introduces yet another facet to his thought, the concept of constitutional homosexuality. In *The Psychological Aspects of the Kore*, published first in 1940 with *The Psychology of the Child Archetype* and eventually combined with essays by Karl Kerenyi to form the volume entitled *Two Essays on a Science of Mythology*, Jung describes the archetypal figure of the Maiden. In the course of examining how this figure—in current Jungian terminology known as the *puella aeterna*—functions for men, Jung states that, since "a man's wholeness, in so far as he is not constitutionally homosexual, can only be a masculine personality, the feminine figure of the anima cannot be catalogued as a type of supraordinate personality but requires a different evaluation and position."[40]

The concept of constitutional homosexuality—that is, a same-sex sexual orientation that is inborn rather than learned—is a venerable idea in psychology. Obviously, if such innate homosexuality could be definitively determined, the clinical treatment of homosexual men and women would take a radically different course. Evidence in support of this hypothesis that homosexuality is constitutional or at least the result of some genetic predisposition can be found in the memories of gay men and women who remember experiencing same-sex feelings and attractions at a time so early in their development that their personalities were still barely formed. Needless to say, any irrefutable determination of constitutional homosexuality is still a psychogenetic chimera; the standby formula of "nature *and* nurture" to explain psychosocial behavior is still the extent of our empirical understanding. All the same, the concept of constitutional homosexuality remains a provocative hypothesis and one Jung himself actively entertained.

Jung's altogether passing mention of this possibility leaves certain questions about what he meant by constitutional, which could indicate either a genetic characteristic or a characteristic acquired so early in development and so firmly part of one's personality as to be unalterable. Also the question of how such constitutional homosexuality could be reconciled with a man's conscious "masculine personality," in Jung's terms, is left similarly open. Does a man's wholeness consist of something other than a masculine personality if he is constitutionally homosexual and if so, of what does it consist?

Jung's research into the symbolism of alchemy forms a major and controversial part of his later writing, and so it is especially interesting to find two references to homosexuality within his exposition of alchemical symbolism. In *The Psychology of the Transference,* a book published in 1946, Jung uses a set of alchemical pictures to explicate the inner process set in motion and brought to completion through the analytic relationship. Jung writes that

> practical analysis has shown that unconscious contents are invariably projected at first upon concrete persons and situations. Many projections can ultimately be integrated back into the individual once he has recognized their subjective origin; others resist integration, and although they may be detached from their original objects, they thereupon transfer themselves to the doctor. Among these contents the relation to the parent of the opposite sex plays a particularly important part, i.e., the relation of son to mother, daughter to father, and also that of brother to sister.

Then, in a footnote, he writes, "I am not considering the so-called homosexual forms, such as father-son, mother-daughter, etc. In alchemy, as far as I know, this variation is alluded to only once" and he then quotes the *Visio Arislei,* an alchemical text from Basel dated 1593, "'Lord, though thou art king, yet thou rulest and governest badly; for thou hast joined males with males, knowing males do not produce offspring.'"[41] Jung cites this same passage from the *Visio Arislei* again later in the article when examining the process by which a human being emerges from an infantile preoccupation with self, symbolized in the alchemical texts by brother-sister incest: "The union of 'like with like' in the form of homosexual relationships is to be found in the 'Visio Arislei' (*Art. aurif.*, I, p. 147), marking the stage preceding the brother-sister incest."[42]

As is usual with Jung's alchemical writings, there is at first more obscurity than illumination. The point of these references to homosexuality, occurring as they do within a discussion of the alchemical symbolism of incest, appears to be developmental. The theme of the article as a whole is to map out, through the imagery of alchemical texts, the stages a personality goes through, within analysis, as an individual progresses toward psychological wholeness. Thus the stage in which a union of "like with like" occurs is seen to precede a union of "like with unlike." Such a statement, therefore, though initially abstruse, does no more than repeat what Jung has already said elsewhere in a different way: homosexuality, the union of "like with like," is a forerunner of a true union of opposites, the "like with unlike" whose alchemical symbol, as we have seen, is brother-sister incest.

The final mention of homosexuality in the *Collected Works* continues the examination of the archetypal symbolism of incest and its relationship to the archetype of the Self. In *Aion: Researches into the Phenomenology of the Self* and published in 1950, Jung seeks "with the help of Christian, Gnostic and alchemical symbols of the self, to throw light on the change of psychic situation within the 'Christian aeon.'"[43] More simply stated, in *Aion* Jung intended to examine the psychological transformation of consciousness wrought by the symbolism of Christianity and its archetypal connections with the Self. To this end, Jung begins by explaining his concepts of ego and Self and uses his concept of anima/animus to demonstrate one way in which the ego and Self remain distinct from one another but related. However, Jung notes that frequently a personal sense of self—ego in his terminology—is not sufficiently developed and "then there appears before you on the psychological stage a man living regressively, seeking his childhood and his mother, fleeing from a cold cruel world which denies him understanding."[44] Jung continues the description of this psychological situation:

> The fragment of the world which he, like every man, must encounter again and again is never quite the right one, since it does not fall into his lap, does not meet him half way, but remains resistant, has to be conquered and submits only to force. It makes demands on the masculinity of a man, on his ardour, above all on his courage and resolution when it comes to throwing his whole being into the scales. For this he would need a faithless Eros, one capable of forgetting his mother and undergoing the pain of relinquishing the first love of his life. The mother foreseeing this danger has carefully inculcated into him the virtues of faithfulness, devotion, loyalty, so as to protect him from the moral disruption which is the risk of every life adventure. He has learnt these lessons only too well, and remains true to his mother. This naturally causes her the deepest anxiety (when, to her greater glory, he turns out to be a homosexual, for example) and at the same time affords her an unconscious satisfaction that is positively mythological. For, in the relationship now reigning between them, there is consummated the immemorial and most sacred archetype of the marriage of mother and son. What, after all has commonplace reality to offer, with its registry offices, pay envelopes, and monthly rent, that could outweigh the mystic awe of the *hieros gamos?*[45]

Jung seems almost to have come full circle here, interpreting the son's homosexuality as a regressive phenomenon, a "defective adaptation to external reality," a sign of psychological immaturity. Also indisputable, though, especially in light of the alchemical passages just examined, is Jung's connection of homosexuality with mother-son incest, and thus with the self as a symbol of wholeness, the very consummation of psychological maturity.

In Jung's view, the archetypes of the collective unconscious are always ambivalent, possessing positive and negative aspects, and therefore have power that can act as boon or bane for the individual life. Thus, on the one hand, the archetype of wholeness, as symbolized by the incestuous *hieros gamos*, or sacred marriage, can be constellated in an inappropriate way, as just seen, through a regressive retention of childish symbiosis with the all-providing mother. On the other hand, this archetype can be constellated in an appropriate way that satisfies both the demands of outer reality and the inner urgency toward oneness that the archetype possesses, a true and mature union of inner and outer opposites.

Pertinent to our interest is the further step Jung seems to take concerning homosexuality, a step suggested in *The Psychology of the Transference* and reinforced here. The homosexuality Jung mentions here is not simply the result of a mother complex, a problem of the personal unconscious. Nor is it the result of a disturbed relationship to one's anima/animus, a problem of the collective unconscious. Here, homosexuality has its own inner meaning in the incestuous image that holds sway over the man's soul, an image whose power lies in its connection with the Self, the archetype of wholeness. This view of homosexuality, therefore, looks beyond the anima/animus to the archetype of the Self, and sees such homosexuality as being a wrong-headed attempt to have psychological integration without personal cost.

With this tantalizing connection of homosexuality with the hermaphroditic archetype of the Self, we have come to the end of the first leg of our journey, having examined one by one all the references to homosexuality within the *Collected Works*.

REFERENCES TO HOMOSEXUALITY OUTSIDE THE COLLECTED WORKS

A short excursion is in order here, for written references to homosexuality by Jung exist outside of the *Collected Works:* in his letters to Freud dating from his early career and in the two volumes of letters edited by Gerhard Adler; in the autobiographical *Memories, Dreams, Reflections*, written by Aniela Jaffé and not included in the *Collected Works* at Jung's request; in the *Dream Seminars* and finally in that collection of interviews with Jung entitled *C. G. Jung Speaking*. For a number of good reasons, we will forgo looking at most of these further references with the detail and application brought to all the passages above. First, we have worked hard and long and deserve at least a bit of a breather. Second, our purpose here is not scholarly and the academician dedicated to thoroughness may use the references at the end of this chapter to do what we will forbear from doing now. Third, there is really nothing in these further references that contradicts or adds much new to what we have already seen in the *Collected Works*. However, certain passages provide a more personal glimpse into Jung's attitudes than may have been revealed in his other publications and these obviously are interesting to note.

For example, the correspondence between Freud and Jung from 1906 to 1914 contains several minor refrences to homosexuality. However, in the letter dated February 20, 1910, Jung writes to Freud:

> A case of obsessional neurosis has deserted me at the climax of homosexual resistance. This brings me to my real question: the sequence and course of resistances. . . . It seems that homosexuality is one of the richest sources of resistance in men, with women it is perversions or variations of sexuality *sensu proprio* (variations of coitus, etc.). The homosexual resistances in men are simply astounding and open up mind-boggling possibilities. Removal of the moral stigma from homosexuality as a method of contraception is a cause to be promoted with the utmost energy. Here we have a new hobby-horse to ride through the history of culture—contraceptive methods in ethnology: monasteries, self-castration (castration rites among the Australian aborigines). Homosexuality would be a tremendous advantage since many inferior men, who quite reasonably would like to remain on the homosexual level, are now forced into marriage. It would also be excellently suited to large agglomerations of males (businesses, universities, etc.) Because of our short-sightedness we fail to recognize the biological services rendered by homosexual seducers. Actually they should be credited with something of the sanctity of monks.
>
> I still don't know when I have to go on military service and so am not master of my future.[46]

The extravagant tone of this letter as well as Jung's juxtaposition of homosexuality as one of the "richest sources of resistance" in men alongside his wish to award homosexual seducers with the "sanctity of monks" make this letter hard to interpret. That Freud's response to this letter is missing from this correspondence makes a judgment on Jung's seriousness all the more difficult. Certainly there is humor, intended or not, in the concept of "contraceptive methods in ethnology," not to mention the humor of Jung's comment on homosexuality's suitability for "large agglomerations" of men followed by his anxious mention of his own upcoming tour of duty. Nevertheless, despite his manifest overstatement, familiar attitudes of Jung's appear here as well: his advocacy of destigmatization of homosexuals; his acknowledgment of both positive and negative sides to homosexuality individually and culturally; and his view of homosexuality as immature and inferior.

In a letter dated September 12, 1929, to Walter Robert Corti, a younger Swiss educator, Jung writes that

> the young are experimenting like young dogs. They want to live experimentally, with no historical premises. That causes reactions in the unconscious, restlessness and longing for fulfillment of the times. . . . When the confusion is at its height a new revelation comes. . . . This follows psychological rules. Wyneken is also homosexual. (Trial!) The young today can be forbidden no stupidities since they thereby increase the salutary confusion. People like you must *look at* everything and *think* about it and communicate with the heaven that dwells deep within them and listen inward for a word to come. At the same time organize your outward life properly so that your voice carries weight.[47]

Without the letter from Corti to Jung, one cannot really know what Jung meant by the reference to Gustave Wyneken, a progressive German educator tried and condemned for homosexuality. "Also homosexual" could perhaps refer to feelings in that direction which Corti had revealed to Jung or might be just one more example of the experimentation in which Jung saw the youth of that time indulging. The avuncular tone of Jung's advice here and his own open-mindedness toward this "salutary" confusion reveal Jung as a person. That homosexuality is mentioned in this context may indicate that Jung may have identified the greater visibility of the behavior as a sign of the changing times and thus, as a sign of an impending "new revelation." As we will see, Jungian theorists wonder the same thing, understanding the greater visibility and participation in homosexuality and homosexual experimentation as part of a swing of the pendulum away from patriarchal models and toward inclusion of more matriarchal values in life and culture.

Jung's next letter containing a reference to homosexuality, dated May 1951, was written nearly twenty years later, to R. J. Zwi Werblowsky, the author of *Lucifer and Prometheus*, a book for which Jung wrote the foreword.[48] This letter is Jung's response to his initial review of the book and contains a lengthy discussion on homosexuality.

Taking issue with Werblowsky's definition of *hubris* as a "hypertrophy of masculinity," Jung also doubts whether Werblowsky can assert that Greek homosexuality also derived from such overdeveloped masculinity. "Homosexuality is more a social phenomenon which develops wherever a primitive society of males has to be cemented together as a stepping-stone to the State. This is particularly evident in Greece." Jung's observation that homosexuality served conscious, political goals for the Greeks is another example of his willingness to deal with the issue of homosexuality on other than purely psychological grounds.

Jung writes further in the next paragraph:

> Nor can one impute without qualification a contempt of women to homosexuals. Very often they are good friends to them. For instance, a young homosexual bachelor is a welcome guest among women of uncertain [sic] age, and he feels happy in their company because it surrounds him with mothers. Most homosexuals are suspended or potential males still clinging to their mother's apron strings.[49]

Jung's left-handed defense of homosexuality simultaneously attacking the stereotype of the male homosexual's misogyny while nevertheless characterizing "most" homosexuals as something less than complete men—shows a confused view of the matter. Even within Jung's own argument, one could wonder about the level of contempt such "suspended or potential males" might feel toward the women on whom they putatively depend for mothering.

More instructive is that Jung again identifies male homosexuality with an issue of the feminine. Though countering Werblowsky's contention that the castration complex is connected with homosexuality primarily, Jung sees the castration complex much more connected with the meaning of such rites as Jewish circumcision, namely, the attempt to bridle *concupiscentia*, human lustfulness, by way of symbolic castration so as to increase human dependence on divine forces rather than on mortal powers. As the meaningfulness of these rites declines, the symbolic castration no longer fosters a religious attitude of dependence on God but rather

> regresses to dependence on the mother. . . . It is, however, correct to say that homosexuality comes in here indirectly as the result of an almighty mother complex. The mother-fixated son, because of his "aloofness from women," is constantly in danger of autoerotism and exaggerated self-esteem. The characteristic arrogance of adolescent youths towards the female sex is simply a defence mechanism against domination by the mother and can hardly be interpreted as hybris.[50]

Excluding a similar reference to Greece in a letter in 1954 to a young Greek girl as well as an inconsequential reference to Plato as a homosexual in a letter to Hugo Charteris in January 1960, this review of Jung's references to homosexuality in his letters shows essentially many of the same ideas—phrased much less guardedly, to be sure—put forth in his writings meant for publication. Paramount among these attitudes are the identification of homosexuality with a mother complex in individuals and with matriarchal consciousness in the case of culture. While not subscribing unthinkingly to empirically unsupported stereotypes and keeping a somewhat open mind about the function of homosexuality (the hyperbole of his letter to Freud notwithstanding), Jung nevertheless maintains the view that homosexuality is a state in which one is less than fully developed, though it is not without positive benefits.

The last source to be examined is Jung's autobiography, *Memories, Dreams, Reflections*. More a result of a collaboration between his secretary, Aniela Jaffé, and Jung himself than an autobiography in the conventional sense, *Memories, Dreams, Reflections* is a chronicle of Jung's inner life and was a project that grew on Jung only after a long period of resistance to such a summing up. Therefore, it represents perhaps the most personal of all documents examined and is appropriately the last document on our excursion outside the *Collected Works*, since Jung himself finished revising the text only days before his death in June 1961.

Homosexuality is mentioned twice in *Memories, Dreams, Reflections*, both times in the chapter entitled "Travels," in which Jung describes his travels to other countries, and both those times in reference to time spent in Africa. Noticing with interest a number of homosexual couples during his 1920 trip to North Africa, Jung writes:

> I felt suddenly transported to the times of classical Greece, where this inclination formed the cement of a society of men and of the *polis* based on that society. . . . My dragoman confirmed my impression of the prevalence of homosexuality, and of its being taken for granted, and promptly made me offers. The good fellow could have no notion of the thoughts which had struck me like a flash of lightning, suddenly illuminating my point of observation. I felt cast back many centuries to an infinitely more naive world of adolescents who were preparing, with the aid of a slender knowledge of the Koran, to emerge from their original state of twilight consciousness . . . to become aware of their own existence. . . .[51]

Personal as this observation might be (despite Jung's forbearance from detailing the thoughts that struck him "like a flash of lightning" on being propositioned by his guide), the point of view toward homosexuality is, as one can see, no different from what we have already encountered.

The second reference in the autobiography moves to a more theoretical plane in the context of Jung's extensive 1925 tour of Kenya and Uganda.

> I asked myself whether the growing masculinization of the white woman is not connected with the loss of her natural wholeness . . . ; whether it is not a compensation for her impoverishment; and whether the feminizing of the white man is not a further consequence. The more rational the polity, the more blurred is the difference between the sexes. The role homosexuality plays in modern society is enormous. It is partly the consequence of the

mother-complex, partly a purposive phenomenon (prevention of reproduction).[52]

The sober tone of this passage lends some credence to the theory that Jung's letter to Freud was not entirely tongue-in-cheek and that Jung in fact did look on homosexuality as serving a contraceptive function in culture.

In contrast to the writings contained in the *Collected Works*, Jung's letters and his autobiography present Jung's personal attempt to deal with homosexuality on the level of cultural psychology, putting forth his ideas on the function homosexuality serves for an entire society, rather than for individuals, and on what the positive and negative results of such functions may be for both society and individuals.

To say that Jung had anything near a theory of homosexuality is a gross overstatement. Yet Jung's remarks on homosexuality throughout his life elucidate characteristic ways he approached the phenomenon as well as characteristic themes he saw implied by homosexuality on the individual and collective levels. The next chapter will organize Jung's thoughts on the basis of what we have already read, examining both the theories and the attitudes he put forth, attitudes and theories that his followers have pursued in sometimes surprising ways.

3. Jung's Attitudes and Theories on Homosexuality

A CONTRADICTION SEEMS to arise when we take a close-up view of Jung's writings on homosexuality, as we did in the previous chapter. The one side of the contradiction is that Jung, never much the theorist anyway, is hardly a major theorist on homosexuality. The intention, however, in consulting Jung's writings on homosexuality is not to review a major theory of homosexuality but rather to examine in what ways Jung might provide a *tertium non datur,* as he was fond of saying, a third way forward between behavioral and psychoanalytic theories of homosexuality, in the context of the "salutary confusion" about homosexuality, to use his own phrase, which characterizes the present historical moment. In this way, we arrive at the other side of the contradiction. Despite the relatively meager quantity of time and attention Jung devoted to homosexuality—meager considering the thousands of pages in his *Collected Works*—typically Jungian theories of and approaches to homosexuality do emerge in his writings quite clearly. Succinctly put, our review of Jung reveals both that he did not say very much and, in fact, that he said a great deal that is of particular use in dealing with individual gay men and women, as well as homosexuality in the abstract.

Because Jung's intention was never to put forth definitive theories, we would be applying an inappropriate standard to his thought if we looked exclusively at what he wrote on homosexuality theoretically. Though we shall look at whatever theories seem couched in the writings we have reviewed, initially, at least, a more appropriate way to grasp what Jung did say would be to look not at his theories of homosexuality but rather at that aspect in his writings that perhaps comes through more clearly: his attitudes toward homosexuality and homosexual individuals. In this regard, one can discern at least five prominent attitudes Jung takes toward homosexuality, some explicit in his writings, some implicit but equally obvious in the course of the discussions we have reviewed. These five attitudes differ in their emphases certainly, but no one of them inherently contradicts any of the others, and as a whole, four of the five represent useful ways of approaching homosexuality and gay individuals today.

The first attitude made clear in Jung's various writings is that, in his view, *homosexuality ought not to be a concern of legal authorities.* This attitude seems based on two thoughts: first, that homosexuality by itself does not reduce the "value of the individual as a member of society" and, second, that laws making homosexuality a criminal offense are useless and inhuman, and, in fact, promote crimes such as blackmail. Though one can hardly characterize Jung as an agent of social reform, neither can one deny his underlying attitude of social tolerance for homosexuality.

This attitude may at first glance appear entirely consonant with the more politically conscious, depathologized attitude of contemporary psychological thought. However, the rationale for Jung's attitude, which lies mainly in his acknowledging the unenforceability of such laws and their potential for increasing illegal activities, is found in utilitarian arguments; Jung uses no psychological theory here but rather basic common sense. Likewise, Jung's claim that such statutes are inhumane to homosexuals cannot be said necessarily to stem from any enlightened view of homosexuality on his part.

As mentioned earlier, in defining homosexuality as a sickness or psychological deviation, psychiatrists often considered themselves as "protectors of deviants who had suffered at the hands of society and the more traditional forces of social control."[1] At a time when religious attitudes had greater social and political force, homosexuals themselves had even welcomed their reclassification as "sick," if only to escape the harsh legal consequences of being "criminal" or "morally depraved."

Given the date of Jung's writings as well as certain statements of his own in those writings, to assume that Jung did not consider homosexuality sick is unwarranted. His attitude that criminal penalties against homosexuals are unhelpful is based more on the "therapeutic vision" of early-twentieth-century psychiatrists who, without much objective data on the real lives of gay men and women and without any valid political analysis of their social role, could not see the psychological harm caused by even such a "progressive" view of homosexuality as a sickness. On the other hand, to dismiss Jung as politically naive or psychiatrically arrogant is also unwarranted, since there are indications that he did have a wider consciousness of the context of psychological disorder.

Much of Jung's tolerance seems based on his second attitude toward homosexuality: *Homosexuality is best understood when put in a historical and cultural context.* For Jung, classical Greece, in which homosexuality served a social and political function, is a constant point of historical reference, whether he is dealing with individual cases, as in the case of the boy who dreamed of the well at Lourdes, or with larger issues of theory, as in "The Love Problem of a Student" or his letter to Werblowsky. Jung supplements this historical perspective with a wider cultural perspective in which the contemporary social function of homosexuality is an issue to be examined along with any strictly psychological issues raised by the behavior. Examples of this cultural perspective are found in "Woman in Europe," his letter to Freud, and the two references to homosexuality in *Memories, Dreams, Reflections.*

Once again, one must be careful not to read Jung through contemporary, ideological lenses simply because his attitudes appear close to more contemporary views. Indeed, Jung's historical-cultural approach gave him a more comprehensive view of homosexuality as a psychological phenomenon, but nowhere does it result in Jung becoming a homophile activist in any sense. On the contrary, Jung's continual reference to homosexuality in Greece as a point of reference leads him to identify homosexual activity with "primitive," less psychologically conscious societies. Though he and Freud might ride the "hobby-horse" of contraceptive methods in ethnology, Jung's wider cultural perspective does not keep him from doubting the value of what he called the masculinization of women in contemporary society. As far as the positive social functions of homosexuality, such as educative homosexual relationships between older and younger men or the true exchange of intimacies between "high-spirited, intellectual" women, Jung appears pessimistic and uncertain that positive values can be maintained by homosexuals within society.

Whether or not Jung can be made to fit gay liberationist molds of enlightenment is obviously not the real issue. Despite the ideological motivations for his attitude—motivations that are at best unclear—his placement of homosexuality in a wider historical and cultural context represents one extremely useful way of approaching homosexuality. Jung did not see homosexuality as some sort of modern aberration; rather, his clear-headed affirmation that homosexuality is and always has been a universal part of human sexuality in all times and in all cultures results in a more objective and less narrowly individualistic understanding of gay people.

The third attitude Jung takes toward homosexuality is *to distinguish an individual's homosexuality from other aspects of the individual's personality.* This approach is clearest in his case discussions, in which Jung goes beyond the patient's homosexual behavior and feelings to look at other aspects of the individual's psychological development. This approach is also implicit in Jung's more theoretical discussions, such as "Psychological Aspects of the Mother Archetype," in which Jung holds that a mother complex resulting in homosexuality may also foster other positive and negative personality characteristics.

This attitude is undergirded by more than simple kindheartedness or denial. Rather, it appears as a manifestation of Jung's rigorous empiricism, his dedication to maximum therapeutic objectivity, for which all theoretical assumptions must be suspended (as far as is consciously possible) until all data are collected and evaluated. This attitude also seems related to a less obvious but no less important principle, typical of Jung and analytical psychology: the principle of valuing the whole of an individual's personality over any single part. The result of this empirical objectivity and dedication to wholeness is to minimize the importance of an individual's homosexuality and thereby place this aspect of a person's life in perspective.

In the social and clinical climate of the early twentieth century, this distinction functioned to Jung's inestimable benefit. Instead of being blinded to all other aspects of a homosexual patient, Jung was able to go beyond the social and clinical prejudices of the time and achieve a true understanding of an individual's whole psychology. Clearly, his case discussion of the woman with the crab dream and the boy with the well dream indicate a distinct concern with vital aspects of these two individuals' personalities that many other clinicians would have missed in concentrating on the homosexuality as the sole focus of treatment.

However, in today's social and clinical climate, in which the pathology or abnormality of homosexuality has already been challenged, Jung's distinction between one's sexual orientation and the other aspects of one's personality may no longer be necessary or helpful. If homosexuality is accepted nowadays as merely one variation along a continuum of sexual orientation, politically progressive psychologists might argue that such a distinction would in fact work to the detriment of understanding gay people, on the grounds that it would, in effect, slice individual gay people into psychological pieces, with their homosexuality over here to be separately evaluated, their religious beliefs over there, and so on, as if each aspect did not interact with and mutually influence all other aspects. Such a distinction would be unnecessary and irrelevant in a climate of acceptance and growing neutrality toward homosexuality. In fact, one might argue that to generalize at all about the positive or negative function of an individual's homosexuality is to tread on dangerous ground.

Yet the distinction Jung makes between one's sexual orientation and the other aspects of one's personality is a prudent move if it serves us the way it served Jung, by preventing us from assuming right away that homosexuality is *the* problem for an individual. This distinction, however unnecessary and misleading at times, nevertheless may free us, as it did Jung, to see the true place sexual orientation holds in any given individual's life. Obviously, for some people, their homosexuality represents a vital core of their being, a way of being in the world, an organizing principle. For others, their homosexuality represents a marginally important factor in a life built around other concerns. To refrain from assumptions about homosexuality and to see it simply as one of many aspects of an individual's personality can only work to all our benefits.

By far the most important attitude Jung takes toward homosexuality and certainly the most Jungian is the fourth one that comes through in his writings: *An individual's homosexuality has a meaning peculiar to the individual in question, and psychological growth consists of becoming aware of that meaning for the individual.* This attitude is explicit in the case discussion of the boy with the well dream and in Jung's more theoretical discussion in "The Love Problem of a Student." Once again, this attitude seems related to Jung's dedication to making psychology as scientific, that is, empirical, as possible, a goal that required abandoning unsupported theoretical generalizations and paying careful attention to all the available data before making judgments or propounding theories.

The presumption of meaning can be called Jungian in that it assumes the psyche is a purposive phenomenon and that all aspects of an individual's psychological life—even those that seem outwardly regressive or pathological—serve the end of psychological growth. Obviously, this view of psyche is, in some ways, more a philosophical statement than a psychological observation, even though Jung found empirical support for it in his research on the structures and dynamics of the unconscious. The very concept of science in the modern sense of the term presumes a rational understanding of the universe, and Jung continually adhered to the principle that only the rigorous application of rational methods could bring one closer to an understanding of apparently irrational phenomena. Also clear in this attitude toward homosexuality is the characteristic individuality of Jung's psychology, in which the individual soul is the unit of psychological study. For Jung, this individual approach was the only one possible in his role as a clinical psychologist and represents the reason that Jung never really considered himself primarily a theoretician.

The effect of these dual assumptions was to show Jung that homosexuality was as variable as each individual is from every other individual, that each of these various homosexualities contained the seeds of positive growth and the threat of negative effects on the individual personality. Since homosexuality has a meaning peculiar to each individual, one must face the challenge of understanding the meaning of one's homosexuality for oneself alone and make a moral decision concerning how to act out this meaning in one's everyday life.

If this philosophical attitude seems almost too rational to be true, the fact is that Jung himself, though recognizing potentially positive aspects of homosexuality, nevertheless presents only cases in which the homosexuality is a misunderstanding of an otherwise appropriate need or has a purely regressive meaning. Moreover, as is clear from the review of his writing and as we will see in the following discussion of Jung's theories on homosexuality, Jung hardly refrained from making theoretical generalizations conerning the meaning of homosexuality.

Whether or not Jung remained faithful to his own philosophical assumptions is not the immediate issue. Of all of Jung's attitudes toward homosexual patients and homosexuality in general, the presumption of individual meaning seems the most far-reaching. Such a presumption allows gay people to find within their own stories a reason, a goal, and a direction, regardless of the suffering or the fulfillment that their homosexuality has brought into their lives. It permits those of us who know gay people professionally or personally to assume that their homosexuality is not simply some cosmic accident but rather every bit as important as the sexual orientation we ourselves possess. It also lays on the doorstep of gay people a psychological task of no mean measure, a task that ultimately will not be solved simply by political action or social agitation: the task of uncovering and realizing, individual by individual, the meaning of and reason for loving men or loving women. This individual task will remain for gay people even after AIDS has been cured, even after homosexuality is legal in all states of the union, even after social prejudice has been utterly eradicated from the hearts and minds of the world's population. To live our meaning is the spiritual task that Jung makes the very soul of his psychology, and for this reason, it is important to see how this soul of Jungian psychology, this attitude toward self-realization, might also come into the lives and loves of contemporary gay people.

These four attitudes that Jung held toward homosexuality— social tolerance, placement of the phenomenon in a historical and cultural context, distinction between a patient's homosexuality and other aspects of his or her personality, and especially the presumption of meaning—have much to recommend themselves. Despite the relatively scarce attention Jung seems to have paid to homosexuality, one is startled to see how infrequent such sane and sober attitudes are in many contemporary discussions of homosexuality, which sometimes have a political shrillness at once off-putting and senseless. Thus, in forgoing quantity for quality, we have gained much: *what* Jung says is perhaps a far more important corrective to contemporary views on homosexuality than *how much* he wrote.

But we did say that Jung held five attitudes, not just four. The fifth major attitude Jung takes toward homosexuality is that *homosexuality is a result of psychological immaturity and, consequently, abnormal and disturbed.* This attitude seems based partly on the previously mentioned therapeutic vision of psychiatrists: better sick than criminal, better childish than sick. Yet the view of homosexuality as psychologically undeveloped is based on something more than a misguided vision of psychiatry's therapeutic social function. Such a view presumes that objective psychological maturity exists and, most important, that heterosexuality represents that psychological maturity.

Given the preexisting Western religious ideology that gives primacy to heterosexuality, to identify Freud's theory of universal psychosexual stages of development as the sole source of this view of heterosexuality is absurd. More accurate is that Freud unwittingly restated in psychological terms ideas concerning human sexual development that had religious and not scientific bases. Indeed, the research that forced a reconceptualization of homosexuality in psychological theory centered precisely on the issues of normality and maturity.

Kinsey's ground-breaking research on human sexuality, consistently replicated by the Institute on Sex Research, which he founded, showed human sexuality as a phenomenon with myriad variations, psychological and behavioral, with genital heterosexual behavior only one of many possibilities.[2] Ford and Beach's research on animal behavior in the 1940s and 1950s showed that homosexual behavior between adult male monkeys occurred with signs of arousal and satisfaction and even in the presence of available females.[3] Evelyn Hooker's various articles and research with nonpatient homosexuals seemed to reveal considerably less than universal maladjustment on the part of homosexuals and, indeed, opened the question of whether the pathological agent for disturbed gay men and women was their homosexuality or, more probably, the severe social and moral prejudice against gay people.[4] These empirical studies, and many more not cited here, resulted in a revision of psychoanalytic thinking on normality and abnormality by such noted practitioners as Judd Marmor, who began to understand heterosexuality as a culturally determined norm and not a biologically determined imperative.[5]

To be sure, many psychiatrists and psychologists still hold to the ideal of genital heterosexual behavior as the goal of treatment, perhaps no longer because heterosexuality is biologically determined, as once believed, but precisely because heterosexuality still represents the dominant cultural value and any deviation from a dominant cultural value is sure to carry along with it a modicum of psychological distress. These psychologists in good faith believe their task is to reduce such distress and to help homosexuals adjust to the social norm around them. However, the explosion of empirical research on the lives and development of homosexuals makes any intrinsic evaluation of heterosexuality as superior to homosexuality difficult to maintain. The APA's removal of homosexuality from its list of mental disorders, even unwanted, ego-dystonic homosexuality, reinforces this revision of psychological thought on heterosexuality as normal or mature.

Jung's attitude toward homosexuality as psychologically immature or infantile is based on a teleology that sees human sexuality resulting invariably in genital heterosexual practice. Such a view is neither accurate empirically nor useful in the contemporary context, which involves looking more and more at normal variations in human sexuality. In Jung's defense, he developed, over the course of his career, a much more sophisticated understanding of psychological maturity than the mechanical view reflected in these early writings. His later views on the psychological development of the human being, or, in his terms, the individuation process, will bring the question of the individual's relationship to the personal and archetypal feminine to bear on the examination of whether homosexual practice is a manifestation of maturity. Although Jung never gives an example of homosexual practice in a highly individuated human being, his view of homosexuality as intrinsically infantile is open to serious question.

The reason for leaving this last, most questionable attitude of Jung's toward homosexuality until the end of our discussion can be found in the way this attitude dovetails quite neatly into what could be called Jung's major theory of homosexuality. His view of homosexuality as immature or infantile is based on a particular set of theoretical assumptions that we will now thoroughly examine and critique.

JUNG'S THEORIES REGARDING HOMOSEXUALITY: ARCHETYPAL VIEWS

Before delving into Jung's theories in particular, a brief excursus on the role of theory in the psychological study of homosexuality is in order, since the modern situation is a great deal different from the situation in Jung's time. As already outlined, the gay liberation movement and its political and social analysis of homosexuality in modern culture is responsible to a large extent for the revision of clinical thought on homosexuality since Jung. Using more and better empirical research, progressive psychologists and gay liberation activists joined together to demonstrate that negative social attitudes, in particular the hatred and fear of homosexuality called homophobia, are actually more to blame for mental illness among gay people than anything inherent in homosexuality itself. By removing the label of illness from homosexuality per se, psychologists found that one of the primary ways they had come to approach the phenomenon, that is, in terms of finding a cause for homosexuality, was no longer a relevant or urgent concern. One searched for a cause, or etiology, of homosexuality only if one were concerned primarily with providing a cure and reversing a condition seen as pathological.

Because of this traditional link between etiology and cure and because homosexuality has been considerably depathologized in contemporary times, the etiology of homosexuality as a focus of research has fallen far behind research on what one might call the phenomenology of homosexuality. In ordinary language, we look less nowadays at how people *become* gay and more at how gay people actually *are* individually, in couples, and in groups. If there are normal variations within sexuality, homosexuality among them, the search for a cause is irrelevant and our energies are better spent on learning from the real lives led by contemporary gay men and women. Thus, what has always been the major theoretical emphasis in psychology has now shifted.

As is clear from our review of Jung's writings, Jung was hardly driven to find a cure for homosexuality. If the great majority of his remarks on the subject have an etiological bent, one has the feeling that scientific curiosity rather than a fixed and firm belief in homosexuality's invariable pathology is the reason. Nevertheless, Jung's motivations are once again unclear, for his theories do concentrate mainly on providing a possible explanation for the causes of homosexuality.

Moreover, however irrelevant his etiological theories may be, Jung's ideas have influenced a whole generation of subsequent thinkers in analytical psychology. Insofar as Jung held not one theory of homosexuality but rather three, the fact that only one of these three theories has been significantly developed since Jung's time and his other two theories have been all but ignored is especially interesting. Finally, we will learn a great deal from examining what it is about Jung's theories that is helpful or unhelpful, coherent or contradictory. The point of examining Jung is not so much to canonize or execrate his theories, but rather to learn from his clear-sightedness and to become aware of his shortcomings so as to avoid them ourselves.

The first theory, and the one that appears most widely in the literature reviewed, is that *homosexuality is nearly always a result of a particular relationship with the feminine.* In his early writings, before an elaboration of more archetypal and sophisticated views, Jung saw a homosexual's relationship to the feminine primarily as an unresolved dependence on the personal mother, for men as well as women. This theory of dependence on the personal mother was then widened by Jung as he became aware of the existence of the anima. In light of this development, Jung then saw that homosexuals appeared to be acting out an identification with the contrasexual element of their personality and projecting their personas onto same-sex others, pursuing this projection through their wish for erotic relationships with other men or other women. However, the historical and cultural perspective Jung adopts widens this connection to the feminine further, beyond the anima, to the realm of matriarchal consciousness.

The link between homosexuality and the feminine in Jung and in Jungian theory constitutes the only position that one might dare call the Jungian theory of homosexuality. Though homosexuality has never been a major source of concern among analytical psychologists since Jung, Jungian writers who do mention homosexuality almost invariably do so in the context of its connection with the feminine, as we will see in the next chapter. For Jung and for those of his followers whose writings on homosexuality we will examine, their purpose in writing was most definitely not to set out and consolidate a theory of homosexuality. Their views on homosexuality can therefore hardly be taken out of the context of their larger writings and done justice; their intentions must be respected, their limitations acknowledged, their attempts honored and understood. The fact remains, however, that the link between homosexuality and a "problem with the feminine" is primary for Jung and Jungians. This view, this Jungian theory of homosexuality, is marred by serious flaws.

The first problem with the link between homosexuality and the feminine is that, despite all the positive human qualities that result from a mother complex, anima identification, and unconscious matriarchal psychology, homosexuality based on such factors can be characterized only as immature psychologically. Psychological autonomy means growing out of the world of mother, not acting out an indissoluble connection, whether on the personal or collective level. Though Jung and Jungians, in approach, tend to be considerably less harsh in their judgment of such dependence, to see homosexuality as a result of a problem with the feminine is to call homosexuality a disease in somewhat nicer, more sophisticated terms. Clearly, this link between homosexuality and the feminine is the basis for the fifth attitude of Jung's, which we have examined, his view of homosexuality as immature or infantile.

The second problem with this view is the familiar issue of what one must do theoretically with female homosexuality in order for it to be comprehensible within a theory that links homosexuality and a problem with the feminine. In some places, Jung seems not to see any conflict in identifying homosexuality in women with a mother problem. The case of the woman with the crab dream and the case of the young girl with sexual feelings for her teacher both seem based on an incomplete or unsatisfying relationship these females had with their mothers, for which their homosexual feelings and relationships were compensating. Thus, for lesbians, the mother complex at the root of their homosexuality would seem to be a problem of distance from their mother, rather than enmeshment, to which Jung seems to ascribe male homosexuality.

However, if male homosexuality is frequently the result of anima identification based on an underlying mother complex, one would expect female homosexuality to be explained by Jung as an animus identification based on an underlying father complex. In the references Jung makes to female homosexuality in "Woman in Europe" and in his autobiography, which are not strictly psychological writings, Jung indeed seems to worry that the masculinization of women in modern society results in homosexuality. However, Jung sees the masculinization of women as owing primarily to socioeconomic factors that force women to assume traditionally masculine social roles in the workplace, and not necessarily to any individual problem with the masculine.

Thus, Jung explains female homosexuality either in the same terms as male homosexuality, as a disturbed relationship to the mother, or in primarily cultural terms, as a psychological response to changes in gender roles. At best, this theory of female homosexuality is confusing. Is lesbianism a psychological or cultural phenomenon, both, or neither? At worst, this theory is inconsistent with his own explanation of homosexuality in men as being a result of anima identification.

One might put aside female homosexuality and the theoretical problems it presents for Jung since, after all, Jung never claimed to be writing a theory of homosexuality and psychology's track record in dealing with women's experience has never been all that impressive. However, a strange situation results from explaining even male homosexuality in terms of the feminine. Male-male behavior is seen to be an expression of both men's inward femininity or their search for the mother or their matriarchal psychology. Thus an exclusively masculine phenomenon is explained in exclusively feminine terms.

This is an exceedingly odd and ultimately untenable theoretical situation; here the hidden gender definition and heterosexual bias of Jung's thought comes to the fore. The problem with Jung's thought on this point is that he confounds three entirely independent variables of sexual identity: gender, sexual orientation, and sex role. Collapsing these three distinct features into a single undifferentiated concept results in the traditional definition of a man as an anatomically male creature who is heterosexual and fulfills the cultural requirements of masculinity. This conflation forces one to view homosexuality as a major failure in a man's individuation, requiring etiological explanation and psychological cure: By definition, homosexuality violates a heterosexually biased conception of what masculinity is. The only explanation for the anomaly of homosexuality is that it represents a perverse psychological wish to be a woman, for woman is of course similarly defined as an anatomical female creature who is heterosexual and fulfills the cultural requirements of femininity. The latter half of this definition of woman ostensibly supplies the etiology of male homosexuality. Creatures attracted sexually to men are women, or, if they are not women, they must have an unconscious wish to be women.

Since Jung's time, as we have noted, greater social consciousness, more astute political analysis, and more sophisticated empirical research in the social sciences have shown that anatomical gender is determinative neither of sexual orientation (otherwise, homosexuality and bisexuality would be nonexistent) nor of sex roles, which are fundamentally social constructs and not psychological imperatives. Just as sexual orientation is a fluid phenomenon—Kinsey's scale is the demonstration and result of this discovery—sex roles vary from individual to individual, from culture to culture, though obviously anatomical maleness and femaleness do not.

What is at issue here is not that some gay men might have a problem with the feminine. Some undoubtedly do, as do many heterosexual men; in this regard, Jung does not comment idly on the origins of Don Juanism in heterosexuals. Rather, the real problem is whether male homosexuality can be explained exclusively as a problem with the feminine. Can we consign to darkness the influence of the father and his masculinity in the psychological development of gay men and women? Can that influence only be a negative one, the influence of absence and disappointment? Is it impossible to imagine that male homosexuality might be the result of an identification with masculinity and not simply the result of an identification with femininity? In examining the rich and varied phenomenon of homosexuality, male and female, can we ignore masculinity and all its archetypal roots? Obviously, the answer to each of these questions is no.

Because Jung and some of his followers unconsciously assign

sociocultural gender roles to what are inherently psychological phenomena, we are left with a one-sided theory of homosexuality if we simply accept these assignments and do not go any further to develop a truly comprehensive way of thinking about the personal and archetypal factors inherent in human sexuality. Jung's theory that homosexuality is the result of a peculiar, disturbed, and immature relationship to the feminine is only part of the story. As is usually the case with Jung, we must not take this one part for the whole phenomenon or the whole of Jungian thought.

This theory, however major a role it has played for Jung and Jungians, is nevertheless not the only one Jung put forth. His second theory of homosexuality is the one located in his later writings, especially in his exploration of alchemical imagery. According to Jung, homosexuality may result from an incomplete detachment from the original archetype of the Hermaphrodite, the unbroken state of nondifferentiation that comes, psychologically and mythically, before all else.

This theory of homosexuality, which has received considerably less emphasis than the first and almost no further development in analytical psychology, holds much more promise. Although still seeing homosexuality as less developed or immature, Jung brings up the possibility that homosexuality may be a reaction to one-sided sexuality, a way of enacting the archetype of the Androgyne, a symbol of wholeness, the Self. The promise of this view is the very same promise that Jung mentions in "Concerning the Archetypes." Just as homosexuality may be a healthy response to a one-sided sexuality, understanding homosexuality as a phenomenon with its roots in archetypal and psychological androgyny may be a healthy theoretical response to a one-sided view of homosexuality as exclusively allied with the feminine. In fact, given analytical psychology's emphasis on the *coniunctio* or union of opposites in psychological growth, it is highly significant that Jung mentioned the possibility that homosexuality might be one form of the *coniunctio*.

Because of the sketchiness of these references and the complete lack of development of this view, whether Jung meant to value homosexuality as positive or negative in its hermaphroditic identification is open to debate. Though Jung was certainly not the first to discern the fundamental bisexuality of human sexual response, even if he was probably the first to see its archetypal roots as clearly, there is reason to doubt that Jung would promote any form of archetypal identification as a positive step in an individual's psychology. After all, an identification with the Androgyne can be every bit as regressive as progressive psychologically. To play out an androgynous self in the world can be a way to take refuge in primal symbiosis and defend against the painful differentiation of feelings and identity required by individuation, or it might be an embodied sign of psychological and emotional integration, evidence that one has indeed acquired a true and constant inner self, an ability to respond to men or to women on any level, emotionally, spiritually, sexually, without threat to or damage or loss of one's soul. For these reasons, Jung's suggestions concerning the role of the Hermaphrodite in homosexuality are the most tantalizing and perhaps the most potentially revolutionary of all his theories.

The third theory of homosexuality to which Jung gives credence is a theory of constitutional homosexuality, that is, *a homosexual orientation determined by genetic or biological factors*. This theory of homosexuality, one end of the continuum between nature and nurture and an idea that Jungian writers have virtually ignored, is ultimately adverse to the ethos of clinical psychology, which is predicated on the possibility of change. In the climate of greater hostility and lack of information before the political movements of the 1960s, the theory of constitutional homosexuality was welcomed by homosexuals, since its acceptance would relieve them of the harsh moral judgments and criminal accusations that sought to make them responsible for their sexuality. At that time, the issue of etiology overshadowed all other issues, but today, with the advent of the gay liberation movement, the cause of homosexuality, genetic or otherwise, has become and remains largely an irrelevant psychological concern. Thus, Jung's third contribution to a theory of homosexuality, that homosexuality may be constitutional, may be true but may never be particularly transformative.

The only transformative kernel in the theory of constitutional homosexuality is the symbolic aspect of the observation: an individual's sexual orientation appears so fundamental and unchangeable as to appear to be biologically determined. In Jung's references to constitutional homosexuality, he seems to be speaking from his intuition of how fundamental one's sexual orientation seems to be, especially where he speaks of the inverse relationship between a masculine personality and constitutional homosexuality. However, the metaphor of constitutional homosexuality has limited impact these days, since the relative unchangeability of one's sexual orientation is, for the most part, accepted in psychology.

How do subsequent analytical psychologists follow Jung's act? What leads do Jungians take from the attitudes and theories we have seen, and how does their thought develop when they meet gay people in their psychological practice or when they consider homosexuality as a universal form of human relationship? How do Jungians deal with the many political, cultural, social, and religious issues that are attached to homosexuality, and how do they look to Jung to give them direction or guidance? Around these questions the next chapter will unfold.

4. Jungians and Homosexuality

TO SOME EXTENT, exploring what Jung's followers have to say on homosexuality reverses the good news and bad news of our look at Jung's references to homosexuality in the *Collected Works*. On the positive side, the brevity and scarcity of references allowed one to follow Jung's thoughts with relative ease. On the other hand, the brevity of the references made it necessary for us to work harder to delve more into what Jung said, rather than how much he wrote on homosexuality.

With Jung's own attitudes and theories now mapped out, we find ourselves in the opposite situation as we explore Jungians' attitudes and theories on homosexuality. Here, we are faced with what one might call the Jungian legacy (though *curse* may be a better word)—a lack of theoretical focus. Since clearly Jung did not set out to develop a coherent theory of homosexuality but, as we have seen, dealt with sexual orientation only in conjunction with other issues of interest to him, we shall find that Jung's followers cannot help but develop their own ideas on homosexuality along many, and sometimes divergent, theoretical lines. Though such a situation is typical of Jungian theorizing in general—where overarching or comprehensive theoretical positions are eschewed in favor of less sweeping and more individual points of view—this fact does not make our job any easier, and, unfortunately, neither can we expect to find all references by Jungians to homosexuality in one place, as was the case with Jung. As we track down the developments of Jung's ideas and attitudes toward homosexuality, we must go here and there, to the major Jungian journals, to books on topics sometimes only remotely connected with homosexuality, to psychological analyses of myths, fairy tales, and legends where same-sex relationships may or may not occupy the foreground. If the scholar's problem with Jung is how little he wrote on homosexuality, the predicament in dealing with Jungians is how much has been written in so many places from so many different viewpoints, which forces us to organize, curtail, sum up, and even pass over many provocative tidbits to avoid getting lost in the oceanic literature of analytical psychology.

Given this situation, one must constantly keep in mind that the following exploration may best be compared in two ways to examining a living organism beneath a magnifying glass. First, it is always possible to magnify the subject more greatly, which would reveal and encompass more data. The review of literature that follows is not meant to be a minute scrutiny of every known Jungian theory on homosexuality, but rather an amplification meant to show how major Jungian writers, primarily in the English-speaking world, continued to develop the theories and attitudes that Jung espoused in his own writings. Second, just as when one examines a living creature, a literature review is an examination of something that is ever changing, in a continual process of enhancement and development. This examination of Jungian ideas on homosexuality is unfortunately fixed in real time and does not exist on the immortal plane of the collective unconscious. Thus the latest word on homosexuality found here in the literature, the various ideas just beginning to be developed, the promising currents of exploration and thought will undoubtedly be developed and amplified in the coming years. Indeed, the purpose of this book is to provide a touchstone or reference point for subsequent research and development in the field of analytical psychology and to spur further creative theorizing on not only the history and origins, but also the meaning and purpose, of love between men and between women. Literature reviews, and this one in particular, can function as they should only if their generalist character and planned obsolescence are acknowledged.

But now for the good news (which, interestingly enough, resembles the difficulties we will encounter): A great deal has been written on homosexuality by analytical psychologists from wide-ranging perspectives, some helpful, some not so helpful. The purpose in examining the various viewpoints is to isolate characteristically Jungian ways of approaching homoerotic relationships and homosexuality, and in this regard, even the not-so-helpful ways some Jungians have viewed homosexuality may actually be quite informative, since they bring to light how old conceptualizations, faulty ideas, or theoretical biases have obscured a true picture of the lives and loves of gay men and lesbians. A certain amount of sifting will need to be done to separate that which furthers our understanding of homosexuality from that which does not. As with all sifting, removing the chaff and retaining the living kernels of growth can be a delicate, artful process, and this is especially true with a subject so highly controversial psychologically, politically, religiously, spiritually, socially, and personally. However, the purpose of this examination is not primarily to critique; we are interested much more in those typically Jungian ways of approaching same-sex love that challenge contemporary views by going further, past the merely personal involvements of man with man, woman with woman, to discern the archetypal and transpersonal patterns being enacted in our passions and commitments with men and women.

Various ways of proceeding suggest themselves, but perhaps the clearest and most useful way is to stick to chronological order. For this reason we will begin with the first generation of Jungian analysts and what they wrote on homosexuality, and then go on in the second part of this chapter to survey the growing literature of sexuality and human relationships being produced by the second wave of analysts and writers familiar with Jung's work. Of course, to split the Jungian community into two generations is at least as artificial as any other method (for example, to organize by Jungian schools or by various theoretical views of homosexuality); since many of the analysts who knew Jung are still alive and writing today, there is not really much of a generation gap. Yet, as we shall see, those analysts who knew Jung or whose professional lives paralleled his in time tended to stay fairly close to certain of Jung's own ideas, while contemporary analysts (whose views we will examine in chapter 5) tend to hold more diverse theories about sexuality and homosexuality in particular. The reasons for this division are not that hard to fathom. For the most part those analysts who knew and studied under Jung were Europeans living in the early part of the twentieth century; many of the contemporary analysts who have turned their attention to issues of sexuality and Jungian psychology are North Americans who have lived through the enormous social changes of the 1960s and 1970s and seen the civil rights movement, feminism, and gay liberation leave indelible marks on psychological thought. Nonetheless, the division of first-generation from contemporary analysts ought not to be exaggerated, since its purpose is mainly didactic and individual exceptions abound.

With such an embarrassment of theoretical riches, a certain amount of sifting and discrimination must take place, and yet, to do only that smacks of the very reductionism Jung stood so firmly against. Thus, alongside our sifting, we will now and then attempt to blend as well—to see how certain views on homosexuality may be rounded out by other ways of thinking, to explore ways in which the many preliminary observations of the lives of gay men and women made by Jungian analysts may be developed into fullness, to bring to bear on later Jungian views of homosexuality other concepts put forth by Jung that lead to greater understanding.

HOMOSEXUALITY AND THE ARCHETYPAL FEMININE IN THE THOUGHT OF THE FIRST GENERATION

Of Jung's many followers, Erich Neumann holds a place of considerable importance, not only because of his long association with Jung himself but also because Neumann's writings provide important theoretical expositions of Jung's ideas. In the literature of analytical psychology, Neumann's works hold a central place because of their erudition and because of the depth of their intellectual understanding. Alongside *The Great Mother*, a work that can only be called monumental in its breadth, *The Origins and History of Consciousness* remains Neumann's most enduring contribution to Jungian thought, and so it is interesting to note that homosexuality is mentioned once in this work, in a footnote.

Neumann's purpose in this book is to trace the stages in the development of human consciousness out of unconsciousness, a process that is represented imaginally and mythologically by the ego's emergence from what Neumann calls the "uroboros," a primordial condition of self-contained unconsciousness symbolized by the circle of the snake devouring its own tail. Neumann's thesis in his work, based on creation myths from around the world and bolstered by his experience as an analyst, is that, as the ego consciousness differentiates itself from uroboric unconsciousness, the ego begins to experience this primordial unconsciousness both as the life-giving origin of its very existence and as an all-devouring threat to its newly won autonomy. This ambivalent experience of the unconscious by the emergent ego consciousness, Neumann finds, is often given imaginal shape in the ambivalent figure of the Great Mother, who, in bestowing all life, therefore holds both life and death, existence and nonexistence, in her all-powerful hands. For true autonomy to occur, therefore, Neumann sees that, mythologically, the domination of the Great Mother must be shaken off by individual ego consciousness, and he describes two subsequent stages in which this process occurs: first, what Neumann calls "the separation of the world parents," in which the opposites of masculinity and femininity emerge from the matrix of uroboric unity, and second, "the hero myth," in which the ego aligns itself with the principle of heroic masculinity in order to free itself from the dominance of the matriarchy.

Although this is perhaps an overly simple exposition of material that Neumann presents in great and persuasive detail, it is important to see that Neumann discusses the emergence of the hero within a very particular context, one in which the primordial Great Mother holds sway and from which masculinity must free itself through great struggle and strife. Thus, Neumann writes, "Male societies, secret societies and friendly societies originate in matriarchal conditions. They are the natural complement to the supremacy of the matriarchate," and in a footnote he mentions that "even today we almost always find, in cases of male homosexuality, a matriarchal psychology where the Great Mother is unconsciously in the ascendant."[1]

Now this altogether minor reference to homosexuality is of little theoretical interest in and of itself. Neumann's comment on the inner psychological situation of most homosexual men is actually not that far from at least one of Jung's theories concerning homosexuality and consequently seems to share implicitly in one of Jung's attitudes as well: Homosexuality, as a result of an identification with the archetypal feminine, represents a lack of psychological development and can be considered immature. This footnote therefore presents nothing new, nor does it intend to.

However, what this single footnote does point out is the danger in taking a single footnote too seriously without reading Jung fully on the subject of homosexuality. Without the foregoing review of all of Jung's writings on homosexuality, we would not know that Neumann's footnote here echoes but one theory of Jung's concerning homosexuality (homosexuality as a problem of unconscious feminine identification) and but one attitude of Jung's (homosexuality as developmentally immature). Nor, without reading Jung fully on the subject, would we know that Jung actually had somewhat more positive and potentially fertile ways of imagining the meaning of homosexuality in the life of the individual. To focus on a single footnote or a single writer or even a single passage in the literature of analytical psychology presents a danger, and as we shall soon see, even Jung's closest associates held a kaleidoscope of views.

For example, we read in Jung's longtime associate Jolande Jacobi's *The Way of Individuation:*

The influence of the intellectually independent and mature woman, who in this way became a dominating force and often pushed the father's authority into the background, can have an exceedingly oppressive effect on her children, particularly on boys. One knows countless cases where this influence unconsciously and unwittingly prevented the development of the masculine ego to full responsibility. The man then remains fixated on the level of a pubescent, not infrequently has homosexual leanings, and remains a *puer aeternus*, an infantile adult, for the rest of his life.[2]

And later in the same volume, seeming to follow Jung's lead in understanding how an inadequate masculine or feminine persona may create a dynamic of shadow projection, she writes,

The shadow qualities may appear personified in dreams. They often appear in projection, as the qualities of some object or person with whom there is a correspondingly strong positive or negative tie. Mostly they are projected on persons of the same sex as the projicient, as can be observed among brothers and sisters or pairs of friends (this is particularly striking in homosexual relationships). . . .[3]

In discussing the Jungian conception of the symbol in *Complex/Archetype/Symbol in the Psychology of C. G. Jung,* Jacobi again seems to characterize homosexuality as a problem of inadequate masculinity or femininity:

Or let us consider another problem which has taken on a particular urgency today, that of homosexuality. If it is taken not concretely but symbolically, one may discern in it a striving for union with an element of like sex, i.e., with the psychic aspect of oneself that has been experienced too little or not at all. Only then, fortified by this "increase" in his own sexual factor (whether male or female) does such an individual feel himself secure enough in his sex to be able to approach the opposite sex. Consequently his desire for a homosexual relationship is justified, but he misunderstands it by taking it in a biological and sexual, rather than a psychological and symbolic sense. To project it upon another individual, to experience it as a homosexual drive, is to misunderstand this desire and fail to see its profound meaning. Where this occurs, it can never come to a real fulfillment and can never, as it might with symbolic understanding, lead to an inner assimilation and resolution of the conflict.[4]

Thus it would seem that Jacobi simply develops to fullness a view that Neumann's footnote seems to imply: homosexuality as a problem, a misguided attempt at constituting for oneself true masculinity or femininity damaged by matriarchal domination, a problem of shadow projection, a kind of undesirable acting out. All of these theories and attitudes, as we know, are to be found in Jung and indeed are not among his most positive considerations of this phenomenon. Yet in the very next sentence Jacobi writes,

Aside from the small percentage of individuals who may definitely be designated as homosexual in a physical sense, there are no doubt certain types who come into the world with a homosexual psychic structure and who therefore can be "cured" by no form of treatment, psychotherapeutic or other.[5]

These brief excerpts from Jacobi's longer works are especially interesting since Jacobi is the author of one of the few contributions to the Jungian literature specifically on homosexuality, an article in the *Journal of Analytical Psychology* entitled "A Case of Homosexuality."[6] Although this piece is not cited nearly as often as some of the other articles on homosexuality published in Jungian journals (especially an article by John Layard to which we will turn later), the article is noteworthy for several reasons. First, it focuses on homosexuality as a major topic of exploration, something we have not yet seen either in Jung himself or in the Jungian literature. Second, it covers homosexuality both theoretically and clinically in the form of a detailed case study of the analysis of a young gay man over a period of some years, giving one a very clear sense of how one world-renowned Jungian analyst dealt with a homosexual client over a long period of treatment. Third, and perhaps most interesting given the time in which this piece was published, the high positive regard and understanding she shows her analysand and her conclusions regarding homosexuality all reflect that which is most unique and powerful in Jung's own clinical and theoretical perspectives.

Jacobi again follows Jung's lead in many ways. She mentions in the first paragraph of her case study Jung's suggestion that homosexuality is "nature's way of attempting to regulate the excessive rise in the birthrate."[7] Likewise, she includes a brief historical note concerning the existence of homosexuality in ancient Egypt, Crete, Greece, and Rome and in the Christian Middle Ages, putting the phenomenon into that historical-cultural perspective so typical of Jung himself. She goes further than Jung, however, in this regard. Because of the date of her writing, she has available to her some of the empirical research on human sexual behavior that brought about the contemporary revision of thinking on sexuality and homosexuality. In particular, Jacobi is familiar with Ford and Beach's research on patterns of sexual behavior, with the English translation of Magnus Hirschfeld's work on "sexual anomalies and perversions" (the outdated language belies Hirschfeld's quite nonjudgmental approach to homosexuality and other variations in sexuality), and, finally, with Kinsey's famous study *Sexual Behavior in the Human Male*, from which she cites the statistics that "37 per cent of all men in the United States have had homosexual experience at some time" and that "in the case of young people during adolescence (60 per cent, according to Kinsey, ibid.), homosexuality is widespread, although the practice is given up in most instances upon reaching adulthood." On the basis of this research, she takes issue with the prejudicial stereotype of homosexuality as resulting from adolescent seductions: "In my opinion—and many authors confirm this—the so-called seductions to which many young people are exposed only initiate permanent homosexual practice if the individual was already constitutionally predisposed to homosexuality."[8] Here again we hear an echo of Jung, in particular his theory of homosexuality as a constitutional condition and the lack of judgment which Jung and Jacobi seem to share.

Thus, if one takes Jacobi as an example of subsequent Jungian thought on homosexuality, there is much to be commended. She has neither shut her eyes to contemporary empirical research nor seen it necessary to jettison some of Jung's more positive attitudes and theories, such as the potentially helpful biological function homosexuality serves in human life, the ubiquity of homosexual relationships in modern and ancient history, and the basic nature of a homosexual orientation for certain individuals.

Lest one should get the idea, however, that Jacobi has turned into a gay liberation advocate, the section of her article that follows this introduction balances the rather positive views of homosexuality by looking at "causation" and focusing on what could only be called negative explanations. Etiological theories, as we have noted, can have only a negative tinge, since they are linked to the medical model of curing a disease by determining its cause. Despite Jacobi's obvious goodwill, her review of the etiological theories of her time reads like a list of psychopathologies. Among those factors that seem, in her experience, to "contribute significantly" to homosexuality, Jacobi notes families with histories of psychological disturbances, disturbed relationships to parents (especially strong mothers and absent or harshly rejecting fathers), fear of women or sexuality, something she calls a "general fear of life resulting from maturational failure," and, finally, absence of "feminine company," as in prison or the military. She then goes on to note Freudian psychoanalytic views concerning the neurotic nature of homosexuality, its relationship to paranoia, and the complex disturbances of ego in homosexuals and continues with Medard Boss's existential view that homosexuality is a "narrowing of the entire mode of human existence" and the result of a weak ego.

From Jung, she quotes a personal communication to the effect that

> homosexuality had to do with a shadow problem; that is with a repressed, undifferentiated element of masculinity in the man and of femininity in the woman which, instead of being developed on a psychological level from the depths of the individual's own psyche, is sought on a biological plane through "fusion" with an-

other man or another woman, as the case may be. This takes place either through identification with the mother in order to be loved by the father, or by seeking fusion, or identification, with the father in order to gain greater strength to possess a woman. In the case of most homosexuals, both forms occur alternately, according to whether the feminine or masculine role is assumed in homosexual relations. It is known that the integration of the shadow, and thus the masculinity which is lacking, gives a feeling of security and strength, and results in the courage necessary to approach the other sex.[9]

The result of conflating such a plethora of views is, as one can see, utter confusion. These one-sidedly negative explanations of homosexuality make one wonder if such etiological theories may not simply be fantastic psychologizing in the service of restating the cultural value of heterosexuality as the approved social norm while attempting to thrust on homosexuality heterosexuality's own shadow: familial disturbances, fear and hatred of women in a patriarchal culture, and the psychological immaturity that can be hidden in a conventional heterosexual relationship because of its culturally approved status.

This section of Jacobi's paper exemplifies precisely why etiological research on homosexuality has fallen out of favor in recent times. First, it is virtually impossible to undertake such research in a culture that values heterosexuality without starting from a basically negative point of view. Second, the complicated interaction between, on the one hand, the environmental influences that come to bear on psychosexual development, gender identity, and sex roles and, on the other, whatever constitutional predispositions may exist in any individual renders any conclusions little more than imaginative speculations. Freudians have their network of etiological mythology, existentialists theirs, and Jung and Jungians their own, and no camp can definitively prove that its views are any more empirically truthful than those of the rival mythologies. Indeed, the explanations Jacobi lists are often self-contradictory. If an absent father and an overly present, harsh father can both cause homosexuality, if homosexuals seek both fusion with women and fusion with men, little clarity is gained on the specific causes of homosexuality. Surely every boy with such a father has not turned out to be homosexual, nor does a heterosexual male's search for fusion with women or his sense of camaraderie with his male companions at a touch football game generally come under the category of psychopathology. Such theoretical excogitations, however fruitful for one's imagination, are not the result of a scientific process of inquiry and so these theories of causation are of little use in treatment. This obviates the need for developing an etiological theory at all.

Jacobi, to her credit, seems to sense the can of worms that is opened when attempting to determine causation for a phenomenon as complicated as human sexual behavior and in the section entitled "Prognosis and Treatment" she moves swiftly away from these contradictory and somewhat fabulous etiological theories to consider homosexuality from the point of view of the individual patient, which has always been analytical psychology's strongest suit. She minces no words when acknowledging the psychological effect of social prejudice on gay men and women:

> In many instances, homosexual men share the psychological fate of immigrants, of illegitimate children, of members of minority groups or other types of outsiders. They almost always feel themselves to be rejected, even despised, and they have corresponding inferiority complexes, leading often to feelings of persecution that may be justified since they are condemned on the basis of religious and moral principles.[10]

And she offers with utmost seriousness the conclusion that "on the basis of my experience . . . there are homosexuals whose constitutions are such that there is no possibility of their being anything other than what they are, whether it is a question of heredity or environment." Working from this conclusion, she is of the opinion that

> it is no wonder that in the cases where a homosexual eventually marries, the marriage may not work out satisfactorily in the sexual sphere. . . . This naturally provides no gratification for the woman who is longing for eros. So one should not be too ready to assume that marriage for men with a homosexual past or with homosexual tendencies provides the proper solution. Too many dangers of destroying the married life are entailed. It would be even less desirable for such a marriage to be undertaken as a cover for homosexual practices.[11]

Having seen "about 60 homosexuals for one or two consultations or for lengthy treatment," she puts forth with great modesty her goals for treatment:

> Evidence of unequivocal homosexuality is soon given by the dreams of such individuals. . . . I soon decided *not* to discuss tendencies or experience with my patients, but rather to concentrate on the psychological task of their maturation, without concern for their continuing to seek men's company. . . .
>
> Homosexuals are often artistic, or intellectually gifted, individuals. It has been my immediate aim to awaken this aspect in these often despondent, unhappy, self-persecuted and self-despising persons in order to endow their lives with meaning, to establish them firmly in a satisfying profession and to raise their self-esteem.
>
> In this way, they were able to break away from the ruinous pattern of chance encounters in the sexual sphere, which unfortunately lead frequently to the most saddening and sordid form of homosexuality, and devote their affection to one man in a lasting and also fruitful relationship. I have thus experienced time and again where it was not possible to effect a transformation to heterosexuality—and it has been possible with certainty in perhaps only six cases (10 per cent) of those I have seen, at least a spiritually higher state could be attained which once again made their lives meaningful and worth living.[12]

The case Jacobi discusses in this paper is that of Werner, a "timid, soft and pale young man," twenty-four years old when he first consulted Jacobi. She saw him for varying lengths of time over the course of approximately eight years. As she puts it, "Both sides of the family had histories of severe psychological disturbance" and "there was no member of the family that did not show some abnormality."

As for Werner himself, he "was an idealist and a dreamer—as are so many homosexuals." At age sixteen, he had a homosexual experience on vacation with a roommate and considered his proclivity for masturbation and homosexual fantasies a sexual "derailment." Continually disappointed in his attempts with girls, "finally he came to hate women," and yet lived out his homosexuality in fantasy only, without any physical experiences. He came to Jacobi with the hope of "becoming 'normal' and of being able to fall in love with a woman." Jacobi reports a series of Werner's dreams early on during their treatment, dreams that allude to both a negative mother complex and homosexual fantasies about a neighbor, and their conversations centered primarily on childhood memories and his attempt at a heterosexual adaptation. After an operation for phimosis, which was followed by a long period of pain and bleeding (Jacobi does not call attention to the obvious expiatory significance of the patient's voluntary submission to such an operation after an unsuccessful attempt to seduce a coworker's wife), Werner, she reports, was somewhat less conflicted and shame-ridden about his homosexual desires. For her part, she says:

> I took no stand and let him—though with heavy heart—continue to fight his battle, anxious as to what the outcome would be. I reflected that he needed to feel free, uncriticized and accepted by me as he was and that I should not interfere.[13]

The period following the operation found Werner more actively pursuing men "out of longing to have platonic discussions," and with the onset of a prolonged bout of insomnia Jacobi encouraged Werner to paint his insomnia. Her suggestion of painting was a breakthrough in treatment, allowing Werner to contact feeling, life, and instinct through the medium of art and bringing him much inner satisfaction. Her interpretations of Werner's many paintings, based largely on his own words, have much more to do with what one might call Werner's individuation process, his process of becoming more inwardly centered and at peace with himself, than with issues of sexual orientation, which in his outer life vacillated between heterosexual disappointments and platonic fascinations with men. In a statement that may be taken as Jacobi's principal attitude toward Werner's analysis, she writes:

> Without criticizing or preaching, I accompanied him on the right paths, as well as on what I took to be the wrong ones which he followed. I pointed out the advantages and disadvantages of all that confronted him, and tried, with genuine sympathy, to stress the final, prospective aspects of all his sufferings and experiences. He felt that I believed in him and in his chances. Slowly, he became aware he did not have a place in the outer world, but in his

own inner world "between being a man and woman," that basically he was a homosexual. His relationship to men was examined closely and he perceived that when he loved he pursued his partner constantly with jealousy, nagging, curiosity and romantic ideas, but that at the same time, he made a victim of himself, in purely masochistic terms, since he singled out sadistic men as his best friends. . . . He then began an earnest struggle with his shadow. This was early in 1951.[14]

Jacobi is careful to report the various details of Werner's treatment and growth that do not have to do directly with his homosexuality: the development of his interest in music, his love for travel, advancements and setbacks in his career, his separation and individuation from his family, the development of an inner religious strength and prayer life. When not in treatment, Werner maintained regular contact with Jacobi through letters and nonprofessional visits, and the two major changes of Werner's life that Jacobi reports have nothing to do with sexuality—his attainment of financial stability and his ability to be "an open, happy and sociable person." After a final period of analytic work, in which he struggled to integrate the shadow side of his masculinity and relinquish the victim role at the hands of sadistic men, Jacobi reports his settling on a successful career at a concert hall and mentions that while preparing her paper she telephoned him for news on his life. In his words, she reports:

> "Things are going marvellously; I'm very satisfied and would never have imagined that I could have worked as I now have to. But it's wonderful to be able to do it. My private life has also settled down. For two years now I have had a very dear friend, a Spaniard, with whom I have much in common artistically. With him I have been able to reconcile both sides of my life. I love him physically, it is true, but that is secondary. The important thing is our spiritual contact."[15]

In conclusion, Jacobi states her judgment that she considers his case a "relative success." She continues:

> When one has treated as many homosexuals as I have, one becomes modest. . . . These individuals require, in particular, a great deal of love, understanding and protection, perhaps much more than others. They are unfortunate individuals, but in most

cases are highly gifted. If this latter aspect of their personality can be awakened, the chances for recovery are better; if this awakening does not occur, such individuals are subject to depression and neurosis. I was deeply grateful that Werner was able to free himself from this threat. Could I wish for anything more than his statement that he was happy and content in his work? Great progress had been made and considerable maturity achieved. However, whether Werner ever finds his way to a woman lies in the hands of fate.[16]

We have examined this article at great length to point out that in following Jung's lead, Jacobi abandons all theoretical presuppositions and allows her patient the individuation process that is his and his alone, focusing not simply on the homosexuality but on all the other facets of Werner's life that need development and consolidation. Even with regard to the homosexuality in the case, she shares Jung's attitude that the expression of the homosexuality is much more at issue than the homosexuality itself. For example, the patient's sadomasochistic wishes and relationships are not seen as characteristic of homosexuality per se, but rather understood as issues derived from an unintegrated shadow masculinity that needs contact with the patient's conscious ideals and spiritual development. Though she certainly makes no secret of the value she places on heterosexual relations, never does this value intrude on the treatment, and she is quite satisfied that Werner has found a companion who has made him happy.

Still, for all her sensitivity and care, she remains a woman of her time. We notice that Jacobi, in spite of the literature at her disposal, does not question the value she places on heterosexuality and tends to characterize homosexuals as a class in somewhat pathetic terms: "unfortunates," "soft," "overly feminine," "sensitive," "weak." Both the case she chooses to present and the way in which she presents it give support to Jung's idea that homosexuality is the result of a problematic unconscious identification with the feminine, resulting in psychosexual immaturity. She shows little consciousness, despite her own historical survey, that homosexuality may be a normal variation of human sexuality, and she does not question Western culture's condemnation of homosexuality, though she does arrive at the conclusion that the low self-esteem and neuroticism gay patients present may be justified given their status as despised outsiders in society. Jacobi is certainly far from homophobic, and she is thoroughly involved in her own way in helping gay men and women come to terms with who they are, and not who they have been told to be. Yet she lacks the critical sociocultural perspective that would allow her to change her own way of thinking on homosexuality, rather than focus on how her homosexual patients may or may not change. This omission of a sociopolitical analysis that would put the analyst's own cultural values into question first seems to be the downside of analytical psychology's exclusive and overriding concern with the individual and the archetypal, especially as it applies to homosexuality. The result, evident from even such a positive case study as this one, is that a judicious and talented analyst such as Jolande Jacobi may come off as faintly condescending toward the very patients she so clearly cares for and hopes to help.

This same difficulty appears in the work of another analyst long associated with Jung, M. Esther Harding, who is similarly positively disposed to homosexuality and who tends to focus on female homosexuality in her works. For example, in the revised edition of *The Way of All Women*, a book on the psychology of women and feminine individuation, Harding's chapter "Friendship" contains three references to homosexuality. First, in discussing the relationship between Eros and friendship between women, she comments:

> Attraction between members of the same sex, based on a feeling rapport, is a usual condition among both boys and girls during their adolescent years, when these friendships form their closest emotional ties; they are living through a homosexual phase which is entirely normal. Later in life, friendship and love for some member of the other sex usually displaces this earlier love but the phase of emotional development which gives rise to these friendships is not confined to early youth. The instinctual love of which it is a manifestation may yield its *primary* place to another instinctual bond, but love for friends usually persists throughout life and is often of great importance in the emotional experience of the individual.[17]

She further remarks that "in these modern times when the period of immaturity is greatly prolonged, the emotional develop-

ment of young people is often correspondingly retarded. . . .
Retarded development of this kind will account for a certain number of homosexual friendships among women, but hardly for all."
She goes on to notice how in certain periods of time, such as the
Greece of Plato's time and the chivalrous Middle Ages, friendships between men served to create an "increase in the strength
and significance of the manly virtues and a corresponding de-
crease in the purely physical involvement of men in instinctual
satisfaction with women."[18]

The echo of Jung rings clearly here. Homosexuality is not condemned or treated reductively, but neither is it implied that it is
a mature choice. Yet later in this same chapter Harding points
out the imprecision of the word *homosexual* and comes closer to
some of Jung's more positive attitudes:

> The word *homosexual* is used today, however, in many senses, so
> that in any discussion of friendships between two people of the
> same sex it is necessary to make clear exactly what is meant.
>
> The emotional involvement in a friendship may be intense in
> its character and yet be without physical expression. For love be-
> tween women does not necessarily involve physical sexuality.
> Viewed from one angle such a friendship would not be called ho-
> mosexual. Yet for women who have no sexual expression in their
> lives the repressed instinct is bound to color their major relation-
> ship and give it that quality of emotionality which is the earmark
> of erotic involvement even though no overt sexual acts or even
> conscious sexual impulses are present. . . . In other cases the
> love between friends may find its expression in a more specifically
> sexual fashion which, however, cannot be considered perverted if
> their actions are motivated by love.
>
> There is unfortunately no word in general use which makes
> clear the distinction between these two situations. If it were not
> for the sinister connotation which clings to the term *homosexu-
> ality*, it might not be necessary to make a clear-cut distinction,
> but it does not seem right to refer to friendships of either charac-
> ter by a term which is linked in the mind of the public with de-
> based practices and criminality, for they are often of a high moral
> and ethical quality. Yet in the absence of any other term, *homo-
> sexual* must serve.
>
> In judging of any sexual relationship, whether homosexual or
> heterosexual, it must always be borne in mind that the quality of
> the emotion involved is the criterion of value rather than the na-

ture of the accompanying physical expression. It is necessary to be cautious how we apply the term *perversion*.[19]

However, at the end of this chapter on women's friendships she writes:

> The increase of homosexual friendships among women must be considered as a transitional phase of civilization. Perhaps it is *womanhood* that is passing through adolescence in regard to individual development. This trend in society is, perhaps, a symptom of human evolution, while in each particular friendship, the friends may become mature—rounded out psychologically—through this very experience.
>
> These movements must be regarded without prejudice. We must seek their psychological goal and significance—their creative quota—and not regard them from the *a priori* standards with which they conflict. . . . Marriage represents an adaptation to the sexual and reproductive instincts of humanity and is, without question, a mature adaptation on the biological plane. But the step back is, as we have seen, related to a movement directed toward a psychological development in women by which a more conscious and differentiated relationship becomes possible. The movement is biologically a regression, but psychologically has a progressive significance. . . . Regarded from a psychological and cultural angle, it reveals itself as a *reculer pour mieux sauter*—a drawing back to get a fresh start. For through this step many a woman in the past has succeeded in escaping from the condition which demanded that she live only as a man's counterpart. . . . This movement of society may foreshadow the development of the woman of the future—indeed of womanhood itself—out of the condition of psychological one-sidedness which her unconscious relation to man has imposed, into a freer life in which she will find herself as a conscious and complete individual.[20]

The feminist bent of these statements is unmistakable, and Harding's passionate plea for neutrality and clear-sightedness was undoubtedly influenced by her own relationships to women, in which she experienced the Eros of which she writes. Yet, one sees in these passages what we have previously seen in Jung: how extraordinary tolerance and an intense appreciation for the goodness and potential in even "regressive" phenomena can coexist with faintly damning appraisals of homosexuality as immature, retarded, adolescent. While such nondogmatic thinking does permit the kind of room for individuality and positive development that both Jacobi and Harding advocate—trademarks, as it were, of Jung's own clinical approach—the larger theoretical issues concerning homosexuality and its place in the modern Western world go untouched. In characteristically refraining from making definitive statements or from taking to heart critical perspectives derived from fields outside of individual psychology proper, Jacobi and Harding do a disservice to their own goodwill.

The late 1950s saw the appearance of a trio of articles by Jungian analysts on homosexuality and related topics in the *Journal of Analytical Psychology*. The most important and most frequently cited of these articles is John Layard's, entitled "Homo-Eroticism in Primitive Society As a Function of the Self." As Layard states in the first paragraph, his research focuses on the concept that the "organization of primitive society [is] an externalized form of what we think of as the self," and his intention in the article is to elucidate its "homo-erotic aspect."[21]

Layard's thesis is that the network of interrelationships that form the kinship organization of what he (in imitation of Jung) calls primitive societies may be understood as "an externalized psychic mandala," with the inner psychic wholeness and structure of the individual represented in the outward social structure of kinship relations. As he states it, "They, the inner and the outer, are the dual manifestations of the same all-embracing phenomenon of human development, which in this case has its external manifestation in the kinship system and its internal manifestation in the psychic organization of each individual composing it. . . . Our present concern is with the basic pattern, and in particular the homo-erotic side of it: that which, so often unperceived, builds up society."[22]

Layard goes on to describe the way primitive communities in Australia arrange marriages according to two principles, the first of external endogamy (marrying within one's own community), the second of internal exogamy (marrying outside of one's own social group within the tribe), so that each marriage at the same time represents a union of patrilineal and matrilineal opposites while avoiding any literal incestuous relationship between husband and wife. Layard focuses on a pattern he calls near-incest, the double marriage of men from two different social groups who exchange sisters for wives, a pattern that, when continued over generations, creates an extraordinarily complex, mandalalike set of interrelationships that simultaneously creates and avoids incestuous pairings.

In looking at the rigor of this kind of arrangement, Layard writes:

> Society, that is the kinship mandala, is thus so much more important than the individual that children, while free to make any temporary sexual unions they like so long as they do not publicly violate the framework of the incest taboos, have no say whatever in the choice of a marriage partner.
>
> This being the case, the whole of collective society, though implemented by the men, functions as a "male mother" demanding total obedience from her sons. It must be borne in mind in what follows with regard to homo-erotic relationships that grow up under these conditions that, though these may appear on the surface to be "accidental" in the psychological meaning of the term, they are no more so than are the pathological homosexual relationships which grow up in our own society as a result of personal as well as of impersonal factors in contrast to the collectively dominating "male mother" constellated in the kinship system.[23]

The homoerotic relationship to which Layard refers is the pair of brothers-in-law who are related through marriage to each other's sister and each of whom is at the same time his wife's brother and his sister's husband. Significantly, the so-called homoeroticism of this brother-in-law relationship has very little to do with any homosexual desires of the two brothers-in-law for each other; rather, it is implicit in the way

> each fulfills the other's sister-incest desire. There is thus, apart from any other considerations, the closest bond between them [the brothers-in-law] of the greatest ambivalence. On the one hand they are affinal allies, each being the other's wife's brother. On the other hand (though this is of course repressed) as sister's husbands, they are the intensest sex rivals, each having supplanted the other in the fulfillment of his own sister-incest desire.[24]

In contrast to this near-incestuous, homoerotic relationship, Layard goes on to discuss true homosexual relationships between men and boys. In social systems where polygamy causes a dearth of wives, the betrothal of unborn infants to guarantee men "wives" sometimes results, when the infant turns out to be a boy, in a "marriage" between man and boy. Layard relies on the "prudish delicacy" of descriptions by English anthropologists of the Victorian era to allude to certain vague initiatory rites involving anal intercourse, semen rubbing, and hair exchanges. Yet another form of true homosexual relationship Layard reports as occurring between

> the hopeful bridegroom and the prospective bride's brother . . . if the girl is born but not yet nubile. An elder brother of the girl may become the boy-lover of the man, and will return to his own people when the girl is ready to be married. . . . In this way it is not only sisters who are exchanged for wives, but it may be also their brothers.
>
> We may now see the added complication in the relation between these brothers-in-law: that each, while *after* marriage fulfilling the other's sister-incest desire, by marrying this other one's sister, *before* marriage fulfils it in his own person.
>
> We thus find in this primitive kinship source external evidence of what has long been suspected psychologically regarding homosexual intercourse as an incest-substitute.[25]

This conclusion leads Layard to see the homoeroticism or the expressed homosexuality of such relationships as "shadow-phenomena" with "the incestuous element of man's desire transferred from women on to men, forming that psychic bond between men which is the foundation of society. This may include overt sex relations, or it may not. In the areas under consideration, it does";[26] Layard adjudges such relationships characteristic of "primitive" societies, though not inherently negative. After alluding to ancient Greek society, in which love relationships between men and boys were institutionalized and aided the development of civilization, Layard states:

> There is little doubt that [love] begins in primitive society not heterosexually between men and women, but between men and men, in this case between the man-lover and the boy-lover who is his own sister-substitute and the man-lover's wife-substitute.
>
> It is much later in the history of culture that such love (as op-

posed to purely sexual relationship) gets transferred back on to women as wives.[27]

Expectably, given this context, Layard goes on to discuss in great detail the initiatory symbolism and function of homosexual relationships between older and younger men, such as the belief that the anal injection of semen promotes growth and masculinity and therefore serves both physical and psychological functions in native societies or the way in which the older lover is charged with the education and socialization of the boy-lover, a situation that may result in "extreme homosexual jealousy." As Layard puts it, "such cases obviously verge on the pathological."[28] The novice-tutor relationship in the Small Islands is detailed, including the way in which the initiates are treated as women until a number of trials are undergone over a period of nine months—a symbol for the potential psychic impregnation with masculinity that, for Layard, is at the core of the initiation. Anal penetration by ancestral spirits seems a part of this belief system, representing not simply impregnation with mature masculinity but also impregnation with the collective spirit of the tribe.

Layard ends by recounting the New Guinea myth of the origin of sodomy, in which Kambel, a father god who is both a male originator and identified with the moon, sodomizes his son, Gufa, to promote the son's growth. Layard discusses this myth of divine father-son incest symbolically, pointing out how

> the ultimate purpose of all incest taboo is not only to expand society, but to create within the psyche precisely that which has been tabooed externally. In the case of the matrilineal incest taboo, this is the anima. The anima is for a man, however, mainly a go-between or mediating function for the realization of his own "shadow" or inner masculinity, which is the ultimate goal of his own development.
>
> The patrilineal incest taboo is in fact what all this homosexuality is concerned with, particularly on its fantasy side. . . . The Son thus has the Father both inside him and without, so that we have here adumbrated in this very primitive myth the highest doctrine of "the Father in Me and I in him" with the symbolic semen fulfilling the same function as the Holy Spirit (the spirits of the ancestors) which is the carrier of love between the Father and the

Son. This impregnates and anoints the son, the shadow-figure that at first sight always appears so odd or bad or disappointing but that is known to show forth the figure of the potential Savior under such disguise.

All this occurs in primitive mythology alongside the most flagrant misconceptions and abuses. This is a phenomenon not confined to New Guinea or to the "primitives." We have it flourishing among ourselves.[29]

The point of that last, somewhat alarmed paragraph seems to be that the literalization of this homosexuality, which Layard would like to see remain on a purely psychic level, makes for "misconceptions and abuses." Amazingly, Layard closes by quoting Paul's diatribe from the Letter to the Romans on the psychic-spiritual consequences of homosexuality when it is literally enacted rather than understood as a sacred, symbolic showing forth of the Father God.

While this article cannot be criticized for its scholarship and clarity, the attitudes Layard brings to his material and the conclusions he reaches are highly questionable. A number of presuppositions fairly jump off the page in certain of these discussions. His bias toward Western values is particularly obvious in the use of the word *primitive* to characterize these cultures. This term is a kind of Jungian convention that began with Jung himself and to some degree survives even today in the Jungian literature. Unfortunately, the use of the word *primitive*, no matter how dispassionately intended, implies a specious developmental schema in which nonwhite, non-European, nontechnological cultures are understood as inferior to white, European, technologically developed societies. Layard is explicit about this attitude in a number of places: for example, his characterizing homoeroticism in these cultures as a manifestation of an immature phase of development before sexual desire is transferred "back" on to women, or terming "misconceptions and abuses" those initiatory enactments of homosexuality that are not scientifically based (such as male impregnation, semen used to impart virility, and so on). Should there be any doubt as to the underlying attitude of Western superiority, Layard quotes Paul's condemnation of heathen sexual practices, against which Paul set Christian sexual ethics as a superior example. This attitude, though understated in Layard and perhaps unavoidable given the date of the piece, nevertheless influences how he approaches the homoeroticism he intends to examine. His reminder that such practices are not limited to "primitive" societies but are also "flourishing" among us has the kind of alarmed tone that might make objectivity difficult, and, despite Layard's best intentions the implication is that homoeroticism and institutionalized homosexuality, in the author's opinion, are a "primitive" phenomenon, whether found in native cultures or among more "civilized" people.

Clearly, when one ceases to judge societies on a scale running from primitive to civilized, one is no more justified in characterizing institutionalized homosexuality in native cultures as primitive, undeveloped, or ill-conceived than one would be in characterizing any cultural phenomenon, such as marriage or food rituals, as primitive simply because it plays an important part in native cultures. Further, one is even less justified in leaping to judgments about such phenomena in contemporary culture on the basis of what appears to be their significance in native cultures. Layard does not go this far explicitly, but one must wonder about the purpose of his research into homoeroticism in native society if it is not to be applied to homoeroticism in Western societies. The danger of such facile connections between native cultures and our own should be clear. Even if archetypal parallels between cultures seem obvious, the influence of the cultural values of the researcher and the cultural milieu of the researched peoples cannot be so easily sidestepped. Given the vastly underresearched (for that time) nature of homoeroticism in Western societies, one regrets that Layard and other Jungians did not put their hand sooner to the more relevant task of the archetypal themes that appear to undergird contemporary homoeroticism and the gay culture of the twentieth-century Western world.

Another bias of Layard's, which, as we have seen, was shared by Jung, is the idea that all individuals are born heterosexual and that heterosexuality alone is normative human sexual behavior. Because of this assumption, Layard takes great pains to show how the institutionalized homoeroticism, enacted or not, in the kinship relations that he examines is actually a defense against heterosexual incest wishes, which renders the homosexuality of the male-male relationships subordinate to the incestuous heterosexuality that Layard presupposes. While this explanation of homosexuality as the result of thwarted heterosexual incest wishes may certainly be true of the homoeroticized brother-in-law relationships of the Australian tribes Layard examines, the existence of homosexual attraction as a normal variation in human sexuality opens the door to another interpretation.

Is it not equally possible that the homoeroticism which Layard senses in the double-brother-in-law relationships is actually the primary phenomenon, with the sister-swapping being but a secondary phenomenon determined by the attraction of the men to each other? Later in the article, Layard himself notices how love develops at first homosexually in native societies and only later, if ever, takes heterosexual form. To see homosexuality as the primary phenomenon and heterosexuality as secondary fits every bit as well with the extreme ambivalence of this kinship relationship, in which the two men are seen both as one person and as the intensest rivals (a characteristic of every love relationship), and has a further advantage as well: It accepts the homoeroticism for what it is rather than reducing it to a derivative of heterosexuality. Layard's theoretical contortions on this point seem to come from the idea that all men are created heterosexual and the result of such thinking is that intimate male-male relationships can only be characterized as fraught with shadow, phenomena subordinate to "real" relationships, which, as this heterosexist bias would have it, occur only between man and woman, brother and sister, mother and son, father and daughter. To hold a one-sided position in favor of heterosexuality as normal, especially if such a position is held unconsciously and unthinkingly, necessitates the projection of shadow onto sexual deviations, such as homosexuality. The problem that Layard faces even in this short article, however, is the question of what we are to make of all the initiatory symbolism so clearly designed to strengthen native societies and assure their continuation. Can this be just shadow? Here Layard seems to forget how much this homoeroticism really does serve a function of the Self in native societies, especially in the way that collective masculinity is handed down and made individual through institutionalized homosexual relationships. Why must all this rich homoeroticism be understood—especially by a Jungian—as nothing but sublimation, perversion, or abuse?

If Layard wishes to show how homoerotic male relationships are simply the enactment of shadow issues, a sign of primitive, inferior masculinity, then he is using the wrong set of anthropological data. Clearly much more is occurring in all the other instances of institutionalized male-male homosexual relationships that he reports later in his article. In these, the older-younger male pairings have at least as much to do with embodying a communal sense of manhood, a positive, progressive social function, as with defending the younger men against the engulfment of the feminine and protecting them from their putative desire for heterosexual incest. The creative symbolism of the initiation rituals has at least as much to do with the fecundating power of the male, embodied in the various rites centered on semen, as with the life-giving but engulfing power of the female. Indeed, Kambel, the sodomizing father of the New Guinea myth, is identified both with the feminine symbol of the moon and with the principle of male agency, as first originator and father of all.

Any attempt, therefore, to paint homosexuality simply as a primitive throwback to a stage in human development when men bonded with men to cast off the tyranny of a matriarchal Great Mother (as implied, for example, by Neumann's footnote and its context), as an inferior coupling between childish, matriarchally dominated boy-men who have yet to locate their own phallic powers, will find little clear support in the data Layard reports. In fact, Layard's article serves only to point out the unconscious bias that lies behind such conclusions. By characterizing native cultures as primitive, by holding that heterosexuality is humanity's only normal form of sexual behavior, and by viewing matriarchy as an engulfing, devouring entity to be defended against, Layard's article is considerably less than useful in looking at contemporary homosexuality from an archetypal perspective.

What seems much clearer from Layard's article—and what is supported by all the more recent cross-cultural studies of homosexuality—is that native societies, despite the apparent rigor of their social divisions, do not differentiate between male and female, heterosexual and homosexual, brother and sister, father and mother quite as cleanly or clearly, psychologically or symbolically, as more technologically developed societies attempt to. For this reason, the use of such terms as *homoerotic* is slightly misplaced, implying a distinction between homosexual and heterosexual, male and female that the native societies do not seem to make, in word or in deed. An example of this different set of gender categories is the kinship terms that Layard holds up for our consideration, all male-female composites in which female defines male: wife's brother, sister's husband.

The homoerotic practices, beliefs, and myths that Layard reports tell us a great deal about the way masculinity and femininity are closely intertwined in these cultures and are not nearly so separate or hostile as the modern Western "civilized" war of the sexes would lead us to believe. The fluidity of gender categories and the flexibility of sex roles in these societies, if looked at objectively, should make one wonder more about the rigidity and repression of our own culture and whether our myths truly serve to develop the full masculine or feminine capacities in young men and women. Far from proving the existence of homoeroticism as a defense against incestuous wishes or matriarchal domination, Layard's data seem to suggest that the fluid sexual relations and gender identities of these societies come more out of a connection to the oneness of the androgyne Self than out of any compensatory, shadow-ridden, masculine protest. That Layard did not make this point more forcefully, as the title of the article suggests he might have, is unfortunate.

I have gone into great detail concerning the strengths and weaknesses of Layard's work because the dearth of Jungian literature on homosexuality leads to frequent citation of this piece, especially in support of the contention that homosexuality is a regressive phenomenon linked to the archetypal struggle of the immature male to throw off matriarchal domination through a bonding with other men intended to strengthen such "inferior" masculinity.[30] Examination of this article shows that Layard's patriarchal and heterosexist biases make both his reports of the data and his conclusions of questionable use. Much more usable, from a Jungian perspective, though unfortunately largely ignored, is the more recent anthropological literature on homosexuality and homoerotic relationships in non-Western cultures, often based on the experiences of gay researchers as participants who, because of their own sexual orientation, have access to material long held back from white male heterosexual anthropologists and psychologists.[31] Nevertheless, more up-to-date and creative Jungian thought on the relationships between homosexuality and the homoeroticism of native initiation practices can be found in the excellent collection of articles entitled *Betwixt and Between: Patterns of Masculine and Feminine Initiation*.[32] In chapter 5, we will be looking at this more modern anthropological research along Jungian lines to see what symbolic material the research has uncovered that was, regrettably, not available to Layard at the time of his writing. Ironically enough, as we shall see, what these contemporary researchers find differs little from Layard's experience, which, indeed, forms the basic contention of his article: that homosexual relationships between men serve an important and sometimes central function in native societies.

Before we conclude our survey of the writings of first-generation analysts on homosexuality with Marie-Louise von Franz and her work on the *puer*, the other two articles on homosexuality that appeared in the 1950s in the *Journal of Analytical Psychology* merit some brief attention, though neither is particularly searching or extensive. In "The Therapeutic Function of the Homosexual Transference," by G. Stewart Prince, which appeared in the same issue as Layard's article in 1959, Prince "focuses upon the significance of the latent homosexual orientation for symptomformation, its influence upon the transference, and in particular the part it plays in the therapeutic process."[33] In reporting a series of dreams of a young man in his late twenties, Prince follows the vicissitudes of the idealizing and hostile transferences his patient developed toward him and looks at the homosexual overtones of each, particularly the way the patient's repressed homosexual feelings are infiltrated with anal aggression, which is then defended against through idealization and sexual attraction. Thus, Prince reports no new formulation of homosexuality and, in fact, makes a point of remarking on the similarity of his views to Layard's ideas of homosexual attraction as a manifestation of primitive, inferior masculinity, a shadow-ridden search for "real" masculinity outside oneself. Prince reports that a working through of the anal-aggressive material led to a fairly stable love relationship with a woman, only to have the patient's homosexual feelings and transference to Prince stimulated once again by a chance meeting with an idealized tutor from his student days, just at a time when analysis needed to be terminated by the patient's decision to accept a job abroad. Again, in both the adoption of Freudian-psychoanalytic formulations concerning homosexuality, apparent in the idea of homosexuality as defense against anal aggression, and in its bias toward heterosexuality, Prince's article makes an apt companion piece to Layard's. An all too short but promising discussion of the *various* meanings homosexuality might have, however, appears late in the article, where Prince makes a cursory survey of both Freudian-psychoanalytic and Jungian literature to better understand the symbolism of his patient's dreams and their import for the development of the patient's ego. Nevertheless, this article lacks both the extensive detail of Jacobi's case history and the somewhat broader perspective provided by Layard, thus making it, too, of limited use.

Anthony Storr's article "The Psychopathology of Fetishism and Transvestitism"[34] is not on homosexuality per se. However, in examining the "sexual perversions and anomalies" of the article's title, Storr makes various interesting but questionable points concerning male homosexuality, primarily because many of the cases he describes are cases in which the patients are male homosexuals with various sexual fetishes that range from the expectable (bondage, castration fantasies, compulsive interest in circumcised penises) to the somewhat more offbeat (fetishes concerning fair-haired men and corduroy trousers). In his discussion of these cases of "homosexual fetishism," Storr agrees with a statement by Strauss and Walker in their book *Sexual Disorders in the Male* that "many cases of homosexuality could be interpreted as 'phallus-fetishism,'"[35] and Storr sees the foundation for phallus fetishism in the sense of inferior masculinity and castration that fuels such fetishism, in its characteristic search for a penis substitute. Although Storr can hardly confine such inferior masculinity to homosexuals, acknowledging forthrightly that these sexual perversions are nearly always thought of as heterosexual phenomena, he nevertheless generalizes concerning homosexual men, as in the following passage.

The refined delicate type of homosexual is usually most strongly attracted by a tough, aggressive muscular male, often of a lower social class than his own. . . . It is often a tragic fate for homosexuals to be so attracted by the people with whom they are least likely to be able to make a relationship. This type of homosexual is really being driven to seek through projection what he feels to be lacking in himself. He attributes to his beloved object all the qualities of tough maleness which are unconscious in himself.[36]

Here again we meet what amounts to a stereotype in psychological guise—homosexuals as anima-identified, projecting their inferior shadow masculinity and pursuing it with a compulsive quality common to fetishism—a stereotype with its origin in an unconscious equation of masculinity with conformity to prevailing heterosexual gender roles. Thus Storr's characterization of certain kinds of homosexuality as phallus fetishism is especially interesting, though problematic and bordering on offensive. While such a term may aptly indicate the compulsive quality of many gay men's frantic search for sexual satisfaction, one need only apply this term to heterosexual women's attraction to men and describe female sexuality as phallus fetishism to smell out the inherent problem.

Fundamentally a description of sexual psychopathology, the term *fetishism* can only indicate a negative view of the phenomenon in question, something abnormal, perverted. Thus Storr's unconscious bias against homosexuality shows in his agreement with such a term. Moreover, this description has a distinctly anti-Jungian flavor, a particularly reductive, "nothing-but" type of tone ill suited to describing a phenomenon as complex and enduring as homosexuality. Although Storr does agree with Jung's ideas concerning the positive functions homosexual relationships may have for the participants, particularly the educative function it may serve in relationships between older and younger men, he still is of the opinion that homosexuality represents a kind of immaturity.

To Storr's credit, the bulk of his paper focuses on heterosexual fetishism and transvestism. Contrary to the popular view of transvestism as a sign of homosexuality, Storr is more than aware that the phenomenon is predominant among heterosexual men, and his discussion of the way in which fetishes and transvestism for these men relates to the archetypal Phallic Mother through compensation and identification is fascinating.

The last major contribution to theories on homosexuality from Jung's own pupils comes from Marie-Louise von Franz and her work on the archetype of the *puer aeternus,* or Divine Child, as contained in her book *Puer Aeternus,* which was originally presented as a series of lectures at the Zurich institute in 1959 and 1960.[37] The same caveat is in order at this point as was necessary with Jung. Von Franz's book examines the archetype of the *puer* and discusses homosexuality in this connection. Therefore, what statements she does make concerning homosexuality occur in the context of her discussing something else and can hardly be understood as proposing anything so grand as a theory of homosexuality. Yet the connection between the *puer* and male homosexuality has almost become a cliché in Jungian circles, primarily because such a view is the logical successor to Jung's theory and attitude that homosexuals are feminine identified and therefore psychologically immature.

How closely the *puer*-identification theory of homosexuality is related to the feminine-identification theory of homosexuality (if such terminology does not somewhat overstate the case) and how such a connection automatically turns homosexuality into a problem can be gleaned from the first page of von Franz's book. She describes the phenomenon of identification with the *puer* archetype as one in which "the man . . . remains too long in adolescent psychology; that is, all those characteristics that are normal in a youth of seventeen and eighteen are continued into later life, coupled in most cases with too great a dependence on the mother," and then goes on to cite Jung's connection of homosexuality and Don Juanism as "two typical disturbances of a man who has an outstanding mother complex."[38] Von Franz develops this view a little later in a wider context, when she mentions how

homosexuality . . . is increasing more and more; even teenagers are involved and it seems to me that the problem of the *puer aeternus* is becoming increasingly actual. Undoubtedly, mothers have always tried to keep their sons in the nest, and some sons have always had difficulty getting free and have rather preferred to continue to enjoy the pleasures of the nest; still one does not quite see why this in itself, a natural problem, should now become such a serious time-problem [problem of our time?]." [39]

Thus we see at least two themes that von Franz repeats several times in the course of her discussions: first, that *puer* identification is caused by an underlying mother complex, resulting in psychological immaturity, and second, that homosexuality is one outgrowth of this problem that seems to von Franz to be on the increase in modern times. Both of these points have certain problematic features.

To begin with, all the criticisms of Jung's linking of homosexuality to a problem with the feminine apply equally well to this theory of homosexuality as a manifestation of *puer* identification, since we can see that these two theories are theoretically equivalent; as von Franz points out, the phenomenon of *puer* identification seems to grow out of an unresolved dependence on the mother, both personal and archetypal (Jacobi made a similar point). The difficulty is that homosexuality in this context becomes a problem because it is *defined* as a problem. If there is an unconscious cultural assumption that the only mature and normal form of sexuality is heterosexuality, all other forms of sexuality are a priori deviant, immature, pathological. Thus this theory of homosexuality is nothing much more than a restatement of a cultural stereotype of gay men based on a faulty view of human sexual behavior in which homosexuality is seen as an aberration rather than as a normal and ever present variation in sexual orientation.

This criticism is not to deny, however, that some gay men may be psychologically identified with the *puer aeternus*. But what does this mean if such an identification might equally well manifest itself in compulsive heterosexuality, the Don Juanism Jung and von Franz mention? Does this not imply that homosexuality is *not* necessarily inherently linked to *puer* identification, and that sexual orientation, homosexual or heterosexual, is *not* inherently determined by such archetypal identifications but somehow develops apart from mother complexes and archetypal identifications of this sort?

For this explanation of homosexuality as a *puer*-related phenomenon to be useful and convincing (especially in the context of von Franz's intent that her exploration of the *puer* be used as a guide to clinical work with patients), one needs to see demonstrated that gay men are more prone to *puer* identification than heterosexual men, that it is an expectable archetypal constellation in gay men that somehow determines their sexual orientation. Obviously, neither von Franz nor any other Jungians including Jung make such a claim, because such a claim cannot be made. If both heterosexual and homosexual men can be *puer* identified, then by von Franz's own admission identification with this archetype seems to have no determinative effect on sexual orientation. If the *puer* is an archetype of the collective unconscious, one can expect its appearance in *everyone's* psychology, so its mere presence in gay men's dreams, fantasies, and symbolic self-imagery does not necessarily constitute an identification as such. Moreover, a standard gay liberationist criticism of psychology may be in order here: Analytical patients, in analysis ostensibly because of problematic patterns and relationships, do not constitute a representative sample of the homosexual population, the great majority of which probably never seeks out Jungian analysis. Conclusions about homosexuality in general drawn from work with patients in Jungian analysis at least need to be supplemented by further contact with gay men and women who are outside the analytic situation and by knowledge of contemporary gay male and lesbian communities. In one-sided patriarchal cultures, such as those in the industrialized Western Hemisphere, where the feminine is so harshly devalued and repressed and where an ideology of masculinity holds sway, to find widespread psychological immaturity as evidenced by a frequent occurrence of *puer* identification among analytic patients can hardly be seen as a problem of sexuality.

In fairness, von Franz herself recognized this fact. In response to a question regarding the connection between *puer* identification and psychopathy, she states, "Let's say somebody has a religious problem. That is a problem in itself, but, in addition, the person can be normal or be a psychopath, or a schizoid or hysterical about it. The same applies to the problem of homosexuality, which can be combined with, or free from, other neurotic features, and can be linked with the time-problem [the general problem of our time?] more or less closely."[40]

At this point, von Franz quotes Jung's theory on homosexuality as a natural form of contraception and, in attempting to account for what she senses as an increase in homosexuality, hypothesizes, "Nature might possibly employ such a ruse, and overpopulation is just now our greatest problem."[41] Von Franz seems to confuse the visibility of homosexuality as a form of human relationship with its frequency of occurrence, thus leading her to believe that homosexuality and *puer*-related problems are on the increase as problems of our time. The most probable explanation for her impression, however, is that forms of human relationship that might be called unconventional are now more freely admitted and discussed and are therefore more visible. The statement, later in the article, of her own father concerning the relative rarity of homosexuality in the Austrian army of his day is remarkable not because homosexuality was necessarily rare then but precisely because of its acknowledged existence in such a time and place, which suggests homosexuality is an ever present form of human sexual relationship across time and place.

This discussion of the *puer* has a negative cast primarily because homosexuality seems defined beforehand as a problem by von Franz, either because it may be precisely that which led her patients to consult her or because homosexuality is in fact defined as such in a society that values heterosexuality above all other forms of sexual behavior and relationships. However, it is important not to depreciate the *puer aeternus* or to go away with the mistaken impression that von Franz equates *puer* phenomena with pathology. Jung's article on the Divine Child makes clear the importance of the *puer* in our psychological life and growth. The *puer* is life, potentiality, newness, and spontaneity, and von Franz again and again in her book points out this enlivening and renewing effect of the *puer* when this symbolic figure takes its proper place in the psychology of an individual. These positive characteristics of the *puer* to some extent might account for why gay men are linked closely in the collective mind with the Divine Child.

In a patriarchal culture badly in need of psychological life, potentiality, newness, and spontaneity, those members of society considered inferior by the dominant culture, those on whom the collective shadow is cast, may be forced to carry those *puer* characteristics that our rigid, competitive, industrialized culture cannot yet admit. Thus we find minority cultures in the United States, including gay male and lesbian culture, so frequently embodying those characteristics of the *puer* so badly needed and yet so severely depreciated. These cultures, including black and latino communities, often represent the cutting edge of political and culture developments and may be childlike in their love for spontaneity, celebration, sensuality, and color. Social prejudice, which finds its support in shadow projection, might force gay men and women to play the *puer*, not because homosexuality is somehow inherently puerile but rather because the hatred and fear of homosexuality in our culture denies gay men and women the possibility of being individuated *and* gay. Hence, one of the few accepted psychosocial roles assigned to such "inferior" men and women is that of the child and may account for the occurrence of *puer* identification among gay men and women in contemporary society.

We must note that von Franz does not pathologize the archetype of the *puer* but rather notes that unconscious identification with the *puer* is the real problem. Jung's negative evaluation of *any* archetypal identification has less to do with the content of the identification than with the unconscious nature of the identification. This distinction is important because it opens the way for gay men and women to disidentify with whatever archetypal constellation they have needed or been subtly forced to identify themselves with for whatever reasons—psychological, social, personal, or spiritual—while not necessarily finding their sexual orientations changed in the least. The case studies by Jung, Jacobi, and Storr all suggest that archetypal insights are probably best used nonetiologically, since whether one stays homosexual seems not to have a great deal to do with archetypal identifications. Indeed, we have seen how tempting it is to fall into what might be called archetypal reductionism: homosexuality as nothing but mother complex, anima identification, matriarchal psychology, *puer* identification, phallic fetishism, regression to primitive psychology, or whatever other Jungian term one may choose. Notably, all these terms can be seen as connected with the archetypal feminine, with Jung's own suggestion of homosexuality as linked to the archetype of the Androgyne all but ignored, and with the archetypal masculine unmentioned in any context whatever (except for Storr's phallus fetishism, which is nevertheless seen as a lack of psychological distance from the feminine).

We have seen that this state of affairs may be related to certain unconscious assumptions by first-generation Jungian analysts, assumptions that at the very least are open to question: heterosexuality as the only normal form of human sexual behavior, with the concomitant assumption of homosexuality as an aberration or deviation; homosexuality on the increase in contemporary society; sexual orientation as amenable to clinical intervention and change; a positivistic view of cultural and psychological development, which is seen to proceed in a somewhat clear and unbroken line from primitive to civilized. Many of these assumptions are questionable not simply on logical grounds but also on the grounds that they often ignore or do not use the genius of some of Jung's most important insights and attitudes, especially those we encountered in chapter 3: homosexuality as having an individual meaning, homosexuality as possessing its own cultural and social history, homosexuality as distinct from other aspects of an individual's personality. Many later Jungians' views on homosexuality are not particularly well thought out, nor do they advance Jung's own thinking very creatively; often they resemble restatements of cultural stereotypes in Jungian terminology more than original contributions to a psychology of homosexuality or new insights into the process of individuation for gay men and lesbians.

Perhaps the outstanding characteristic of the literature, however—and one that should temper our criticism a bit—is the noticeable paucity of systematic work on homosexuality by Jungians of the first generation. Among the possible explanations for this state of affairs is that neglect, more than judgmentalism or execration, may be the form of homophobia endemic to analytical psychology. In our examination of more contemporary views of homosexuality from a Jungian perspective we shall see how homosexuality has been addressed more creatively and with greater diversity by subsequent writers.

5. Contemporary Views of Homosexuality from a Jungian Perspective

WHEREAS THOSE ANALYSTS who knew Jung and were his contemporaries remained fairly close to certain of his attitudes and theories with regard to homosexuality, a new tone of discussion concerning homosexuality can be discerned among those who have followed the first generation of Jungian analysts. Because many of these contemporary authors are not analysts trained in Jungian institutes but rather writers using Jung's insights, we cannot call their views of homosexuality representative of the thoughts of Jungian analysts. Still, these writers and analysts have found in Jung's writings on homosexuality a number of provocative departure points for developing views that go beyond the narrow confines of traditional Jungian thought—though even today there is no lack of traditional thought on the subject, as we shall see.

If contemporary writers and Jungian analysts demonstrate a new tone and a new attitude toward homosexuality, much of this is undoubtedly owing to certain changes in social attitudes and psychological theories outside of strictly Jungian circles. Feminist thought and consciousness-raising on the pervasiveness of sexism in modern culture have brought about a virtual revolution in psychological thought concerning precisely those ideas on human personality that first-generation Jungian analysts accepted and used in a confused and sometimes uncritical way. Most notably, feminism has questioned the traditional concepts of masculinity and femininity so compellingly that many contemporary writers find themselves unable to take for granted the accepted definitions of these concepts and must strike out on new paths to deal with homosexuality in a genuine manner.

If their work is to have any credibility or impact, most contemporary Jungian writers must take into account the findings of almost thirty years of empirical psychological, sociological, and anthropological research on homosexuality. This research has affected the literature of analytical psychology in at least two major ways. First, homosexuality is no longer considered a mental disorder by the American Psychiatric Association. Though it is certainly possible to carp and claim that the 1973 decision to remove homosexuality from the list of mental disorders was more reflective of political realities than psychological truth, the result is the same. Homosexuality, even when the homosexual individual finds it disturbing and undesirable (ego-dystonic homosexuality), can no longer be classified as an illness. Second, contemporary social-science research on homosexuality flushes out the hidden biases of previous views of homosexuality, which first assumed homosexuality to be an aberrant phenomenon and then went on to research its causes. Homosexuality, if it is no longer an illness, is regarded much more widely as a normal variation in human sexual behavior, though cultural responses to this ever present form of sexuality may vary a great deal.[1]

Because of these two shifts in attitude toward homosexuality, contemporary Jungian writers and analysts are abandoning their preconceived notions concerning homosexuality more and more and are becoming open to the positive aspects of homosexual relationships and imagery. Though such an attitude of openness toward the individual is quintessentially Jungian and in fact represents one of Jung's major attitudes toward his homosexual patients, we have seen how even the best-intentioned of Jung's followers did not always succeed in shedding their negative preconceptions. Contemporary research and critical thought on homosexuality make such dated biases obvious when they appear in the Jungian literature.

And there is no lack of such biased attitudes and theories in the Jungian literature, even today. Many contemporary Jungian writers continue the tradition of the first-generation analysts by focusing on homosexuality solely as a result of a mother complex and therefore inherently pathological and immature. Examples of this sort of insidious condemnation of homosexuality, carried out by discussing homosexuality in the context of psychopathology, are distressingly frequent in the Jungian literature. The entry on homosexuality in the recently published *Critical Dictionary of Jungian Analysis* does cite Jung's list of positive qualities that a mother complex may bring to a man's personality, but ends the entry by distinguishing "narcissistic homosexuality," which is seen as part of a larger narcissistic personality disorder and a "compulsive search for control and fear of otherness," from "Oedipal homosexuality," which is considered "a version of sexual identity in its own right" and the difficulties of which "are of a cultural or familial nature."[2] The unfortunate choice of terms here leaves the impression that homosexuality is the result of an Oedipal or pre-Oedipal disturbance that may be more or less problematic. The idea of homosexuality as potentially problem-free is not entertained or addressed.

The same kind of tactic, linking homosexuality to the phenomena of psychopathology, mars an otherwise promising article by L. Zinkin in the *Journal of Analytical Psychology*, "'Death in Venice': A Jungian View."[3] Although the article is ostensibly an exploration of Jung's ideas on the individuation process by way of Thomas Mann's novella, Zinkin focuses on the protagonist Aschenbach's fascination with Tadzio, the *puer* figure in the story, and brings in clinical material from his treatment of pedophiles. Unfortunately, even offensively at times, Zinkin makes comparisons between Aschenbach and his pedophile patients, leaving the impression that the character of Aschenbach is suffering not from an individuation crisis but rather from an ingrained disorder of personality and sexual desire that ought to have been treated psychoanalytically. Mann's story is treated in an extremely reductionist manner, and Zinkin's article seems more a perversion of Mann's intention and his characters than a symbolically evocative exploration. More offensive, however, is that Zinkin does not consistently or clearly distinguish between homosexuality and pedophilia; for example, he uses the word *homosexual* in places where *pedophile* would be more appropriate. Given the highly charged stereotypes of homosexuals as child molesters and seducers in our culture, Zinkin's carelessness on this point shows again how some contemporary Jungians, intentionally or not, insist on seeing homosexuality as a form of psychopathology.

Jerome Bernstein's article in a recent collection of papers on initiation, *Betwixt and Between: Patterns of Masculine and Feminine Initiation*, is yet another example of how negative views of homosexuality creep in where one might least expect them. Given the initiatory symbolism that Jung and others have clearly seen in male homosexuality, one might expect Bernstein's piece, "The Decline of Masculine Rites of Passage in Our Culture," to deal with the initiatory function of homoerotic fantasy and relationship. However, Bernstein's sole comment on homosexuality is to notice how "homosexuality is another avenue of escape for men fearing intimacy with women," as if the rich area of male-male sexual relationship could simply be put down to fear of women, psychosexual escapism on the part of immature men.[4]

Bernstein uses as support for this comment a paper on homosexuality by San Francisco analyst Melvin Kettner, "Some Archetypal Themes in Male Homosexuality."[5] Kettner's paper, because it is one of the few pieces specifically on homosexuality by a Jungian analyst, is often cited by other analysts when discussing homosexuality. However, since Kettner's paper was never formally published but was a private presentation to the joint conference of Northern and Southern Californian Jungian Societies in 1967, it is not really all that well known outside of the Jungian community. Kettner's rather harsh and reductive view of homosexuality as a regressive throwback to ancient phallic cults devoted to the Great Mother results in his pathologizing many of the gay male community's rituals and interactions. The paper takes the identification of male homosexuality as a problem with the feminine a step further by focusing on some of the more shadow-ridden and promiscuous elements of the gay male community and seeing these elements as inherent to the "homosexual archetype." Kettner treats gay male culture in the same way in an article, "Patterns of Masculine Identity," published in a collection of papers entitled *The Reality of the Psyche*. He comments in a footnote on the way "leather jacket queens" in the gay community are attempting to compensate for their lack of masculinity by creating a tough, masculine image—rendering them, in Kettner's words, "a curious caricature of the American collective masculine ideal."[6]

In all of these works, the typically Jungian identification of homosexuality as a problem with the feminine makes homosexuality fundamentally a question of psychopathology. Whatever the intentions of the authors of these statements, whether they are homophobic or simply unthinking, their views of homosexuality are theoretical dead-end streets. Homosexuality in these places is defined and treated as psychopathology before its normality, its positive attributes, its individual character are even entertained. Such views leave these Jungian writers decidedly out of the mainstream of current thought on homosexuality and make them seem unfortunately reductionist and focused on psychopathology. Given Jung's criticisms of Freud on these points, it is ironic for Jungians to hold such views of homosexuality.

It may be more fruitful to concentrate on those Jungians who hold fewer preconceptions and negative judgments about homosexuality and who are more open to seeing homosexuality as a positive individual phenomenon. A pair of articles that reflect the dividing line between older Jungians' attitudes toward homosexuality and more contemporary evaluations appeared in 1981 in the *Journal of Analytical Psychology:* Steven Centola's evocative "Individuation in E. M. Forster's 'Maurice'" and K. Marriott's follow-up "Comment" to Centola's article.[7]

Centola, in examining Forster's *Maurice,* first emphasizes that his psychological exploration of individuation themes in Forster's coming-of-age novel applies as much to the title character as to Forster himself, who, in Centola's view, most probably was using the novel therapeutically to express his search for wholeness as a homosexual in a homophobic society. In light of the double function of the novel, therapeutic and artistic, Centola's comment takes on greater force when he says:

> Through his portrayal of Maurice's ordeal, Forster implies that the homosexual's search for wholeness, though more painful, is ultimately no different from that of the heterosexual. It is only after he confronts the dark recesses of his unconscious psyche that symbolise his homosexuality and integrates them into his consciousness that Maurice is finally able to become a whole individual.[8]

With regard to these "dark recesses . . . that symbolise his homosexuality," Centola avoids absorbing the bias that has afflicted other analysts. Centola examines how Forster uses the imagery of darkness in describing Maurice's first intimations of his homosexuality; instead of identifying the homosexuality with the shadow, Centola sees Forster's use of darkness to express the unconscious character of Maurice's homosexual longings. This fine distinction serves Centola well, by allowing him to notice how, little by little, as Maurice discovers the character of his passions and explores them in his relationships with Clive and Alec, the shadow imagery of homosexuality is transformed into the imagery of wholeness.

For Centola, *unconscious* homosexuality, not homosexuality in general, bears the shadow in individuation, and so Centola sees more deeply into the positive aspects of Forster's story of homosexual self-realization, Maurice's coming out, as we might put it today. Rather than denigrate Maurice's adolescent longing for the "ideal friend" as a manifestation of immature masculinity or as an attempt to throw off a mother complex, Centola sees in Maurice's search for his double "a symbol of Maurice's desire to achieve unity of being."[9] Rather than dwell on the unsavoriness of Maurice's encounters with the flamboyant Risley and the ambivalent Clive, Maurice's first lover—that is, rather than attempt to fit these relationships into the mold of shadow projections—Centola points out quite aptly how Risley and Clive function as archetypal guides and guardians for Maurice, showing him the way to his self, a self that is inseparable from his sexual orientation:

> Maurice experiences a type of eternal moment when he accepts his homosexuality, for he momentarily glimpses his true self, "the root whence body and soul both spring, the 'I' that he had been trained to obscure and realised at last." He perceives that he is "neither body or soul, nor body and soul, but 'he' working through both."[10]

Because his sights are set more on how Maurice achieves consciousness as a homosexual than on how Maurice does or does not achieve heterosexuality, Centola misses none of the irony in Maurice's attempts to find a cure by way of hypnosis and psychiatry. As he charts the novel's denouement through Maurice's love relationships with the working-class Alec Scudder, Centola notes how social oppression, in the form of homophobia and class distinctions, works against Maurice's individuation. By forcing Maurice and Alec into an exile outside of society, into the "greenwoods of England," society prevents Maurice from completing the final stage of his initiation, which is, as Centola puts it, "the individual's incorporation of his newly discovered self-knowledge into his society—a stage that provides the stimulation which any culture needs for further advancement."[11] However, Centola sees this more as civilization's loss and, in the final paragraph of the article, he writes:

> Nevertheless, regardless of the degree of his attainment of individuation, Maurice finds comfort, happiness and, most importantly, psychic stability, through the triumph of homosexual love.[12]

In marked contrast to this finely wrought and well-considered examination of the novel, the comment on Centola's piece by K. Marriott completely misses the point of both Centola's psychological considerations and Forster's intention. Leaping from his objection to Centola's idea of individuation as a fixed state, Marriott wonders:

> Just as individuation is not a fixed state, so perhaps homosexuality is not a fixed state either? In the past ten years I have done analytical work with three homosexual men, all of whom were confirmed homosexuals; they *none of them sought "help" for their condition*, yet all of them have profoundly changed.[13]

Just after both Forster's and Centola's demonstration that Maurice's self-realization as a homosexual man was essential to both the psychological and artistic intention of the novel, Marriott's comment here seems out of place, particularly since he then chooses to discuss in detail a case of his in which a homosexual man eventually developed heterosexual feelings and no longer identified himself as a homosexual. Although one might certainly agree with Marriott that "wholeness is all,"[14] and there is plenty of clinical and empirical research that suggests sexual orientation is a fluid phenomenon, the idea that wholeness consists of acknowledging heterosexual impulses if one is basically homosexual is no more than a restatement of a cultural preference for heterosexuality and says nothing nearly so new or original as Centola's article and Forster's novel.

At the other end of the spectrum is a forthright article by sociologist David Walsh that appeared in *Harvest*, the publication of the Analytical Psychology Club of London.[15] "Homosexuality, Rationality and Western Culture" shows precisely how Jungian insights and the modern political-psychological revision of thought on homosexuality may be brought together to both critique and deepen analytical psychology's perspective on homosexuality. For those familiar with the writings of gay liberation activists of the late sixties and early seventies, Walsh's article strikes many familiar notes. For example, rather than focus on homophobia alone, Walsh sees the fear and hatred of homosexuality as derived from a more "general complex of repression in regard to sexuality," a hatred of the body and of sexuality projected most clearly on women and female sexuality, resulting in the misogynist sexism of Western culture. Walsh writes:

> Superficially, the homosexual is almost the classic case of misogyny, but I would argue that the homosexual is a threat to misogyny since the acceptance of homosexuality as an ordinary form of sexual repression [sic] depends upon a rejection of the hierarchical separation of logos and eros and its attendant sex and gender identification. Misogyny and the repression of homosexuality as an aberrant phenomenon, then, go hand-in-hand in western culture. [16]

Walsh goes on to note how negative stereotypes of homosexuals, the "mincing effeminate" or the "butch" lesbian, serve to reinforce conformity to sex-role and gender categories in a society that, in its attempt to repress sexuality, must project this fearful shadow onto individuals who are different—a dynamic that Sylvia Brinton-Perera terms the "scapegoat complex." [17]

Writing before John Boswell's masterful critique of the same concept in his landmark book *Christianity, Social Tolerance, and Homosexuality*, [18] Walsh spends a great deal of time debunking one of the primary rationalizations Western culture gives for evaluating homosexuality negatively: the idea that homosexuality is unnatural, a contention supported by some psychologists and sociologists who find homosexuality both psychologically troublesome for individuals and sociologically undesirable in its challenge to social conventions and traditional values. Walsh casts the concept of nature in terms Jung would have understood:

> Where "Nature" is invoked by western consciousness to analyse the problem of homosexuality, the rationalism of the terms in which it has made the invocation (particularly scientific concepts) forgets how "Nature" is a mythical representation of reality and not an external set of things. [19]

Nature is a myth created by human beings through language to make sense of their experience. As Walsh puts it,

> "Nature" is the telling of the otherness of Being which discloses it as world. . . . Where men have elected to see the *Hand of Nature* at work in the ordering of sexual experience (rationalism), thereby making homosexuality a problem, we need to recover the hand of nature as the *Handiwork of Man*, thereby making rationalism the real problem that needs to be addressed.[20]

Walsh links much of this problematic rationalist, nonmetaphorical understanding of nature to the antisexual character of Judeo-Christian attitudes toward the body and consequently toward sexuality and women. His critique of this tradition and its effects is well within the purview of Jung's criticism of Christianity as a one-sided, Logos-oriented, shadow-banishing system that, in its doctrinal rigidity, has become a dead symbol in need of renewal, renewal that must come from the very aspects of human experience which Christianity has attempted to deny and repress. In Jungian terms, Eros—sexuality, connection, passion, feminine consciousness, and intuition—must be integrated into Logos. Walsh faults Freudian psychoanalysis and Western psychology in general for failing to integrate Eros, despite some promising starts in that direction made by Freud in his acknowledgment of the power of sexuality in human life. In opting for sublimation of the soul's erotic side and subjugating Eros to social convention and control, psychology and sociology, in Walsh's view, have become handmaidens to the hatred of sexuality that afflicts Western Judeo-Christian culture. Walsh sees the hatred of sexuality, not homosexuality, as the true pathology:

> Western culture has all too easily projected a collective problem as a personal pathology. But the material out of which the pathology is woven—the misogynous consciousness—embraces the whole culture. The homosexual is not the bearer of misogyny but its victim. Misogyny is the rejection of eros, and this is precisely what the homosexual who lives out his or her homosexuality has not done, and what the "normal" heterosexual who lives his or her life in terms of cultural stereotypes of masculine and feminine identity is doing.[21]

Two San Francisco Jungian analysts, David Stockford and J. Michael Steele, in a review of *Homosexual Behavior: A Modern*

Reappraisal, are less strident in their critique of psychology's handling of homosexuality but are no less direct than Walsh:

> Jungian psychology is not without its own troubled vision on this subject, which no doubt reflects the fact that mid to late nineteenth century European Judeo-Christian values were common to Freud and Jung. From early Jewish and Christian codes come the punitive laws and austere judgments on homosexuality in the West. Despite their symbolic orientation, Jungians themselves often dwell uncomfortably close to Freud's "anatomy is destiny" view, and Jungian psychology withal remains more developed as a psychology of heterosexual men, as women often note.[22]

Stockford and Steele bring to the Jungian audience of this journal for the first time a review of the newer research on homosexuality that prompted the revision of psychological thought on homosexuality in America. Their article examines the animal studies that show homosexual behavior to exist in many species and to be unconnected with abnormality. They mention Masters and Johnson's research that revealed communication and openness in homosexual couples superior to that in heterosexual couples, and they go to some length to mention the findings of cross-cultural studies of homosexuality, studies that challenge the idea that sex-role patterns are rooted in anatomical gender and that found homosexuality normal and acceptable in many non-Western cultures. Stockford and Steele note the book's unbiased observations of contemporary American gay culture's attempt to construct positive, healthy social and personal identities for gay men and lesbians, and they cite many articles critical of psychoanalytic judgments against homosexuality—negative judgments unsupported by psychological testing, research on gender-identity development, or the clinical experience of many analysts. However, Stockford and Steele's piece remains constrained by the book-review format from going much further in developing these ideas in a Jungian way.

For writings with a psychological rather than sociopolitical emphasis, we turn to James Hillman and Spring Publications, which under his direction has issued some of the more creative and gay-positive pieces on homosexuality in the Jungian literature, at all times retaining a distinctly archetypal perspective.

In the lead article in his collection *Puer Papers*, Hillman discusses the many interconnections between the archetype of the *puer aeternus*, the Divine Child, whom we have met in other Jungian writings on homosexuality, and the archetype of *senex*, the Old Man. Intent on showing how these archetypal dominants, with their own multifaceted characters, are but opposites in the same archetypal polarity, Hillman is eloquent about the duality of *our* consciousness and the unity of the archetype itself:

> This primary polarity [between consciousness and unconsciousness] is given only as a potential within the archetype which theoretically is not divided into poles. The archetype *per se* is ambivalent and paradoxical, embracing both spirit and nature, psyche and matter, consciousness and unconsciousness; in it the yea and nay are one. There is neither day nor night, but rather a continual dawning. . . . Our usual daily consciousness grasps only one part and makes it into a pole.[23]

In this connection Hillman goes on to describe the phenomenology of *senex* and *puer*, what these archetypes look like imaginally, and how their intimate connection with each other is often ignored by an over*senex*ed consciousness among Jungians:

> We must therefore deny again the usual separation into first and second halves of life. . . . It dangerously divides puer and senex. Always the puer is described from within the senex-puer duality and therefore comes out negatively, which also implies a positive senex view of itself.
>
> Let us look at the usual recommendations for the "first-half" of life or "how to cure a puer": analyze the unconscious, reduce the fantasies, dry the hysterics, confront the intuitions, bring down to earth and reality, turn the poetry into prose . . .[24]

One might add to this prescription: Help immature homosexuals grow into mature heterosexuals with spouses and *pueri* of their own.

By using Saturn as his guiding *senex* personification, Hillman demonstrates the true nature of this inculcation of convention and lays bare why the image of *puer*, projected negatively onto the lives and loves of gay men, is so thoroughly rejected by Jungians such as von Franz:

This path of worldly commitment aims to sever the puer from his own vertical axis; it reflects a senex personality which has not itself separated the parental from the archetypal and is thus threatened by its own child, its own phallus, and its own poetry.[25]

Unwilling and unable to divided *puer* and *senex*, Hillman can, with relatively greater objectivity, see more deeply and imaginatively into the archetypal currents that lie beneath one of the primary psychological patterns of many relationships, particularly homosexual love. In a section entitled "The Union of Sames," Hillman shows how, if the dual faces of *puer* and *senex* are at last truly appreciated as a single figure with double aspects, then our ego's insistence on splitting this unity into an apparent duality must be opposed, and, since it is James Hillman who is writing, opposed imaginally. The significance of this "union of sames" for homosexual men and women ought not to be underestimated:

> We seek this merger in our own lives. We seek a transformation of the conflict of extremes into a union of sames. Our time and its longing to be healed asks that the two ends be held together, that our other half so near to us, so like us as the shadow we cast, enter the circle of our light. Our other half is not only of another sex. The union of opposites—male with female—is not the only union for which we long and is not the only union which redeems. There is also the union of sames, the re-union of the vertical axis which would heal the split spirit.[26]

What Centola sees in Maurice's (and Forster's) longing for an ideal friend, a double with whom physical union is but the manifestation of an emotional and spiritual urge toward individual wholeness—what Zinkin pathologizes into pederasty in Aschenbach—Hillman sees contained in the polarity of youth and age. It is noteworthy that Hillman's imagery is male—Saturn and Eros, Zeus and Ganymede, Mercurius, Dionysus, and Christ—especially since the revolutionary points he is making about the identity of *puer* and *senex* are, to some extent, taken for granted in the realm of the archetypal feminine: Youth and age, mother and daughter, Demeter and Persephone are dual faces of a single archetype. That such a point concerning the archetypal masculine should have to be made by Hillman shows to what extent patriarchal overvaluation of ego has alienated men from their own potential for wholeness. It also makes clear why, archetypally, homo-sexuality—this blasphemous union of sames—is perceived as so threatening, psychologically and spiritually, and why its visibility and importance cannot and should not be ignored.

We have looked at Hillman's article so as to see the current of thought in which two other articles, more explicitly about homo-sexuality, occur, and to deepen our understanding of the points that Rafael Lopez-Pedraza and Mitch Walker make in their ar-ticles, both of which appeared in the 1976 edition of *Spring*. In "The Tale of Dryops and the Birth of Pan" Lopez-Pedraza, a Venezuelan Jungian analyst trained in Zurich, uses tales of Apollo and Hermes to flesh out mythologically the points that Hillman made in his article on *puer* and *senex*.[27] He sees in the myth of Apollo and Admetus an archetype of male-male Eros, a direct re-lationship of affection, love, servitude, initiation, and power that the ancients perceived and honored; in the myth of Hermes' love for the nymph of mortal King Dryops he finds an indirect expres-sion of male-male Eros that itself is enormously fructifying, since Hermes' love for Dryops' nymph results in the birth of the god Pan. Attention to these myths of male-male Eros leads Lopez-Pedraza to a confrontation with psychology's negative views on homosexuality:

> Here I would like to question what the psychology of this century has done for psychotherapy with all those conceptual coinages of "homosexuality," "latent homosexuality," "the shadow (or the an-ima) as the unknown in men's relationships," "the negative mother complex" and, above all, "transferential homosexuality," so mis-understood and falsely interpreted. Along the psychological road of this century, the sorcerer's apprentice has been dominant in this respect. The conceptual frame has placed homosexuality within a sterile causalism that tries to understand it in terms of the father and mother. Western culture has evidently lost contact with the archetypes which are behind eros among men. Thus an archetypal view of homo-erotica has been falsified.[28]

Behind the Hermes-Dryops Eros, Lopez-Pedraza sees what one instantly recognizes as a common pattern of male-male Eros, that of "falling in love with another man's fantasy," and Lopez-Pedraza uses Freud and Jung's own relationship to gain insight into how and why their friendship held so fast for years and yet broke down so thoroughly. Moreover, Lopez-Pedraza does not miss the significance of the fact that the child of this Hermes-Dryops union through the nymph is none other than the Judeo-Christian Devil himself, the heathen god Pan, whose sexuality and wildness is the fruit of male-male Eros in the myth. Lopez-Pedraza begins to restore a truer image of Pan here, one less obscured by modern prejudices and religious dogma, and he points out how psychotherapy often, in its search for cure and social adaptation, may miss the appearance and language of Pan and thereby lose out on a real and vivifying connection to sacredness. For psychotherapy with gay men, Lopez-Pedraza minces no words on the importance of recognizing Pan's appearance in the course of analysis:

> My attempt has been to discuss the Image from the viewpoint of an archetypal psychology and particularly to stress the fact that Pan's birth was made possible by two men loving each other through a nymph. The insight that Pan is concerned with the psychotherapy of the body can open a door for a psychotherapeutic approach to the pathologies attributed to him. It can offer, also, a psychotherapeutic approach to the analytical situation in which the patient's homosexuality appears centre-stage. Instead of a homosexuality with no psychological body, this approach could provide that same homosexuality with the body psychology of Pan, son of Hermes.[29]

In this same issue of *Spring*, Mitch Walker, a well-known writer from the San Francisco gay community, offers in his piece "The Double: An Archetypal Configuration" a further development of the thesis Hillman presented in "Senex and Puer," that there exists "a soul figure with all the erotic and spiritual significance attached to anima/us, but of the same sex, and yet not a shadow."[30] Walker uses the Enuma Elish, the Sumerian creation myth, and the relationship between Gilgamesh, the half-god, half-man protagonist of the story, and Enkidu, Gilgamesh's friend, to demonstrate how the double is neither just shadow nor simply a symbol of the ego or the Self. In the myth, Enkidu functions much more positively than the shadow might; though certainly wild and contentious at the beginning of their relationship, Enkidu ultimately functions as a kind of ideal comrade to draw

Gilgamesh's ego forward and show him the way. Yet Enkidu, who is both mortal and expressly created by the gods as Gilgamesh's coequal—"his own reflection, his second self," in the words of the myth—cannot be easily summed up as Gilgamesh's ego or as a symbol of the Self. If anything, Enkidu functions as the anima might for Gilgamesh—appearing in Gilgamesh's dreams as helper and guide, beautiful and enchanting in his wildness, a figure with its own mind and personality and yet one that deeply embodies Gilgamesh's own inner self—and yet it is not the anima, as Jung intended the concept, since the double appears to be of the same sex.

Walker examines the aspects of the double using myth and literature to draw out its characteristic ways and means:

> As these myths suggest, the double is a soul-mate of intense warmth and closeness. Love between men and love between women, as a psychic experience, is often rooted in projection of the double, just as anima/us is projected in love between the different sexes. And as with anima/us, such love may occur within or without the heroic quest. Furthermore, since the double is a soul figure, the sexual instinct may or may not become involved. That is, the double motif may include a tendency to homosexuality, but is not necessarily a homosexual archetype. Rather the double embodies the *spirit* of love between those of the same sex. And the spirit of love in the double is what I see as the supportive ground of the ego.[31]

Walker finds the double figure functioning as the "root of ego identity" and as such, "it may lead one to significant self-realizations. This is the symbolic meaning of its presence in the hero myth."[32]

Going further, he echoes Hillman's intuitions and finds what he calls the "youth-adult" variation of the double motif, in which older and younger persons of the same sex are in partnership with one another, and yet Walker feels that such a youth-adult variation of the double motif need not always embody a *puer-senex* combination. His view is that it is a matter of proportion and equality between the two partners, who may not necessarily embody the one-sided extremes of *senex* conservatism or negative puerility. Thus, Walker does not find Mann's *Death in Venice* an example of his concept of the double but rather sees in

Aschenbach's story an illustration of how the negative *puer* can be called forth when one is identified with *senex*, thus ensuring entrapment in the "seductive power of the youth."[33]

As to the darker side of the double archetype, Walker indicates how nonrecognition of such a soul mate within may lead to its consignment to unconsciousness, so that it gathers about itself the ego's shadow, though it is essentially not shadow. Just as the highly unconscious anima of a man who has ruthlessly attempted to repress all his femininity takes on the destructive, almost evil, mischief-making function of the shadow (the "negative anima" of Jungian literature), the double, Walker believes, follows a similar dynamic if one's homosexual tendencies are rejected. Then the double becomes mixed with shadow and its guiding, ideal, and self-reflective qualities are lost as it becomes instead a competitor, a threat, an unholy Other. Walker wonders if this may not be the archetypal root of homophobia, aided by cultural pressure to reject the "union of sames" (homo-sexuality) and restrict oneself exclusively to the "union of opposites" inherent in hetero-sexuality, the sexuality of otherness.

Walker's thesis is imaginatively and evocatively supported by the mythological and artistic material he adduces. We have seen the motif of the double explicitly represented in Forster's Maurice, whose image of the friend is a helpful, guiding fantasy figure who leads Maurice to realize his own individuality in the face of societal disapproval. While Walker prefers to name this archetypal configuration the double, the same concept has also been discussed in the Jungian literature as the male anima or female animus.

A number of Jungian analysts have expressed impatience concerning the literalistic tendency that creeps into many discussions of the anima and have registered reservations as to whether the traditional concept of the anima/animus is really able to capture the multifaceted nature of an individual's soul guide. Hillman, Edward C. Whitmont, and John Beebe, among others, have suggested that the kind of phenomena that Walker sees in myth and literature leads to the conclusion that at times and for some individuals the anima may wear a same-sex face.

Hillman, in *Anima: An Anatomy of a Personified Notion*, is uncomfortable with having anima carry all of a man's femininity and

sees in the traditional understanding of "anima as a man's feminine soul" a potentially restrictive introjection of outward definitions of femininity. His book aims quite effectively at dismantling
the idea that the archetype of the anima conforms to *our* ideas of
who or what "she" should be—psyche, soul, feeling, Eros—and
he wonders, along with Jung, if it may not be more accurate to
"confine the archetype's femininity to its projected form."[34] His
suggestion that the archetype may be androgynous, essentially
contentless, opens the door to wondering whether the anima or
animus may not at times appear as the same-sex doubles Walker
so clearly delineates.

Whitmont, in "Reassessing Femininity and Masculinity," sees
the strict consignment of masculinity to men and femininity to
women as psychologically false and overly restrictive: The soul
does not follow such tight lines of delineation. If, Whitmont
posits, one acknowledges that both masculinity and femininity
can be found in both men and women, then "it appears to be
impractical and not borne out by contemporary psychological experience in our culture to limit the concepts of anima and animus
to one sex."[35] Furthermore, Whitmont points out that Jung's use
of the two different terms *anima* and *animus* gives the mistaken
impression that there was a similarly great distinction made between the Latin use of the terms when, in fact, the terms were
used interchangeably.

In a presentation entitled "On Male Partnership" at the Nexus
Conference "Friendship, Love and Companionship between
Man and Man, Woman and Woman," sponsored by the Los Angeles Jung Institute in 1987, John Beebe's suggestion is similar to
Hillman's: The anima may not always be a figure conforming to
sex-role stereotypes but, if truly an archetype and a soul figure,
the anima may at times be better understood as a figure—male
or female—who serves the psychological *function* of the anima
as posited by Jung. Male figures, as well as female figures, may
serve the function of anima, and Beebe used the movie version
of *Kiss of the Spider Woman* to demonstrate the soul-guide function that Molina, a gay man, serves for his heterosexual cellmate,
Valentino, in leading Valentino to wholeness through fantasy,
beauty, and feeling.[36]

Moreover, even many traditional analysts find themselves

drawn toward using the somewhat convoluted formula of "animus of the anima" or "animus's anima" to denote what Walker, Hillman, Beebe, Whitmont, and certainly many gay men and women have clearly seen: that homo-Eros, whether enacted or simply fantasized, is not always an example of immaturity or a misunderstanding but rather at times an expression of the soul's inherent oneness with itself, a connection not to an Other in a *coniunctio* of male-female, but rather a lived psychological Self-expression embodied in a man's love for masculinity, outwardly and inwardly, a woman's passion for her femininity, within and without. If it is this *coniunctio* that one feels, then the symbolic inward expression of it can only have a homosexual form and can only be embodied in the male anima or the female animus, Mitch Walker's ideal double, friend, companion, comrade, brother/sister, and lover.[37]

Since men's union with their own masculinity is the subject of Eugene Monick's book *Phallos: Sacred Image of the Masculine*, one ought not to be surprised to find in it one of the most focused discussions of homosexuality in the contemporary Jungian literature. The major purpose of Monick's book is to recover a view of phallos that is undistorted by either the patriarchal triumphalism of contemporary culture or its compensatory counterpart in depth psychology, the Great Motherism that sees all of unconscious experience, including masculinity, as fruit of the deep, dark feminine (Monick offers Neumann as the best example of this compensatory overvaluation of the Mother in depth psychology). By establishing the inseminating male phallos as a coequal creative principle, and not simply something subordinate to the Great Mother, Monick intends to help contemporary men and women toward a more faithful union with phallos—not just the rational, intellectual, Apollonian "higher phallos," the sun consciousness of thought and spirit, but the darker, primeval phallos, the thrusting, wild, Dionysian sexual body experience of "lunar masculinity," which has been so hated and so thoroughly repressed in contemporary Judeo-Christian culture.

With regard to homosexuality, Monick acknowledges, along with Danish psychoanalyst Thorkil Vanggaard, the existence of what Vanggaard called a "homosexual radical," every person's "capacity for some degree of homosexual interest." Monick writes:

Homoeroticism enters the picture when a male's need for masculine affirmation is urge and his hunger for phallos becomes sexual desire. Three distinct factors are involved. One is the homosexual radical present in all men. Another is the emergence of eroticism based upon this radical and upon need. Still another is the acting out of homoerotic desire in sexual behavior.[38]

Which leads Monick, later in the book, to ask explicitly, "Is homosexuality pathological?" His answer is unique in the Jungian literature for its forthrightness:

Were Phallos only an instrument of service to the Great Mother—derivative of her and returning to her in obedience to her magnetic attraction as source—a case might be made for homosexuality as an aberration of basic instinctual energy. . . . It is to be noticed, however, that even the most rigorous psychoanalytic treatment rarely excises phallos from the erotic interest of men with an active homosexual radical. If the psychological situation were a matter only of maternal distancing and the analysand's resolve to take up the cudgels of heroic stance, the "cure" ratio would be much greater than it is. The point is that men, be they homosexual, bisexual, or heterosexual, have an archetypal connection with phallos that cannot—indeed should not—be cured, since it is not an illness. How a man deals with his sexuality is where pathology enters the picture—a question involving collective expectations and judgments and their effect upon the subject. . . . Sexuality, in itself, including the omnipresent homosexual radical in men, is not, and never has been, pathological. . . .
It is as wrong for psychoanalysts to judge where a man should be on the continuum of the homosexual radical as it would be for them to judge his masculinity by the size of his penis.[39]

Besides Monick, the two Jungian writers perhaps best known for their work on sexuality, masculinity, and femininity are John Sanford and June Singer, who, in their many books, have addressed the question of homosexuality and the issues it raises clinically and theoretically in Jungian psychology.

June Singer gives her most thoughtful and extensive treatment of homosexuality in her extremely popular and enduring book *Androgyny: Toward a New Theory of Sexuality.* An entire chapter is devoted to "Androgyny Experience in Homosexuality, Bisexuality and Heterosexuality," and, refreshingly, this section of the book is organized around three case histories, two men and one woman, whose androgynous potentialities became manifest in the course of their analyses with Singer through the emergence of homosexual thoughts, feelings, fantasies, and, eventually, gay relationships. The first man she presents is a patient whose homosexuality had played an important part in his sexual development but who had thoroughly—and unhelpfully—repressed this side of his erotic nature, marrying and having children but finding himself drinking too much and caught up in homoerotic fantasy to a greater and greater degree. Singer helps him, with tact and acceptance, toward allowing this side of himself greater play in his life. She is tolerant of the raw, unfinished, and obsessive qualities of his first gay experiences, and her calmness goes far in enabling him to accept the complexities of his inner and outer life as a bisexual.

Singer is explicit about the way her knowledge of recent research on sexual orientation and the depathologization of homosexuality by the APA made it imperative that she find a flexible and individual approach to these issues with her patients, but this very flexibility, combined with her focus on androgyny, not homosexuality, causes her discussion of the second patient, a woman, to appear to be a strange contrast to her analysis with the bisexual man. This woman, self-identified as a heterosexual and in a relationship with a man when analysis began, became more and more drawn toward women, whom she found more responsive emotionally and sexually, and eventually began a long-term relationship with a woman and came to identify herself as a lesbian. Singer is quite clear on the positive effect of this woman's self-acceptance as a lesbian but seems uncomfortable with this gain:

> I had to ask myself the question, was Ms. B really a homosexual? There were no doubts about it in Ms. B's own mind; she happily identified herself as such. I was not so sure, despite her assertions that she had achieved her first truly satisfying sexual experiences with a woman.[40]

Carrying out a typically Jungian process of archetypal amplification, Singer draws parallels between this woman's lesbian identity and the mythical Amazons, the Greek warrior women.

That Singer does not fall into the trap of archetypal reductionism that afflicts so many Jungian writers on male homosexuality—homosexuality as nothing but a Great Mother fixation, for example—is to her credit as she draws the Amazon parallel. She acknowledges frankly, "Perhaps now, for the first time, Ms. B was beginning to experience her sexuality *as a woman.* In the past, the men to whom she had related had in many ways fulfilled the feminine image. . . . Ms. B's relationship with her female companion was clearly a relationship with someone who was different in kind from herself"[41]—an Other Woman whose more stereotypically masculine qualities, such as assertiveness and the ability to provide financial security, lead Singer to identify this element as the source of the lesbian relationship's positive effect on her patient.

> Surely the stereotypical concepts that are commonly associated with the words "homosexuality" and "heterosexuality" must fall before the experiences of real people such as these. If human beings are released, or can release themselves, from the boundaries of sex and gender, there can be a far wider reaching out in love to people *as people* on the basis of individual needs and desires.[42]

Her examples are meant "to show how necessary it is that in the age of androgyny we eliminate the categorization of people on the basis of their preferences for sexual partners at some given moment in time."[43]

Singer's third case involves a confused young man who finds in a college gay community a temporary home and identity but whose true heterosexual nature eventually emerges after he participates in a transformative experience at a party in which heterosexual and homosexual coupling occurs. Rather than feel self-satisfied or triumphant at effecting a cure, Singer states, "In his case, his excursion into homosexuality had been a step in his psychological and sexual development. This is not to say that homosexuality is necessarily to be equated with immaturity, or heterosexuality with maturity. But in Mr. C's case, the progression was a developmental one."[44]

Singer's thoughts on homosexuality are not without their problems. At one point she makes an unfortunate comparison between exposure to "the seeds of homosexuality" and exposure to the virus of the common cold and cancer cells, thus perpetuating the unconscous link between homosexuality and illness we have seen elsewhere in more deliberate and virulent form. And her focus on androgyny leaves one feeling that she is more satisfied with the bisexual and heterosexual resolutions of her male clients than with the exclusive homosexual identity of her lesbian patient. While her recognition that masculine and feminine "energies of love" (to borrow from the title of her subsequent book) should flow freely, she seems less than supportive of exclusive homosexuality and at times invokes the importance of social convention for the cohesion and perpetuation of civilization.

What if someone's sexual orientation does not fit Singer's androgynous ideal? What if I am exclusively homosexual, never interested in women sexually? Am I to be considered one-sided sexually? Are exclusive heterosexuals to be looked at with equal skepticism, or are they to be helped toward homosexual functioning? A true acknowledgment of individuality must include the recognition that for most people, androgynous bisexual self-identity and sexual functioning is not the norm, nor should it become a new sexual standard. There are true homosexuals just as there are true heterosexuals for whom androgyny does not fit. However, Singer's openness to these questions and the sensitive, well-balanced way she approaches these highly charged issues is unique in contemporary Jungian thought.

Also well balanced, thoughtful, and sensitive is John Sanford's approach to homosexuality in his searching works on masculinity and femininity, though his thoughts on the matter are not without their own problems. For example, in his work on the anima and animus, *Invisible Partners*, he devotes a number of pages to looking at the psychological dynamics of homosexuality, repeating once again the traditional Jungian formula of homosexuality (presumably male) as the manifestation of a desire for contact with the male organ due to a problem with the feminine consisting of either distance from or enmeshment with mother/anima/ Great Mother.[45] However, he is to be much commended for also bringing to his discussion an awareness of the fact that other cultures, notably Native American tribes, had other, more mythologically evocative views of same-sex love. Unfortunately, this mention of the Native American transvestite-androgyne in myth and tribal culture remains undeveloped in Sanford's works.

LESBIANISM IN CONTEMPORARY
JUNGIAN LITERATURE

If there is little on male homosexuality in the Jungian literature, there is even less specifically on lesbianism. One cannot help noticing how in our foregoing walk through contemporary Jungian thought, "homosexuality" has been equivalent to "male homosexuality" for contemporary writers, something not at all characteristic of either Jung or his immediate followers, for whom female homosexuality occupied a place of some focus. (June Singer's lesbian patient from *Androgyny*, discussed in the last section here, is of course an exception.) The equation of homosexuality with male homosexuality is perhaps the best evidence for the rightness of the feminist criticism that psychology, analytical psychology included, uses men's psychology as normative human psychology and ignores female experience as much as possible or considers it only in comparison to men's psychology.

However, the gay liberation movement's distinction between the gay male community and the lesbian-feminist community may also contribute to this situation. Many contemporary women who love women do not define themselves as homosexual, preferring to identify themselves instead as lesbian, a term that, like *gay* used for male homosexuals, implies a consciousness of how homosexual orientation carries political, social, and communal meanings. So one asks, could it not be that contemporary Jungian writers may be making a similar distinction—using *homosexual* to denote male homosexuality and reserving *lesbian* for female homosexuality?

Unfortunately, a perusal of the Jungian literature for specific references to and discussions of lesbianism yields woefully little. Despite the burgeoning literature on women's experience and psychology from a host of talented, insightful, and creative women in Jungian circles, the literature of contemporary women's experience from a Jungian perspective remains largely a literature of heterosexual female experience. Even in books where one might expect to find discussions of women's sexual relationships with other women, such as some of the most popular and widely read Jungian books on contemporary feminine experience—Sylvia Brinton-Perera's *Descent to the Goddess: A Way of Initiation for Women*, Linda Leonard's *The Wounded Woman: Healing the Fa-*

ther-Daughter Relationship, Nancy Qualls-Corbett's *The Sacred Prostitute: Eternal Aspects of the Feminine,* Christine Downing's *Psyche's Sisters: Re-imagining the Meaning of Sisterhood,* Ann Belford Ulanov's *The Feminine in Jungian Psychology and Christian Theology,* Jean Shinoda Bolen's *Goddess in Everywoman,* Sibylle Birkhauser-Oeri's *The Mother: Archetypal Image in Fairy Tales*—there are only brief mentions of lesbianism, usually in the context of heterosexual women's lesbian feelings (and a few very brief statements concerning male homosexuality in Great Mother cults). Jungian-feminist reevaluations of the animus concept, such as those by Demaris Wehr or Mary Ann Mattoon and Jeanette Jones,[46] do not show a recognition of lesbianism the way we have seen contemporary reevaluations of the anima concept to include discussions of male homosexuality. Some may find this a surprising omission, especially since lesbianism was traditionally characterized as animus identification among Jung and his immediate followers.

Two exceptions to this near silence on lesbianism are to be commended, despite their brevity and limitations. Betty De Shong Meador, a Jungian analyst in Berkeley, California, describes in great detail an erotic countertransference reaction she experienced toward a female client in an article in *Chiron* entitled "Transference/Countertransference between Woman Analyst and Wounded Girl Child." Given the scarcity of frank discussions concerning countertransference in the literature and the even more serious absence of nearly anything on lesbianism, one can understand why Meador couches her clinical report in the form of an impersonal fairy tale concerning two women. Likewise, Marion Woodman in *The Pregnant Virgin* discusses the lesbian imagery of a number of dreams of women she has treated.[47]

The major limitation of both these creative and even courageous contributions to the literature lies in the fact that these discussions are not on lesbianism at all but rather on heterosexual women's experience of same-sex attraction. Lesbians, women whose primary (or even exclusive) sexual orientation is toward other women and who define themselves socially and politically by this orientation, remain an unknown population for Jungian writers. Is there a specifically lesbian psychology with its own archetypal themes and experiences? The Jungian literature remains silent and provides no answer—indeed, the question itself has not yet been raised.

In reviewing Barbara Black Koltuv's *The Book of Lilith* for the New York journal *Quadrant,* Karin Lofthus Carrington, comments on Jungians' silence on lesbian experience:

> Koltuv's book does not acknowledge the unique meaning of an erotic longing between women that often occurs in the individuation journey. Jung recognized that a sacred knowing about immortality is experientially transmitted between the mother and daughter alive in every woman. The ancient Greeks honored this transformative knowing between women with both sacred and profane enactments of the erotic at the ritual initiations at Eleusis. However, in modern Jungian thought there appears to be a taboo against speaking too directly or clearly about the importance of women loving women. I wonder if this attitude within the Jungian community is not reflecting a phobia in the culture at large. For if women are gazing into mirrors and into one another's eyes as a way of remembering their wholeness, who will then mirror to men their souls?[48]

So far, it seems, this question may be too anxiety-provoking to answer by exploring the real nature of lesbian experience, except in the context of heterosexual women's brief flirtations with lesbian relationships. One hopes a fuller and more satisfying view of "the importance of women loving women" is forthcoming from the many talented women that populate the Jungian community.

ON THE HOME STRETCH

Contemporary thought on homosexuality from a Jungian perspective remains fragmentary, even scattered. Although various important issues are consistently addressed in many of these discussions—in particular the way conventional definitions of masculinity and femininity, within analytical psychology and without, may no longer be adequate to describe male and female psychological experience—there does not seem to be a great deal of agreement at present on what homosexuality means psychologically or archetypally, or even whether it is a phenomenon to be regarded negatively, positively, or neutrally. Some writers take the traditional Jungian tack of gently worded disdain and indirect pathologization when referring to homosexuality; others clearly reject the idea that homosexuality is inherently pathological and insist on training the spotlight on sociopolitical issues or individual fidelity to self. Some writers, such as Hillman, Lopez-Pedraza, Monick, and Singer, use approaches based on mythological imagery, and others, such as Zinkin and Centola, look at fictional depictions of gay men for psychological insight. But few present the kind of detailed personal accounts of gay people to be found in Jung's cases or even in some of the case studies presented by first-generation analysts like Jacobi or Prince. Gay people and their community, their individuation process, their fantasies, dreams, loves, hopes, and desires—all of these continue to remain hidden, despite the imagination of Jungian writings. Moreover, we encounter next to nothing from contemporary analysts on lesbianism as a psychological or cultural phenomenon, a surprising lacuna in a literature rich in women's studies.

What does not exist in analytical psychology is a comprehensive approach to homosexuality, or to sexual orientation in general, that is at once archetypally based and faithful to the contemporary experience of gay men and women both in analysis and not in therapy, an approach consonant with the more objective social-science research findings on homosexuality over the past twenty years. However evocative and stimulating much of the Jungian literature may be, we have seen how no one has yet been able to put together a contemporary Jungian approach to homosexuality that, if it cannot (or should not try to) explain the mystery and passion of men loving men and women loving women, then at least might deepen our awareness of those currents in our souls which lead in and out of homosexual desires, fantasies, and relationships.

It may be argued that comprehensive theories are somehow against the spirit of Jung and that individuality ought to reign. However, it is clear that the lack of organized thought on homosexuality serves no one, least of all gay men and lesbians whose experiences and value risk being lost without at least some kind of clarity on issues of sexual orientation. The overall effect of such piecemeal work on homosexuality by Jungian writers is to leave more confusion than light and to hide gay experience. Such a result itself seems contrary to Jung's intention of bringing to consciousness what has hitherto been unconscious. The rather positive attitudes Jung showed toward homosexuality and gay individuals are not used to further Jung's work. Individuality cannot reign unless attention is paid to gay experience.

In the next chapters, I will propose and demonstrate how one can meld archetypal insights, contemporary research, and both individual and communal gay male experiences into a comprehensive approach to homosexuality and sexual orientation. In using the best insights of Jung and Jungians on homosexuality, we will discard outdated attitudes and confusing theoretical suggestions to erect a provisional theoretical structure that will bring a bit of order to the *massa confusa*, a structure that, I hope, will provide a home where the many faces of Eros, male and female, gay and straight, conscious and unconscious, can be seen and honored.

6. Toward a Jungian Theory of Sexual Orientation: Gay Men and the Archetypal Feminine

A THOROUGH EXAMINATION of the thought of both Jung and Jungians on homosexuality shows more clearly what has and has not been done in analytical psychology on issues of sexual orientation. Also clear is that there is both a lack of and a need for a coherent theory of sexual orientation in analytical psychology. Ideally, such a theory would take into account specifically Jungian insights concerning the nature of the soul while honoring the real and diverse experiences of modern people, homosexual and heterosexual. Given the greater knowledge of sexual diversity and the present transition in social values on gender, sex roles, and sexual orientation, such a theory would need to satisfy certain requirements to be truly useful in deepening our understanding of the mysteries and wonder of sexual orientation.

First, a Jungian theory of sexual orientation would have to be just that, a theory of sexual orientation, not simply a theory of homosexuality. To be most useful, our theory would need to pave the way for a rich and open-ended understanding of all sexual orientations—heterosexuality as much as homosexuality and bisexuality. As we have seen from the writings of Jung's followers, to isolate and attempt to explain homosexuality by itself, as if heterosexuality were not as unfathomable at times and as much in need of deeper insight in our patriarchal culture, is to fall into the trap of implicit pathologization contained in all etiological theories. A truly useful theory of sexual orientation would go beyond the various forms of sexual orientation and provide an archetypally based way of understanding the full range and psychological import of the Kinsey scale, in terms of both individuals of differing sexual orientations and variations in sexual orientation over a given individual's lifetime.

Second, a Jungian theory would need to be firmly tied to Jung's most far-reaching discovery, the archetypes of the collective unconscious. This requirement is not important simply to toe the line of whatever Jungian orthodoxy there might be; rather, it makes sense because of the fundamental, passionate, and enduring character of one's sexuality, and especially of one's sexual orientation and sexual expression. Such a human phenomenon must have its roots in the deepest level of the soul, however it may be molded by personal and cultural factors. Analytical psychology, perhaps more than any other school of psychology, has the theoretical means at its disposal, in the concept of the collective unconscious, to illuminate the way our sexual orientation forms one of the fundamental pillars of our self-identity, not just in North America but throughout the world and across time.

Third, our examination of Jung and Jungians on homosexuality was not carried out simply for love of academic minutiae but was successful in revealing certain especially helpful attitudes with regard to homosexuality and sexual orientation in general on which a Jungian theory of sexual orientation might draw. Among such attitudes, as we have seen, is the notion that theory is to be used synthetically, to help an individual toward wholeness, rather than reductively or analytically, to split off or trivialize any one aspect of one's individuality. Less abstractly put, whatever the components or aspects of one's sexual orientation, one would need to hold each aspect in equal esteem and see the whole rather than any part.

Since Jung assumes homosexuality has meaning and purpose, a theory of sexual orientation should do likewise. An individual's orientation is not an incidental, unimportant aspect of his or her personality. Closely related to this presumption is the importance of grounding theory in empirical material, the real lives of real people, obtained both inside and outside of the consulting room. Any theory of sexual orientation must consult the enormous quantity of material on the real lives of gay and bisexual individuals and not simply feed on past theoretical formulations. Many may find certain of Jung's theoretical conjectures far-flung, mystical, or unverifiable, but none can deny his attention to real material drawn from the real inner and outer lives of the people he treated.

Last, but just as important, a Jungian theory of sexual orientation must avoid perhaps the most serious theoretical mistake Jung and his followers have made, namely, the way the three variables of sexual identity—anatomical gender, sociocultural sex roles, and sexual orientation—have become confused in analytical psychology, such that the simplistic Western conceptions of man and woman are not questioned as often as they might be. A truly useful theory of sexual orientation needs to honor the myriad personal experiences and archetypal elements that become fused at particular moments in an individual's life to shape that individual's interpersonal expression of sexuality, and, for its archetypal character to be credible, it would need to honor that fusion, however constant or changing it might be, cross-culturally as well as in Western culture. Such a theory would need to take seriously the many questions being raised inside and outside of analytical psychology on the adequacy of traditional definitions of masculinity and femininity, and it would need to bring Jung's own insights on the inherent contrasexuality of men and women to their logical conclusion in people's inner *and* outer lives.

All of the foregoing criteria for a theory seem to present a tall order. A Jungian theory of sexual orientation would need somehow to take completely seriously the variety of sexual expression in our own culture as well as in all others, and at the same time provide a coherent, unitary archetypal explanation for such variety. Moreover, this theory would need to deepen our understanding of the staggering variation among individuals without reducing the phenomenon of sexual orientation into a mechanistic set of how and why. A Jungian theory must always leave room for who and what, the ever personified but ever shifting character of the human soul and its passions. My proposal for a Jungian theory of sexual orientation, one illustrated by the following examination of the various archetypal themes in the lives of gay men, satisfies all of these requirements and has the added advantage of being both simple and elegant: *The sexual orientation of an individual or any group of individuals is determined through a complex interaction of the archetypal masculine, the archetypal feminine, and the archetypal Androgyne.*

The theory of sexual orientation proposed here is clearly very powerful. Nonetheless, it does not go beyond the bounds of current Jungian thought. Whatever newness this theory has lies in its synthesis and its application of preexisting concepts in analytical psychology, and not in any elaborate theoretical innovations. Rather than conceiving of the masculine, the feminine, and the Androgyne as separate archetypal dominants within the personality, this theory posits that *all three* (not just one or two) work together in a sometimes mysterious (though often not so mysterious) way, to produce that particular, archetypally tinged aspect of the personality, an individual's sexual orientation.

For those familiar with Jungian thought, such a suggestion is nothing new with regard to heterosexuality. Jung's theory of contrasexuality demands that a man's femininity be seen as a vitally important part of his soul; indeed, in its incarnation as anima, a man's femininity bears the Latin name for soul. Simarily, for better or worse, Jung and Jungians have understood that the element of masculinity in a woman's personality, her animus, or masculine soul, serves the purpose of integration as well.

Yet with such emphasis on contrasexuality in Jungian thought on heterosexuality, what can be easily forgotten is the synthesizing presence of the Androgyne. Even in Jungian theory, men and women can be seen and experienced as opposites engaged in a battle of the sexes, incarnations of an Otherness. The very term *contrasexuality* suggests conflict. To assume that all sexual orientation contains all three archetypal dominants of masculinity, femininity, and androgyny is to push farther and deeper toward the wholeness that is the teleological thrust of sexuality on its most basic level, Eros in its binding, connecting power. This theory of sexual orientation would, therefore, go past simple contrasexual explanations for various heterosexual phenomena. Heterosexual men are not attracted to women simply because of anima projections, a need to recapture a lost or unconscious femininity. To take the proposed theory of sexual orientation seriously would mean acknowledging that a crucial element in heterosexuality might also be the urge toward fulfillment of the demands of the Androgyne, the wholeness inherent in being both male and female in the act of sexual union. The theory would lead one to wonder whether the Androgyne, and not the conflicting, contrasexual opposites of masculine and feminine, is the god being served in an orientation toward heterosexual union.

I am aware that the notion of an androgynous element in heterosexuality is neither new nor radical. Jung himself went far beyond simple contrasexuality in *Mysterium Coniunctionis* and in

The Psychology of the Transference, in which heterosexual coupling is examined, with depth and breadth peculiar to Jung, as a symbol of wholeness, the end of individuation itself, the union of opposites. June Singer's masterful book on androgyny is certainly, at least for now, the last word. Thus this theory of sexual orientation may not add a great deal to the theoretical and archetypal examinations of the meaning and symbolism of heterosexual relationships already conducted by many Jungians. Heterosexuality, because it has been the dominant cultural value for millennia, needs no apologists, nor perhaps any additional theorists.

My theory may not be stunningly innovative for an understanding of heterosexuality using a Jungian perspective, but it would nevertheless function quite well to challenge any theoretical or experiential one-sidedness that might creep into a consideration of the meaning and function of heterosexual relationships. Given the way that culturally determined sex roles are unconsciously applied to psychological phenomena in Jungian thought, with archetypal entities somehow being straitjacketed into Western sex-role categories and gender-identified behavior, the theory I propose here would be of great use in holding up the true complexity of sexual interrelationships. Should one forget that men are not always just men as defined by Western culture but may at times also be, archetypally and emotionally, women and androgynes, just as women are not always just women but possess a masculinity and an androgyny often repressed by cultural values, a theory that views sexual orientation as a confluence of masculine, feminine, and Androgyne both broadens and deepens a mistakenly narrow view of the dynamics of heterosexual relationships. The great advantage heterosexuality has enjoyed socioculturally, having been the "normal" sexual orientation against which any variations have been judged as deviations, makes the theory proposed here one more contribution to a vast stream of preexisting thought on heterosexuality, though it is an important contribution to hold in awareness, given the often extreme cultural pressure toward repressing diversity and androgyny.

My proposal, however, does not come out of a burning desire to understand male-female relationships but rather to make some archetypal sense of the phenomena of homosexuality, same-sex relationships for which very few unbiased and progressive theories have been advanced. Our sweeping overview of the work of Jung and Jungians on this topic provides ample evidence of how the various archetypal dominants of masculinity, femininity, and Androgyny have been ignored, taken out of context, used reductively, or overemphasized according to prevailing social prejudices against homosexuality. In this theoretical environment, to hold up all three archetypes of the masculine, feminine, and Androgyne and to posit that theoretically *all* must be at work in some combination, however rich or complex the interaction, is of inestimable use in avoiding the especially pernicious one-sidedness that has affected much Jungian theorizing on homosexuality. The Jungian theory of sexual orientation proposed here is perhaps most important for gay men and women, because it not only counteracts this one-sidedness but also places sexual orientation on more neutral ground. Gay men's sexuality is not simply a one-note affair, a flight from womanhood, a feminine identification, androgynous acting out, but rather a polyphonic affair in which Father-Son, Mother-Lover, and the hermaphroditic Self all become actualized and acted upon through physical and emotional connection with another man. The theory works in a similar way for an understanding of homosexual women, whose sexual attraction and connection to other women become a deep interweaving of Mother-Daughter, Father strength, and androgynous oneness, and not only a Demeter complex or an animus-ridden aberration.

To make theoretical conjectures is one thing; to demonstrate their usefulness in organizing the data of experience is another. In the following chapters I intend to examine just how contemporary gay male culture filters and honors all three archetypal dominants of the masculine, the feminine, and the Androgyne, using both clinical and nonclinical material from the lives of gay men to bring forth the rich diversity inherent in male-male erotic relationships. To use a sometimes overworked term, my examination will be organized around gay men's stories—sometimes the fictional stories, the myths, as it were, which gay male culture has developed, sometimes the real inner and outer stories of individual gay men I have seen in therapy.

The focus here is on gay men and gay male culture for reasons no deeper than those of my own personal experiences, the majority of which have been within the gay male community. Although lesbians have numbered among my clients and friends for many years, my respect for women's experiences and autonomy leads me to allow lesbians to speak for themselves on their own archetypal experiences individually and collectively. My regret is that I am unable to redress the painful lack of attention to women's erotic relationships with other women; my hope is that my work on male homosexuality will enable lesbians in the Jungian community and beyond to carry out similar studies on lesbianism.

THE WIZARD OF OZ: A MYTH OF THE ARCHETYPAL FEMININE FOR CONTEMPORARY GAY MEN

We have seen how the appearance of the feminine in gay male experiences has led to the idea in Jung and Jungians that gay men universally suffer from a mother complex and thus identify with the anima and project and pursue the masculine with erotic compulsion, thereby remaining immature and less than fully developed. We have also suggested that this idea is a vast oversimplification of homosexuality and we have seen how this idea is for all intents and purposes identical to calling homosexuality a sickness since it presumes homosexuality's pathology a priori by the way homosexuality deviates from the peculiar conflation of gender, sex role, and sexual orientation that defines masculinity and femininity in Western patriarchal cultures.

However erroneous the Jungian attempts to theorize, we nonetheless see that themes of the archetypal feminine are indeed one element—and a vitally important one—of gay men's experience that cannot be ignored. Certainly, within collective gay male culture the presence of the feminine often comes out in flippant and trivial ways. The camp humor of some gay men, as when they bestow female names on one another; call one another Mary, girl, or sister; or adopt the more outrageous aspects of the patriarchal stereotypes of the feminine sex role (concern with appearances, emotionality, histrionic self-presentation, coquettishness, and bitchy verbal competition) clearly expresses gay men's closeness to collective femininity and therefore challenges one to examine the centrality of the feminine in gay men's experience without treating this phenomenon reductively or in a pathologizing way.

There is no reason to suppose that the feminine as an archetypal dominant in human experience functions any differently in heterosexuals than in homosexuals, and here we must admit that gay men may be just as prone to feminine identification as any other group of people (including straight men). The dangers inherent in any collective identification are as present for homosexuals as for heterosexuals. However, in positing this, is it not possible to conceive of a more conscious, differentiated, and progressive relationship to the feminine for gay men than the heterosexual stereotype of the sissy? Might not we find ways within gay male culture that the feminine is mediated collectively and individually so that she participates in the process of gay male individuation to enable gay men to attain a fuller sense of themselves as men? And what of real gay men's experiences of the feminine in their dreams and their lives?

The Wizard of Oz is a movie that has enjoyed nearly universal popularity since its 1939 release, and it is regarded with special affection and delight by the American gay community. Evidence of this affection is not hard to come by if one knows gay people or is familiar with the gay community. "Somewhere over the Rainbow," the song perhaps most identified with the film, has long served as an unofficial anthem at gay pride celebrations and parades, and the use of the rainbow flag as a gay pride symbol appears to be partly derived from this association. The phrase "friends of Dorothy" is commonly heard slang used by some gay men to refer to other gay men.

Various lines, episodes, and characters from the movie have become a part of gay culture. For instance, during a San Francisco mayoral campaign in which Dianne Feinstein was clearly the front-runner, one of the somewhat tongue-in-cheek candidates in the race was Sister Boom-Boom, a member of the Sisters of Perpetual Indulgence, a group of transvestite "nuns" well known in San Francisco. One of Boom-Boom's posters showed her on a broomstick in the sky writing in large black smoke-letters "Surrender Dianne," using the image of the Wicked Witch of the West from the film to make a humorous point. A gay bar in

Madison, Wisconsin, has a mural at its entrance that depicts Dorothy and her dog, Toto, arriving in Oz as she utters her famous line, "Toto, I've a feeling we're not in Kansas anymore." In various publications of the gay community, one finds a comic advertisement for a record album entitled "Miss Gulch Returns." The impression is that the parodies of the film's songs on the album are to be sung by the Margaret Hamilton drag look-alike who, in the ad, is shown complete with sneer and picnic basket. However, one sure way to see the collective gay male response to the movie would be to attend a showing in a gay neighborhood, where one could count on very vocal audience participation.

The enduring popularity of any work of art suggests the presence of dynamic, collective factors at work psychologically. In modern times, given the decline of written and oral tradition, the rise of mass culture, and the advent of previously unimagined mobility, motion pictures often serve as modern myths, with actors and actresses becoming the projection screens for archetypal contents. One need only look at the near religious fervor that grips the fans of Marilyn Monroe or Elvis Presley to witness the connection between the adoration of film stars and the collective unconscious. Therapists, specifically Jungians, can certainly attest to the prevalence of motion picture imagery in their patients' dreams.

Because *The Wizard of Oz* holds a special place in the heart of the gay male community, one is drawn to the thesis that the film must represent personified archetypal elements of great significance to gay men, that the film is a myth which represents in symbolic form some essential part of gay men's experiences. This is not to imply that this story is the only myth of the gay male community or even the most central. Obviously, other movies whose lines or characters have worked their way into contemporary gay culture, such as *Sunset Boulevard* and *Mommie Dearest*, may also serve a mythic function. Nor, obviously, is *The Wizard of Oz* a myth *only* for gay men.

Of course, the popularity of the film reaches far beyond the gay community, and a Jungian analysis of the film provided by Ann Belford Ulanov suggests that the movie is a symbolic representation of animus integration in the process of feminine individuation.[1] Ulanov's accurate and insightful analysis raises many interesting questions of interpretation when one turns to explore the film's meaning for gay men. How does this myth of feminine development speak to the souls of gay men? What is the relationship between Ulanov's analysis of the feminine and the meaning the movie has for gay men?

If one is to grasp the psychological meaning of *The Wizard of Oz* for gay men and through it the function of the feminine for contemporary gay men, one must take into account the psychosocial context of gay men's development, namely, those sexual mores and attitudes which dominate contemporary Western culture. These sexual mores and attitudes share two salient characteristics. The first is best described by the term *patriarchy.* Patriarchal values identify particular personal characteristics and social roles exclusively with either men or women and tend to value those characteristics and roles assigned to men over those assigned to women.[2] The second characteristic is one that gay liberationists have termed heterosexist. Heterosexism views heterosexuality as the only acceptable, normal pattern for fulfilling human relationships and tends to view all other sexual relationships as either subordinate to or perversions of heterosexual relationships. This view of the primacy of heterosexuality in human development enjoys wide support from nearly every important cultural institution, from the church to the government to the scientific establishment, and has a long but by no means monolithic history.[3]

Whether these two cultural assumptions are adequate or useful in understanding the real, lived experience of contemporary people is an important question. As we have seen in our previous examination of Jung and Jungians, the one-sidedness of such patriarchal and heterosexist values is being called into question more and more by the increasing visibility of individuals and relationships that do not fit conventional molds, and the growing body of knowledge on the completely different value systems that exist in other cultures, such as among traditional Native Americans or in certain Polynesian societies, challenges the Western belief that only patriarchal or heterosexist values work to promote human happiness and social order.[4] Nonetheless, patriarchal and heterosexist values at least presently hold sway in the United States and so these values form the psychosocial context of gay male individuation.

The patriarchalism and heterosexual bias of modern Western

culture seems to create two different but related psychological tasks for gay men, insofar as gay men become aware, consciously or subconsciously, of being attracted primarily to other men. The first task facing gay men is conditioned by the patriarchal view that sexual attraction toward men is characteristic exclusively of women, a gender category that is defined by anatomy and supported by the value placed on heterosexual relationships. For the man who loves men, therefore, the only culturally available self-definition given to him, at least initially, is to see himself as psychologically feminine.[5] How well he comes to terms with this femininity in some positive, individual way determines, for good or for ill, his degree of psychological maturity.

Heterosexual men are hardly exempt from an integration of their own contrasexuality, and this insight remains among Jung's most far-reaching notions. However, a heterosexual man's femininity is not seen socially as determinative of his identity as a man, while in a patriarchal and heterosexist society a gay man's femininity is seen as his identity, both socially and psychologically, because of his sexual attraction to other men. As compared to heterosexual men, therefore, a gay man's individuation process begins with a completely different relationship to the psychosocial definitions of masculinity and femininity; it unfolds in ways that sometimes resemble and sometimes differ from the individuation process of men who are not gay.

Related to this different point of departure for the individuation process, the second psychological task for gay people in a heterosexual world is the process of coming out. Unlike heterosexuals, gay people must go through a special psychological operation of self-consciousness about their sexual and emotional development, because no models of homosexual self-image or relationship exist in the culture at large to support a growing awareness of one's homosexuality. Needless to say, the lack of external cultural supports for homosexuality creates a peculiar and frequently destructive psychosocial vacuum for gay people, who often have a difficult time acknowledging their gay feelings and identity.[6] What have seemed to be manifestations of pathology within homosexually oriented persons are now best understood not as characteristic of homosexuality per se but rather as unfortunate adaptive responses to the fierce prejudice, horror, and hatred shown toward homosexuality in Western societies.

Given these two tasks, one finds that a symbolic analysis of the film as a myth of feminine development is quite relevant to gay men, specifically because of the way gay male sexual orientation has been designated as feminine. In addition, the movie has yet another symbolic theme that speaks directly to the task of coming out, a theme best summed up by noting that "all is not what it seems to be" in Dorothy's visit to the merry old land of Oz. Here the movie touches on another motif relevant to the lives of gay men, the theme of persona creation and development.

GAY MALE INDIVIDUATION AND THE FEMININE

That the gay male community responds so intensely and affectionately to a myth of animus integration should hardly be a cause for wonder. Given the Western identification of male homosexuality with psychological femininity, an identification that some gay men have internalized to the detriment of their sense of masculinity, *The Wizard of Oz* presents to gay men a myth of masculine integration and feminine redemption. One is astonished to see how applicable Ulanov's analysis of the movie is to gay male individuation once one understands that gay men's psychological femininity is not an outgrowth of intrinsic pathology or immaturity but rather the result of internalizing Western sex-role definitions. Dorothy's adventures in the movie give image to many gay male psychodynamics and thereby represent symbolically a way to wholeness.

As Ulanov points out, the film's initial symbols represent elements as necessary to women's individuation as to gay male psychological maturity: the tornadolike storm of feeling that gathers at puberty around Dorothy and her best friend, the instinctive Toto ("whole" in Latin); Dorothy's need to leave home and find her own path; her unwitting and even unwanted jouney into Oz, the Technicolor realm of her unconscious life. Insofar as gay men have internalized a feminine self-definition, they need to set out on the same journey as Dorothy toward the Wizard, a masculine source of power.

For women as for gay men, the journey begins by slaying the Wicked Witch of the West, the power-ridden feminine force that has subjugated Munchkinland, the land of the "little people."[7]

Dorothy's arrival in the realm of the unconscious breaks the witch's stranglehold and serves to constellate the conflict around the feminine in a more differentiated and active way. The now explicit rivalry between Glinda the Good Witch and the Wicked Witch of the West is the symbol of this greater differentiation.

The focus of the struggle, the ruby slippers, is important to note. Ulanov sees in these shoes a symbol of Dorothy's own ego standpoint, that is, Dorothy's own individual point of view and her sense of herself, upon which her personality stands, as it were. But this symbol might be amplified further by the redness of the shoes, a color associated with both passion and feeling. To find one's ego standpoint is a task incumbent on all individuals. Gay men, however, often start with a self-definition largely drawn from patriarchal and pejorative images of femininity. To preserve their sexual passion and feeling as a source of power, gay men often find themselves at the center of an archetypally tinged struggle between good and evil. When understood in this light, one can see why those powerful ruby slippers are what the Wicked Witch covets, what Glinda protects, and what Dorothy must use to find her way forward down the Yellow Brick Road.

A gay male patient, for whom the wedding of a fairly conventional coworker had become a source of irritation, dreamed:

> We are all invited to be in Cathy's wedding and she has supplied clothes and shoes for us to wear. I go to the huge pile of shoes (this is in Whole Earth Access [a store in the Bay Area]) and I choose low-heeled, turquoise-sequined shoes which fit comfortably. I wonder if there will be a teal-blue dress to match with sequins.

Certainly one of the major themes of this dream is the unconscious sense of exclusion this gay man felt in the midst of the preparations for a celebration of heterosexual union. His irritation with the event was even consciously linked by him to the way "gay male relationships don't get honored with this much fuss," and so the compensatory inclusion presented by the dream in the form of being invited to become a "bridesmaid" at Whole Earth Access points toward one way for this man to become part of the wedding—through a connection with his "feminine standpoint," the comfortable turquoise shoes he was able to find to wear. It may be tempting to see in this image a simple adoption of a feminine persona, but the patient had two associations to these shoes. The first was to shoes of a similar color that the patient's sister wore as bridesmaid in a wedding, which points to the patient's using a close, more self-based femininity and not just some collective idea of womanhood. The second association, however, was to Dorothy's ruby slippers, a source of power and strength, that which brings her home to her self. The dream illustrates this gay male patient's similarity to Dorothy in the film, as he searched for a true inner femininity that he could stand on, one that fit comfortably and matched, one chosen by him and not simply assigned.

Ulanov identifies Dorothy's companions on the road as conventional images of the so-called positive animus to be integrated into a woman's sense of self. These initially undeveloped animus fragments, in the form of the Scarecrow, Tin Woodsman, and Cowardly Lion, lack brains, heart, and courage, and Dorothy regards the Wizard as the potential source of these attributes. The quaternity that this group forms is the familiar 3 + 1 pattern often found in fairy tales, and it points to the psychological task at hand for Dorothy, a search for completion.

Once again, women and gay men find themselves on the same psychological path: women because the patriarchal sex-role assignments rob them of a natural ability to see masculine qualities as available to them as women, gay men because patriarchy and heterosexism rob them of a natural ability to see masculine qualities available to them as gay men. The salvation and completion of inner masculinity through the integration of such personal qualities as activity, intelligence, fearlessness, and discrimination—qualities identified in Western patriarchal societies with the heterosexual male—is as important a task for women to accomplish as it is for gay men. Ulanov's analysis rings true. The development of a positive, differentiated inner masculinity is the point of Dorothy's tale, and so the movie possesses undeniable psychological significance for women and gay men alike.

For gay men, however, a connection with the positive side of masculinity may be achieved only once some resolution of the issues of femininity can be found. In casting off society's caricatures of femininity and locating their own passionate nature, their true feelings, the closeness they feel to their own body and its rhythms—in short, in relating to that inner self-based femininity that Jung called the anima—perhaps gay men may not go through all that different a process from heterosexual men in coming to know themselves as men through knowing themselves as women as well. For gay men, as for Dorothy, the point is to bring the feminine and masculine experiences of self together and to know the feminine, not in its outward conventional forms, but rather in its inward power and individuality—a part of "me."

The dangers along the way to the Emerald City are familiar ones from fairy tales and myths. An attack ensues when the Scarecrow attempts to eat apples from the trees of Oz. Too early an appropriation of unconscious contents as "mine" can lead to indigestion and psychological backlash from the autonomous underworld. The delectable and soporific poppy field represents another kind of danger in working with unconscious material, the temptation to fall into its swoon and sleep, abandoning one's awareness and direction. These images speak more of typical collective dangers of the *nekyia,* the journey to the underworld, than to particular experiences of gay men or women. What is relevant to this discussion is how an undeveloped psychological masculinity might tend toward either greed or indolence without a connection to the Self. Persephone's myth gives image to just this kind of masculinity in the figure of Hades, the rapacious hidden god of the shadow realm.

Entry into the Emerald City proves more difficult than imagined, but once Dorothy and her friends are there, the Wizard, an awesome figure, assigns precisely that task which one might expect: Dorothy and her friends are to wrest the phallic broomstick from the clutches of the witch. When we interpret this element of the tale, a difference appears between its meaning for gay men and its meaning for women, thus pointing up the different relationship gay men have to the archetypal feminine and its effect on their identity as men. For women, the negative feminine and her phallic powers are in some way archetypal elements of her fundamental feminine identity and must be depotentiated for further growth to occur; the archetypal witch within must be put in her place and her power relativized. For gay men, however, as men, the witch might be better understood as a symbol of the constricting, withering, destructive power of society's identification of gay men as feminine. The witch and her phallic broomstick are certainly inner figures, archetypal dominants of collective experience. For gay men, though, the wresting away of the witch's broomstick may mean both a depotentiation of this inferior femininity and a reappropriation of the phallic masculinity that has been denied them as gay men. The witch is, therefore, an apt symbol for the spiritual paralysis that occurs when patriarchal attitudes project a negative, witchlike image of feminine voracity on gay male sexuality.

That gay men all too often internalize and act out this sort of femininity is thus psychologically understandable. The historical importance of drag in gay communities, especially transvestite portrayals of witchy, bitchy, larger-than-life phallic females such as Joan Crawford, Bette Davis, and Mae West (and not, for example, Loretta Young, Carole Lombard, Doris Day, and Mary Pickford), can be seen as a manifestation of this internalization. Yet clearly such transvestite portrayals are attempts to do exactly what Dorothy does in her journey: lay claim to the phallic power held hostage by an evil, stultifying, and one-sided femininity. To grab the witch's power for oneself is to break her spell.

This interpretation makes sense of the weapon that Dorothy uses to defeat the witch: water. As a symbol archetypally identified with spirit but also with flexibility, fluidity, motion, and depth, water would obviously be lethal to this priapic witch-bitch, whose rigidity precludes spirit, motion, or life. For gay men, water as a symbol of flexibility has special significance, since flexibility is the best defense against any identification of themselves as exclusively, pathologically feminine. Flexibility and fluidity in self, in love, and in sexual attraction, though anathema to patriarchal attitudes, are the very source and gift of gay sexuality.

As the witch is deflated, so, too, the Wizard, along with his ideal of Wise Old Man masculinity, is eventually revealed as fraudulent. For Dorothy and for women, it seems, an overvaluation of the masculine must be worked through, and this interpretation is supported by the details of the Wizard's exposure in the film. Dorothy's instincts, personified in Toto, show her idealized projection to be just that, a projection. Indeed, he is literally a projection in the movie, since the Wizard Dorothy sees is but an image on a screen. Intimate involvement pulls back the curtain of the projection booth to reveal the real person, whom one meets in passion and companionship. The inflationary image of the Wizard ballooning off into the sky is the direct result of withdrawing this idealized projection. Projecting saviorhood onto men is a dead end and leaves one abandoned.

For gay men, the Wizard's idealized aspects and his eventual exposure may represent much the same psychodynamic situation. After shaking off the tyranny of a feminine self-identification and appropriating to themselves the phallic energy once given away or denied, many gay men fall prey to a frantic search for the ideal man who will constitute for them, in a magical, wizardly way, the powerful, active masculinity that has been the end of their long individual search. The myth of the perfect lover is one that anyone who has worked with gay men clinically can affirm as both an enduring and nearly universal fantasy that appears at one point or another in the gay male individuation process. As Dorothy finds in her relationship to the Wizard, the real person with his faults, his fumbling, incompetence, age, and weakness must be uncovered and disclosed for a true relationship to be found and a true sense of self to be consolidated.

GAY MALE INDIVIDUATION AND THE PERSONA

Another consistent theme of the movie forms an important subtext to Dorothy's adventures and reinforces the mythic importance of the film for gay men: In Dorothy's story, "all is not what it seems to be." The popularity of the movie among gay men is directly related to this theme in the myth, since the transformative recognition that all is not what it seems is, after all, the very heart of coming out as a gay person. In a peculiar and painful social situation in which homophobia works to hide from gay men their individuality and their sexuality, gay men struggle to achieve an autonomous relationship to the collective femininity they have been identified with and denigrated for. In addition to representing some of the *content* of gay male individuation, the movie's archetypal imagery also depicts perhaps the most important dynamic in the *process* of gay male individuation.

The film is saturated on many levels with this conflict between appearances and reality. The cinematic structure of the movie, reinforced by the startling switch from a black-and-white Kansas to a vivid, Technicolor Oz and back to Kansas, is one in which Dorothy's manifest life has correspondences to an inner world. This inner-outer correspondence is taken further when the outer persons of Dorothy's life appear as transmogrified personages in her inner world: The Kansas farmhands are her Oz companions; the traveling professor is the Wizard of Emerald City; the nasty Miss Gulch (whose last name is a sure tip-off to her archetypal role in the tale) could only be the Wicked Witch. The movie as a whole is not simply about Dorothy's adventures in Oz but is explicitly framed by both technique and character to show that Dorothy actually lives in two worlds that are different from each other but also mysteriously, delightfully and frighteningly interconnected.

The same theme is recapitulated in Oz, because each Oz character is somehow fundamentally not what he or she seems. The Scarecrow scares no one. The Tin Woodsman is rusted. The Cowardly Lion is an oxymoron. Glinda and the Wicked Witch have two aspects. The beneficent Glinda has withheld important information from Dorothy on how to use the slippers' power to get home to Kansas, and the Witch of the West is but one half of a nefarious pair. Even the witch's fierce palace guards are half human, half monkey, and they turn out to be hapless victims more than evil monsters. Dorothy is confounded throughout Oz, confronted with flowers that talk and trees that fight back. Appearances in Oz continually belie the reality beneath.

Naturally, the capital of this dynamic interplay between what is and what seems is the Emerald City. The foursome's entry into the city is immediately followed by a carriage ride behind a chameleonlike "horse of a different color" that changes color from shot to shot in the film sequence. Before seeing the Wizard, Dorothy and her friends must undergo an elaborate makeover in a busy art deco–style beauty salon. The gifts the Wizard bestows on the Scarecrow, Tin Woodsman, and Lion are but external tokens of inner qualities—a diploma for intelligence, an honorific heart-watch for love, a medal for courage. In this way, these gifts ironically emphasize the Wizard's ineffectuality and, as Ulanov notes, the necessity of inner development rather than outer achievement.

This counterpoint between appearances and reality is basic to the movie's thematic and visual structure, and the psychological factor at issue in this counterpoint is one of Jung's distinctive contributions to psychology, the persona. Jung used the term *persona* to denote that part of the personality which an individual presents to others in a social context, the external face or mask determined by one's role, external attributes, or professional activities. For this reason, Jung considered one's persona a segment of the collective psyche, since it is formed and conditioned by collective expectations and values, and he spoke of the persona in somewhat derogatory terms:

> It is, as its name implies, only a mask of the collective psyche, a mask that *feigns individuality*, making others and oneself believe that one is individual, whereas one is simply acting a role through which the collective psyche speaks.
>
> When we analyze the persona we strip off the mask, and discover that what seemed to be individual is at bottom collective; in other words, that the persona was only a mask of the collective psyche. Fundamentally, the persona is nothing real: it is a compromise between individual and society as to what a man should appear to be. He takes a name, earns a title, exercises a function, he is this or that. In a certain sense all this is real, yet in relation to the essential individuality of the person concerned it is only a secondary reality, a compromise formation, in making which others often have a greater share than he. The persona is a semblance, a two-dimensional reality, to give it a nickname.[8]

Jung also acknowledged, however, that the choice of the persona was perhaps more complex and individually determined than one might at first think, and he did recognize that a suitable persona is a psychic necessity. Nevertheless, perhaps because of his own introversion or his concern with inner individuality, Jung described the persona in negative ways: a means of concealment, a hindrance, a sacrifice to the external world, and a divisive element in consciousness.[9]

Jung considered the persona a compromise formation, a mediator between the ego and the external world of consciousness, much in the way that the anima or animus serves as mediator between the ego and the unconscious. Jolande Jacobi writes that the positive function of the persona is to "build up a relatively stable facade adapted to the demands of present-day civilization. An elastic persona that 'fits well' belongs to the psychic wardrobe of the adult man, and its lack or its rigidity is an indication of psychic maldevelopment."[10] This split view of the persona permeates Jungian thought on the subject: The persona is necessary for psychic functioning and yet false, a hindrance to true individuation; it is a psychic formation that stabilizes and protects but needs to be stripped before inner work can begin. Such ambivalence about the persona might account for the scarcity of any extended discussion of the persona in the Jungian literature, and especially the absence of any extended discussion concerning its helpful or positive function.

This attitude toward the persona is a drawback when attempting to examine the psychological development of individuals whose social position is that of outsider, as with gay people. No group more than gay people faces persona issues so directly. As the mediator between outside and inside, the persona is the place in the personality in which a compromise must be forged between collective values and individual needs. Since patriarchy and heterosexism typically assume anatomically specific behavior patterns for boys and girls at birth, a masculine or feminine face comes to be pasted on children according to gender, with heterosexuality indiscriminately expected as the developmental norm. Gay men's inner homosexual feelings develop at odds with collective expectations of heterosexual masculinity and do so in a way that can easily be hidden and denied, and yet, in coming out as a gay man, an equally false persona of inferior femininity can be applied to the now acknowledged homosexuality. In these ways, one essential psychological situation for gay men is also one of the basic themes of Dorothy's myth. All is not what it seems for gay men beneath society's ill-fitting mask of heterosexual sex roles or its assignment of inferior femininity.

The predominance of heterosexual sex roles as an unconscious psychosocial assumption in Western culture creates a situation for gay men in which the imposed heterosexual persona binds and restricts. If gay men have not acknowledged their homosexuality, then this mask of collective expectation all too often distorts the true movements of Eros that gay men experience within and serves to hide their real individuality even from themselves. If

gay men have acknowledged their homosexuality, then a heterosexual value system attempts to account for this anomaly by
identifying male homosexuality with inferiority and femininity.
The suffering created for gay men by these double binds, by this
gulf between "what I am" and "what I seem to be," often acts
like Dorothy's tornado, picking gay men up and putting them
down on the Yellow Brick Road to individual authenticity.

For gay men to fail in shucking off society's persona, to fail to
come out and affirm their homosexuality inwardly and outwardly,
is to retain the collective armor of social convention, often with
deleterious effects. The creation of a suitable persona, a persona
that represents and contains one's inner life but does not conceal,
a persona that protects while remaining flexible and resilient, is
one of the most important psychological tasks facing gay men in a
homophobic society. Moreover, it is a task intimately bound up
with issues of what it means to be a man and what it means to be
connected to the feminine in our society. Naturally, the gay male
community reflects and supports this central concern with the
persona creation in myriad, rich ways.

Leather, especially black leather, is the preeminent, post–gay
liberation clothing material and seems related to persona dynamics. After all, what better physical symbol for the kind of persona
that gay people need in a homophobic society than the revealing,
protective sheath of a second skin whose flexibility is matched
only by its strength? What better focus for community celebration than the twin feasts of Halloween and Carnival, where persona creation and persona exhibition have become enacted rituals of archetypal masks and flamboyant costuming? What better
field of human endeavor for gay people than the arts, where the
dialogue between form and content lies at the heart of all creation? What community of people loves camp, irony, and sarcasm
more than the gay community, delighting in exposing "what is,"
unseemly or laughable, behind "what seems"? What better and
more enduring cultural institution than transvestitism? In contrast to transvestitism as an individual *sexual* practice, whose
practitioners, research has shown, are predominantly heterosexual, crossdressing has historically been a *cultural* act for gay
people. The decline in respect for drag queens in the gay community is related to the rise of a more sophisticated political

analysis of antigay prejudice, prejudice to be opposed through more authentic visibility so as to create genuine, rather than defensive, personae for gay people in society and thereby assure psychological and social freedom.

Obviously, the popularity of Dorothy's story among gay men is evidence that this myth of persona strikes a deep chord in the souls of gay men. The persona task for Dorothy in the movie is to see beneath "what seems" in Kansas in order to know more fully "what is" in Oz. The movie, which is the tale of her stripping off her persona to find her soul, is a story of transformation. Kansas, once stifling, now has new depth and richness. Moreover, her sojourn in Oz requires that she accomplish the same persona-removal task there. She must see beneath the ineffectuality of her male companions to aid them in developing true intelligence, heart, and fearlessness. She must unmask the Wizard, find the witch's vulnerability, and go beneath Glinda's bright surface to uncover the wisdom that will bring her home. All these tasks have deep symbolic resonance for gay men who must, in Malcolm Boyd's words, "take off the masks"[11] and make a journey behind the inhospitable outer face of convention to find the color, life, and power of their sexuality within. Dorothy's search symbolizes gay men's own search to see through the falseness of who they seem to be and to fashion a mediating persona that will reflect who they are. Gay men *are* Dorothy's friends in that they, too, must find their way home to a true self in the world.

However, for gay men, the persona themes in the movie are intimately connected to the film's other mythic theme, the relationship between femininity and one's identity as a man, for not only the persona of heterosexuality is imposed on gay men but also the persona of inferior femininity. The struggle to cast off this persona and be initiated into a true inward femininity can be seen in the dreams of gay men in therapy, dreams of impressive feeling for the men involved:

I attend my own wedding as Princess Caroline of Monaco, taking Philippe Junot as my husband and as she/I leave, Philippe and I are mobbed for our autographs. I enjoy it a great deal.

I am taking the place of the princess in a crowd of people at a huge celebration in a medieval town with a big high cathedral from which the procession and crowd is coming from very far away. A sea of people. I am Jane Wheelwright. It is then Oxford Street [patient's home] and I am walking down the street from my house when I pass a festive crowd of wedding revelers, among whom is Deirdre [black friend of patient] in a long flowing gown of many colors and patterns—a Japanese wedding gown made of silk. I say hello as she passes me.

Steve [patient's professor-friend] is in a class teaching and I am among the students. Phrases need to be translated into German and I haven't a clue how to do it. The class suddenly turns into a pool shrine, a grotto of sorts, with a bunch of older men who are attempting to swim in the water, though the tile around it is very slippery. This is Pocahontas's pool and sacred. A few of the older men carefully go in, but I follow quite ably.

[The next dream of the same patient:] I am in the service of a modern-day Arab ruler and am enjoined to perform the ritual of Isis for him at a small altar in a hotel room. At first I do it out of a book, anointing myself and the pillars of the shrine with pine oil from translucent alabaster jars, but then learn to perform the ritual naturally, doing it without the book by candlelight before the king, who is powerful and erotically attractive.

My aunt is describing a commune to me where her son lives in Santa Barbara, the women of which belong to a cult whose rituals have sexual overtones. At night, the women touch their noses to a picture of a beautiful blonde woman, which gives them or their mother an orgasm. I see two women do this (a flash of light occurs at the point of contact) and then I try it.

These "big" dreams, with their wedding and feminine-initiation symbolism, illustrate how the stereotype of gay men's misogyny gives the lie to the way in which gay males' contact with the feminine actually occurs on an intrapsychic level and how such contact results in an affirmation of gay men's masculine identity, as in the dream of the Arab king and the Isis ritual, or the way in which becoming Princess Caroline also means becoming one with the masculinity she marries. By knowing femininity in the direct way depicted in these dreams—swimming in Pocahontas's pool, engaging in ritual worship of the feminine, becoming the princess in the wedding, greeting the goddess in her many-colored robes—these men were clearly learning to relate to the same kind of powerful feminine self that Dorothy finds herself searching for and finding in the film.

The popularity of the Oz myth and the intertwining themes of the feminine and the persona may point up in a more sophisticated way the exact relationship gay men have to a collective femininity. Dorothy finds her feminine self, her home, through integration of masculine qualities, just as gay men find a true femininity, not simply the outer collective persona of denigrated heterosexual femininity, through the same process of masculine integration. To say this in another way, Dorothy's task of discriminating between inner and outer femininity, between individual and collective images of the feminine, occurs through contact with her inner masculinity, a process that parallels gay men's experience when they take off the mask and come out to declare their homosexuality as part of their masculine identity.

Although gay men's relationship to the feminine may at first resemble that of heterosexual women, who must also come out from behind similarly constricting images of femininity, a gay man's inner contact with the archetypal feminine, as in the dreams just related, results in something perhaps not all that different from the experience of heterosexual men: a greater sense of one's fullness and wholeness as a man. More specifically, just as finding one's masculine wholeness through greater relationship to the archetypal feminine forces at work in one's soul does not seem necessarily to result in homosexuality for the heterosexual male, neither should one expect heterosexuality to result for the gay man when he develops a more mature, workable, and intimate relationship to those forces in the soul represented by Glinda, the Wicked Witch, and the Wizard of Oz. What does result, for both gay men and heterosexual men, from the integration of one's despised femininity is the kind of personality enlargement that Jung saw as the end of the individuation process.

Indeed, a mature relationship to the archetypal feminine, in my personal and clinical experience as a gay male therapist, results rather in a greater sense of self-acceptance *as a man and as a homosexual.* This acceptance of oneself as a gay man enables the kind of closeness and intimacy between women and gay men that many heterosexual men notice (and perhaps envy) and that many women find enormously enjoyable and freeing. It is certainly possible for women and gay men to relate to one another in a purely collective way, using the exaggerated and stereotypical images of inferior femininity pasted onto both groups as a vehicle for undifferentiated relationship with one another (the stereotypes of the "dizzy queen" and the "fag hag" are one way this kind of relationship can be imagined); true intimacy between women and gay men, however, results when both have looked within and seen the deep connection that exists for both of them in the depths of their inner and outer femininity. Far from exhibiting their supposed misogyny, gay men who have seen and lived their femininity *through their homosexuality* perhaps know the archetypal feminine in a way that may not be available to men who have not been subjected to such collective stereotyping and who do not live in a gay male community that supports enactment of the feminine in so many ways, individually, socially, and ritually.

None of this is to say that what Jung and Jungian writers have seen and called feminine identification in the lives of gay men is completely wrong or false; gay men, as well as heterosexual men and women, can most definitely be identified with collective femininity in the way suggested by Jung and his followers. Such feminine identification, however, is neither archetypally inherent in homosexuality nor its cause, because identification with the feminine may be a result of the internalized homophobia and the generalized hatred of women that resides in current cultural conceptions of masculinity and femininity. Gay men are indeed able to develop an inner relationship to the archetypal feminine without either losing their masculinity or changing their basic homosexual orientation. Because the gay male experience of the feminine is so unique, perhaps more attention ought to be paid to the appearance of the feminine within the souls of gay men. Still, for all its uniqueness, the gay male experience of the feminine, when she can be seen or felt as a real inner presence, may not be all that different from any other man's struggles with his feminine side. A gay man's anima may be just as close or distant, fickle or helpful, poisonous or nourishing. The anima may carry the Great Mother in both her helpful and destructive aspects, or she may resemble the personal mother of more immediate experience. In truly seeing the feminine in the lives of gay men, we see both her sides, but in ways that force us to acknowledge both the uniqueness and the commonality of the gay male soul.

7. Imagery of the Archetypal Masculine in Gay Male Culture

BECAUSE CONVENTIONAL SEX roles and gender definitions assign the status of woman to gay men, it has been difficult—for gay men perhaps more than anyone—to understand male homosexuality and masculinity as mutually inclusive. We have seen how Jung and his followers tended to identify male homosexuality with femininity, through the concept of a mother complex, an anima identification, or matriarchal psychology, such that gay men's relationship to the archetypal feminine has been distorted and pathologized. By reinterpreting the symbolic import of *The Wizard of Oz* for gay men, bringing to the film a full awareness of the cultural prejudice against homosexuality and its effect on gay male identity, we have seen that there are other—and potentially more positive—relationships that gay men have to femininity, personally and collectively, besides the unhealthy dynamic of identification or bondage to the Great Mother.

It goes without saying that if gay men's relationship to the feminine has been seen in such distorted and negative terms, then views of gay men's relationship to the masculine, personally and collectively, can hardly be less distorted. Our review of what Jung and his followers have written on this relationship between gay men and masculinity showed that very little concerning the archetypal imagery of the masculine in male homosexuality has been explored without gay men's masculinity quickly being assigned to the realm of adolescent strugglers. The imagery of the masculine that appears in gay men's lives is interpreted as a kind of inchoate, immature, and undeveloped masculinity that is still essentially dominated by the mother and the anima.

Jung's and Jungians' failure to discern and appreciate the masculine themes in gay men's lives, individually and collectively, is all the more incredible given the very nature of male homosexuality—which is essentially a male-male phenomenon—and given the contemporary gay male urban subculture in the United States, which is first and foremost a culture rife with the themes and images of the archetypal masculine. Two aspects of American gay male culture in particular exhibit the collective imagery of the masculine in a highly developed, explicit way: gay male erotic literature and the sadomasochistic "leather" culture. Both of these institutions serve a very powerful psychological function in bringing archetypal themes of masculinity into the lives of gay men, whose masculinity has been consistently denied them and impugned throughout their development. Our analysis of the inner meaning of *The Wizard of Oz* suggests that the rawness, exaggeration, and shadowy quality of the masculinity portrayed in gay male erotic literature and in the imagery of the gay S&M subculture has as much to say about the cultural repression of male-male Eros as it does about the inherent nature of male homosexuality.

It may be fashionable and interesting to go far afield to gather the imagery of homoeroticism from foreign cultures, modern and ancient, to discern collective themes and mythologies, but our quest for such exotic material might have less to do with any academic necessity than with our uneasiness in acknowledging homosexuality as a living, breathing reality right under our noses. Layard's wry comment about such practices not being restricted to Polynesia but "flourishing among ourselves" says a great deal about why the enormous mass of collective imagery from the contemporary gay community in America has been largely ignored by analytical psychologists, and yet such material is there for all eyes to see.

One source of such imagery is the huge quantity of homoerotic stories published monthly by dozens of major gay male periodicals, material that is invaluable in discerning certain features of what homosexuality may represent for the contemporary gay man. In the first place, the intention of these erotic stories (almost always accompanied by artwork and nude photographs) is the provision of intense and gratifying sexual fantasies for gay men, one assumes, for the purposes of self-pleasure. These stories will not serve their function unless powerfully charged themes, symbols, and imagery are used. Further, these stories are by definition collective, published and distributed for millions of gay male readers, so the themes, symbols, and imagery used must have a wide archetypal meaning and charge (otherwise surely the magazines would go out of business).

Because the stories, with their exclusively erotic purpose, are not created out of any conscious intention to portray themes with psychological meaning or collective mythology, they are, one might say, psychologically ingenuous. If the authors of homoerotica argued that they meant to make grand symbolic statements about the nature of being human, we would have to either remain skeptical or confront these authors with their artistic failure, for while these stories may be many things, they are not great literature.

Homoerotic stories like these might be seen as the modern equivalent of fairy tales, which, however archetypally rich or revealing when subjected to psychological interpretation, nevertheless remain ingenuous, simple, and entertaining folk stories. Because the psychological interpretation of fairy tales has become almost an industry in depth psychology and because the reinterpretation of folktales for psychologically sophisticated modern audiences has entailed considerable literary adaptation and may be done with great artistic flair, it may be easy to forget that the original folktales—like the gay male erotic stories we will be examining—were raw and unfinished products, more like collective dream fragments bound together around important mythological elements (mythologems) than like the modern novel, with beginning, middle, and end and carefully drawn individual characters. Both fairy tales and gay male erotic stories consist of stock characters, recurring plots, and collective imagery and themes that have no set or definitive form, and both seem drawn primarily from the everyday fantasy life of a group of homogeneous individuals living in a like-minded community and culture. While gay male erotica certainly existed before the advent of the gay liberation movement, it is only since this movement that such material has been made acceptable enough to become visible and available to a general public. As such, gay male erotic stories are an expression of contemporary gay consciousness much in the same way folktales expressed important psychological themes for the folk culture in which such tales were told.

In using various erotic stories in workshops on the archetypal symbols of homosexuality, I have come across people, gay and straight, who find such stories offensive and disturbing, either in principle—believing that sexuality is sacred and therefore ought not to be turned into a consumer product for mass consumption—or more specifically because of the somewhat fantastic or violent nature of the sexual encounters often portrayed in these stories. To such objections I usually reply that my purpose in examining these stories is purely psychological; whether one finds these stories sexually exciting or lurid and distasteful, the fact remains that they are packed with the symbolism of homosexuality, and it is this symbolism that we are after. I usually further point out that the Grimms' fairy tales and Greek myths, to use two examples, are at least as fantastic and violent as any gay male erotic story one might read; our purpose is to take the events portrayed in such material not literally but rather symbolically.

The last and perhaps most important argument for availing oneself of such material is that the images and symbols of masculinity contained in these stories find counterparts in both the dreams and fantasies of gay male patients in therapy and the gay community in general. The chicken-or-the-egg question here—whether such literature creates and fosters such fantasies for individuals and the community or whether such literature grows out of the individual and communal unconscious of contemporary gay men—is somewhat irrelevant, since our purpose is not to establish sociological cause and effect but rather to amplify the imagery of homosexuality using material from the real lives of contemporary gay men.

That imagery is overwhelmingly masculine. The erotic photography in these magazines portrays men of every imaginable shape, size, and type, from caricatures of masculinity—enormous bodybuilders or men who fit cultural standards of masculine beauty so perfectly as to seem unreal—to men of somewhat more ordinary and mortal appearance—the boy next door, the all-American jock, the suit-and-tie businessman. These erotic stories reflect the emphasis on masculine imagery by the distinctly male concern with the role identity of the characters. Although many of the protagonists have individual names and are drawn in discernible or distinct ways, one can read any dozen stories and find that the men are almost indistinguishable from the role they play or the job they hold. These are not individuals but types—the sailor, the athlete, the construction worker, the army sergeant, the college football player, the high-school coach.

Many of these types embody the fulfillment of the contemporary culture's masculine ideal: strong, productive, handsome, self-assured, and always intensely sexual. Notably absent are men who would not embody the masculine ideal. There are few effeminate florists, transvestites, or pimply computer hackers populating this gay male collective universe.

Much has been made of the male initiation imagery seemingly inherent in male homosexual relationships, not only by Jung and Jungians but by many gay researchers. For example, therapists Andrew Mattison and David McWhirter discovered that the longest-lasting gay male relationships involved individuals with an average age difference of between five and sixteen years.[1] A number of gay anthropologists and sociologists have discovered similar patterns of *puer-senex* relationships cross-culturally and across time: the often mentioned Greek pattern of homosexuality, in which youths and mentors shared both education and sexual intimacy, can be found in other cultures such as those examined by Layard. The stereotypical fear of gay men as child seducers and abusers seems related at least in part to the initiatory dynamic that is often embodied in the simultaneous opposition and conjunction of age and youth in gay male relationships.

Thus it is fascinating to find gay male erotic literature rife with this initiatory symbolism. Many stories graphically portray the conjunction of youth and age, a *puer-senex* dynamic of some sort. A striking number of stories portray youthful males as either having sex with or fantasizing about having sex with older male members of their family. Every possible male-male incestuous combination or near incestuous combination can be found: father and son, uncle and nephew, older and younger brothers, older and younger cousins, older and younger brothers-in-law, father and son-in-law. The titles of some of these stories are enough to suggest the material: "Brothers Do It," "Father Blows Best," "Life With Father," "Meathead" (an allusion to Archie Bunker and his son-in-law Mike from the TV show "All in the Family"), "Ben's Brother."

If this weren't demonstration enough of the importance of initiatory symbolism in collective gay male imagery, then the number of stories describing some sort of teacher-student relationship ought to convince one. Again, almost every imaginable combina-

tion is portrayed: coach and athlete, army private and command-
ing sergeant, college student and extracurricular tutor, fraternity
pledge and house leader, boss and employee, new employee and
old hand. The titles suggest the content: "The Coach Taught
Me," "Frat House Rush," "Teacher's Pet," "A Teacher's Touch."

A great many stories concern gay men seducing heterosexual
men and initiating them into the glorious pleasure of homosexuality. These stories, with such titles as "Banging Straight
Butt," "Mr. Straight," and "Breaking in a Hustler," portray at
least one dynamic frequently seen by therapists in male patients,
especially in urban areas with a large and visible population
of gay men: the phenomenon of gay men—usually highly ambivalent about their homosexuality—who find themselves fasci-
nated with heterosexual men, or ostensibly heterosexual men—
usually highly ambivalent not about their heterosexuality but
about their masculinity in general—who again and again find
themselves being propositioned by gay men in various places
and circumstances.

Besides intrafamiliar old-young couplings, student-mentor relationships, and straight-gay male interactions, the fourth kind of
initiatory story one frequently finds in gay male erotica is the
coming-out confessional. If written in the first person, coming-
out stories often relate the first time the protagonist had sex with
a man and realized he was gay. Unlike other types of initiatory
stories, coming-out stories often describe not an interaction between older and younger males but rather an erotic encounter
with a "brother" or "double" character, as in Forster's novel
Maurice.

One story I use in workshops precisely because the various initiation themes are used and developed in a very charged and at
times complicated way is "Cop Brothers," by one Bud O'Donnell,
which appeared in *Honcho* magazine (March 1985). The story
concerns the sexual awakening in late adolescence of Brick
Andrews, who, in the absence of his father, becomes involved
erotically with the brothers next door, sons of the hypermasculine cop Matt Patterson. As brother-doubles of Brick's own age,
the Patterson boys initiate Brick into the joys of gay sex. This activity is recounted as a flashback, attendant on the main plot,
which focuses on Brick's relationship to the older cop-father

Matt, who returns home accompanied by his own brother Steve one day because he (Matt) was injured on the job. So we have two brothers of an older generation, Matt the cop and his brother Steve, and two brothers of a younger generation, Matt Patterson's sons, all of whom eventually have sex with Brick. The sexual encounter between Brick and Matt occurs as Brick cares for the injured cop, bathing him and eventually using the sexual techniques he learned from Matt's sons to seduce the powerful and handsome older man. This encounter between Matt and Brick is discovered and then joined by Matt's brother Steve. Of course the descriptions of these various threesomes are detailed and explicitly sexual, but it is important to notice that the rigid adoption of sexual roles in these couplings (triplings? quadruplings?) does *not* occur. This gives the lie to the recurrent stereotype of gay men dichotomized into passive and active types, a stereotype completely unsupported by my own personal and clinical experience or those of my gay male colleagues. In the story, young Brick gives and receives fellatio, just as the older Steve penetrates and is penetrated anally. In an interesting surprise ending, we find in the last paragraph that the story is actually a masturbation fantasy of Steve Patterson's, whose orgasm in the shower awakens his "cop brother" Matt, asleep in the next room. Thus the intrapsychic nature of this erotic fantasy is made quite explicit in the narrative: The story itself is a fantasy within a fantasy.

What is clear from this story is that the archetypal imagery of initiation found in Layard's cultural researches survives even today in the collective fantasy life of gay men as embodied in gay erotica and that the imagery of these stories is undeniable and archetypally masculine. The masculine polarities of *puer* and *senex* noted by Hillman are explicitly acknowledged, and the story's structural elements attempt a reconciliation of this polarity, as the youthful Brick moves from sexual contact with his brother-double-peers into a relationship with older, more powerful and phallic figures, representative of both male authority (a policeman) and a wider community of men (cop brothers). The masculinity represented by these figures is equally complex and multifaceted, as the men in this story move freely between strength and weakness (the injured policeman), between phallic penetration and phallic receptivity (exchange of fellatio and anal activity), between teaching and being taught (Brick as initiate with the younger brothers, Brick as the initiator with the older pair).

One can see how the imagery of masculinity in this story, especially the themes of initiation into the polarities of masculinity and their reconciliation through sexual intercourse, can take more extreme form in the imagery of the sadomasochistic subculture of the gay male urban community. S&M sexual practices commonly involve the enactment of roles by the participants, commonly referred to as top and bottom, master and slave, dominant and submissive, in which the top man controls, dominates, and manipulates the bottom man both physically and psychologically. Physical control in S&M rituals is generally accomplished through immobilization (using bondage with ropes or other materials, gagging, blindfolding, harnessing, collaring, physical suspension) and is often the prelude to the gradual infliction of various forms of pain or discomfort, such as spanking, whipping, beating, punching, intense stimulation of the genitals (cock and ball work) or nipples (tit play), and penetration of mouth, anus, or penis with body parts or other instruments (toys), sometimes against the will of the bottom. Psychological control of the slave may involve the master inflicting verbal abuse and ritual humiliations (such as what is referred to as raunch, being urinated or defecated on, being forced to ingest urine or feces, being forced to eat out of dog food bowls, and so on), alternating with expressions of care and concern that such measures are needed to discipline or mold the bottom man into a "good slave." Because of the psychological and sexual charge of such extreme masculine imagery for gay men, and because of the obvious shock value such unbridled collective masculinity holds for most conventional heterosexuals, the imagery of S&M has become among the most visible and influential among urban gay male communities in the United States and abroad since gay liberation. Gay publications and advertisements are rife with stern-faced, mustachioed and bearded master types, looking grimly out from their mirrored sunglasses atop their black motorcycles, clad in black leather cap, jacket, and chaps. The terminology and slang of the S&M culture is common parlance among gay men, especially in large cities but, because of the availability of gay publications and the mobility of the gay male community, among rural gay men as well.

One story I use in workshops to illustrate the collective masculine imagery of sadomasochism is "Revenge of the Captive," by Robert Ralph, from the January 1985 issue of *Mandate* magazine. The story occurs on an unspecified Caribbean island after a military takeover. The narrator, the finance minister for the new military government, has made plans to flee the island with Ernesto, a famous soccer player and the beautiful son of one of the minister's former companions in government, whose flight from the island the minister had helped arrange. However, the sadistic chief of police, El Jefe, finds and captures Ernesto before the minister can spirit him off the island. Without knowing of the minister's secret disloyalty or of his plans to flee with Ernesto, El Jefe invites the minister to participate in a sadomasochistic interrogation of the handsome, masculine soccer star. Thus the plot of the story embodies the *puer-senex* polarity of the masculine archetype—the old regime versus the new, the older generation versus the younger. Standing between these oppositions is the figure of the finance minister—a government official for the oppressive military dictatorship who nonetheless is secretly in love with the son of an opposition member and is planning to help him.

The top-bottom polarity, derived from this *puer-senex* opposition and characteristic of sadomasochistic fantasy and enactment, is incarnated in the persons of El Jefe and Ernesto. The soccer player is brought into the room, stripped, and tied up with his arms above his head, legs spread apart. Completely vulnerable in this position, Ernesto and his physical beauty, especially his athletic strength and psychological forbearance as the interrogation begins, occupy a great deal of the narrator's attention (and quite a few paragraphs of purple prose). El Jefe's torture is primarily sexual in nature and carried out by means of a phallic instrument surely unique in the annals of archetypal imagery, a cattle prod with adjustable voltage, which El Jefe uses to pleasure Ernesto against his will until he reaches climax, which is characterized in the story as a humiliating lack of self-control on Ernesto's part. The minister's conflict between saving his beloved Ernesto and blowing his own cover is finally resolved as he takes action against El Jefe, forcing him by gunpoint to write out safe passage for him and Ernesto and then proceeding, with Ernesto, to tie the sadistic chief of police up and use the electric phallus on him, thus taking the revenge of the story's title.

We see in this S&M imagery a particular subspecies of the polarity inherent in the archetype of the masculine, that of dominance and submission, control and lack of control. The narrator is in control as a government official but lacks the control needed to accomplish his will; he is manifestly dominant but simultaneously forced into submission. Similarly, El Jefe's dominance ends in submission, and Ernesto's submission, which consists of phallic activity induced through electrical stimulation passively endured, eventually ends in dominance and the "revenge of the captive." Like the participants in S&M rituals, the imagery of the story plays with the eminently phallic polarities of activity and passivity, erection and flaccidity, bondage and freedom, dominance and submission. However offensive one might find such explicit depictions or enactments on whatever grounds, one thing is nevertheless undeniable: The imagery is derived from the archetype of masculinity through and through.

In using these stories to draw such themes explicitly (perhaps too explicitly at times) and in acknowledging the hypermasculine character of the stories' symbols, we grapple with urgent questions of what masculinity is, how to reconcile the seemingly irreconcilable opposition inherent in maleness, and what it means to relate sexually, emotionally, and socially to another man. These stories and their stark collective imagery of young-old, teacher-student, dominant phallic power and passive, slavish submission graphically describe for gay men the very conflicts that they live daily in attempting to fashion self-identities and workable intimate relationships to other gay men in a society where patriarchy has distorted both femininity and masculinity. The flexibility in sexual roles depicted in these stories, the bringing together of opposites in sexual union and kinship relations, the power and rawness of the sexual and aggressive drives that men feel in their bodies and souls—all these themes seem to serve the same mythic function that *The Wizard of Oz* serves for gay men with regard to their femininity; these fairy tales, however, move gay men toward a recognition of the power and passion of their own masculinity.

If I have insisted on showing the masculine character of this homosexual imagery by using such graphic examples, it is because unwittingly assigning such material, when it emerges in the analysis of a gay man, to a problem with the feminine will lead the therapist to miss the true import of the imagery: namely, that these themes properly belong to the archetype of the masculine, not to the matriarchal world of the phallic Great Mother. The difference in interpretation can be great and in the interpretation—or misinterpretation—can lie the success or failure of a gay man's therapeutic experience. For example, a gay man entering therapy to resolve a number of control issues, including procrastination and a creative block around his painting, brings in the following dream:

> I am at a protest rally in a gay neighborhood. A transvestite is on the doorstep of a Victorian house, shouting epithets and acting outrageously, as a line of policemen close in on the crowd of us. We help the transvestite escape by passing her through windows and out the back of the house. The cops seem threatening but I strike up the acquaintance of one who seems friendly. I invite him to join me for a cup of coffee and he accepts. I intend to educate him about homosexuality, and I get into his patrol car. We are talking very amicably as he drives, until I realize that suddenly no one is at the wheel and he has rigged the accelerator so that the car will go faster and faster and there is no way I can stop it. He is going to kill me and there is nothing I can do. I wake up in terror.

Given the patient's presentation as overly controlled and inhibited, one might make the quick and dirty interpretation of this dream that, in consigning the transvestite Androgyne to the back of the house, that is, to the patient's unconscious, the patient becomes vulnerable to the authoritarian masculinity complex, which seems friendly enough but actually has murderous intentions. The solution to such one-sided masculinity, one might suggest, would be to foster a more conscious relationship to the feminine, to bring back the wholeness of the Androgyne in order to temper the *senex*-savagery of the patient's authoritarian inner masculinity. One might further conclude that the patient's homosexuality is a problem of distance from femininity, which is unconscious and unavailable to him, or that his homosexuality is a compensatory attempt to mitigate the fierce father-authority complex raging within by seeking out sexual connections with men—homosexuality as compensating for a fear of masculinity and a passive, captive feminine stance.

What such interpretations miss, and what the homoerotic imagery of the gay stories brings to our attention, is that there are polarities of dominance and submission within the archetype of the masculine itself; issues of femininity may not be involved at all. It may certainly be true that greater contact with his inner feminine side, his anima, may be helpful in dealing with the authority complex portrayed so fiercely in this dream, but the patient's homosexual orientation makes it more likely that the work that needs to be accomplished is to develop greater contact with the *fullness of the patient's own masculine nature.*

The one-sided masculinity that many see embodied in homosexuality, especially in the hypermasculine persona of so many contemporary gay men, may indeed be one-sided but not necessarily because of the absence of the feminine. Passivity, submission, receptivity, endurance—these are not inherently feminine qualities but are, as the imagery of gay erotic literature makes clear, qualities of what could be termed "lunar masculinity," the quiescent phallos denied and repressed by one-sided patriarchal identifications of masculinity with dominance, control, and penetration. Because gay men's sexual orientation places them a priori beyond the pale of conventional definitions of masculinity, gay men may perhaps be in a better psychological location to break through this one-sided priapic masculinity and to discover the side of the masculine that receives, that reflects, that inseminates, and that rests. This kind of masculinity is the proper compensation for the raging authority complex of the patient, not a prescription of heterosexuality or a series of anima-relation exercises.

One can see that, by failing to recognize the masculinity of male-male Eros, one may end up working in ultimately unsuccessful ways with gay male patients, such as by imagining that the patient just described might do better seeing a female analyst because of the near complete lack of inner feminine presence indicated in his dream. To fail to recognize the presence of phallos for precisely what it is in gay men's inner and outer lives, not a sign of feminine identification but rather a symbol of a gay man's very self, is to risk completely misinterpreting the meaning of certain features of a gay male patient's life. For example, if this patient subsequently reported sadomasochistic fantasies of bondage and dominance, in which he was active and passive at various times, unfamiliarity with the cultural presence of such imagery in urban gay communities might lead an analyst to conclude, à la Melvin Kettner or Jung before him, that the archetypal imagery of phallic worship and ritual indicates some sort of enthrallment to the Great Mother, a mother complex forcing the patient to project his masculinity and then pursue it with erotic compulsion. In assuming instead that gay men are men and therefore masculine, first and foremost, but that this masculinity, because of both cultural and archetypal factors, is highly ambivalent, one has quite a different picture of the function of any sadomasochistic fantasy enactments and the role of the patient's homosexuality in them: The fantasy of tying up and dominating or being tied up and dominated might symbolize attempts to get at the whole of the male self, in both its passive and active forms, to experience one's male self through the activity and passivity of another man, through male initiation, not through the enactment of a feminine role or through the otherness of women.

Dreams of another gay man over the course of five years of analysis have similar themes and imagery:

> A policeman is tied up to a chair back, his legs spread wide with high black boots, his ass open and vulnerable. I find him this way, a victim of an initiation.

> I am in a forced-sex scene with three men who have my hands tied behind my back and have not let me eat in a day. They take turns fucking me and it is enjoyable. One man, however, the oldest and most masculine and sensual of the three, lingers kissing me, with a collection of pills in his lips, until I, greedy, hungry, and excited, swallow them. The sex stops and the man seems to be waiting for some result, which occurs when I climax. I turn bright purple! It seems the little purple cube I swallowed is on

the market and turns people purple for up to 72 hours at moments of intense excitation. I am furious, incredulous, amused, and aroused at this humiliation and wonder how long the effect will last on me and what arrangements I will have to make to hide myself.

At home, Andrew [heterosexual high-school friend of the patient] has come to visit me while Mom and Dad are out. He comes close to me on the couch and then gradually lays down on his back between my legs. I stroke his hair and chest, feeling his tits. He takes off his shirt, telling me that he has gone to a male sensitivity group, but it is clear to me that he wants to have sex. I take off my jeans and shirt and give him a quick kiss. That is when I feel how nervous he is—he has never had sex with a man before.

The male cop from a TV show is lying on a couch naked. Another man and I tell him how beautiful his arms and chest are, big biceps and chest, big full round nipples, big sensuous lips. He gets off on being told this, how sexy and hot he is. We start to touch him—I with some trepidation since he is straight—but his narcissistic pleasure overrides his heterosexuality and he clearly enjoys our attentions. The other man sucks his nipples as I rub his arms and pecs. I reach down and find he has a hard-on and begin to suck him off. He loves it.

David [a policeman and family friend of the patient's parents] is outside on the patio at the beach house when he starts asking me very pointed questions about who my friends are, do I go out with women, etc. I tell him that most of my good friends are men in the theater and the arts. He then draws me under the covers of the lounge chair we are sitting on and tells me to kiss him, which I do, but he cuts the kiss short. I try to turn him on by sucking on his nipples, kissing his neck and ears, but he is still pretty defended. When I ask him whether he is gay, he says no. I think in the dream that he has a long way to go to deal with his homophobia and his marital situation and I plan on seducing him, calling him to go out with me, and so on.

The point of using these stories and case reports is to demonstrate that homosexuality may be as much an expression of masculinity as of femininity. The presence of initiatory imagery in gay men's inner lives, mirrored in the strong initiatory bent of many of the S&M rituals enacted and fantasized by gay men, may, as we have seen, be understood as an outgrowth of gay men's psychological immaturity, a lack of initiation into manhood, which is now being sought outside of oneself, in a concrete sexual act with another man. This was clearly one way Jung understood the presence of this initiatory material, and Jungian analysts have done little to develop or change this view. One could focus on the scenario of seducing the straight male in these dreams and erotic stories as evidence for such an interpretation, with such seductions serving to "impregnate" gay men with the missing masculinity they seek.

However, if one acknowledges that homosexuality is a variation in human sexual behavior rather than a pathological condition with some underlying cause, and if one possesses a clearer vision of how the irrational fear and hatred of homosexuality combines with patriarchal definitions of masculinity to rob gay men of their identity as men, another hypothesis seems equally likely: that the masculine initiation of gay male sadomasochistic rituals is a reflection not of individual pathology but rather of the failure of patriarchal society to provide men, and gay men in particular, with an inward and outward initiation into full manhood. The drive to reclaim one's masculinity, to find one's power and dominance, to experience manhood through submission to men and endurance of bodily pleasure and pain, to play with restriction and freedom in relationship, these are issues with an extra measure of importance for gay men, who feel the lack of male initiation perhaps most keenly, drawn as they are by their very selves to erotic relationship and fulfillment with other men. Thus we see the gay man in the last three dreams acting as the initiator, the one with greater knowledge and expertise being approached by heterosexual men who ask for initiation into a fuller experience of manhood. Intrapsychically, the patient and I understood these dreams to indicate the way the male-male Eros of his homosexual experience needed to be brought into contact with the driving, authoritarian, and sometimes critical father complex that pushed him into overachievement and competition with other men. However, the collective meaning of these dreams is perhaps more powerful. It seems that the gay man's experience of male Eros is urgently needed by the heterosexual men of our society and that heterosexual men need to be taught the lessons in masculinity learned by gay men—that men can live in their male bodies and love them; that men can be powerful and tender with each other and not simply reserve their Eros for their relationships with women; that authority is as much an inner issue as an outer role; and that the world does not disintegrate when men love men.

Because of the initiatory push in homosexuality, one can see why a gay man's drive to find his masculinity often takes the symbolic (and sometimes concrete) form of sadomasochistic sexual rituals involving the essential polarities of the archetypal masculine. We have seen these polarities and themes throughout the erotic stories and dreams: The opposition of old and young, dominance and submission, restriction and independence, physicality and spirituality, authority and obedience, and strength and weakness all appear in graphic, sexualized form in the collective and individual lives of gay men. However, are these themes not also present in every NFL football game, in every hostile corporate takeover, in every negotiation on disarmament, and in every heterosexual male friendship? Is the S&M imagery of gay male erotic literature really any more shocking than the violent and exaggerated masculinity of professional sports stars, corporate raiders, gun-happy military men, or sadistic fraternity hazings? Shouldn't the emphasis in psychology be put on how all men, regardless of their sexual orientation, find themselves on a search for wholeness as men in a society that prizes only one half (and not always the most palatable half) of archetypal masculinity? If male homosexuality is a shadow issue, isn't it time to acknowledge that it is the shadow of *heterosexual masculinity*, which attempts to contain this fearsome male Eros by projecting it onto gay men rather than owning it as its own? Perhaps it is time to see in the lives of gay men the masculine wholeness that homosexuality represents, the attempt to enact and live the extraordinary richness of archetypal masculinity through physical and emotional connection to another man. The individual and collective imagery examined here certainly points to a fuller and therefore a potentially more anxiety-provoking view of the masculine than the one dictated by social convention. For this very reason, the imagery of masculinity in the gay male community ought not to be ignored.

The predominance of exaggerated collective imagery and the

presence of initiatory symbolism may be an effect more of homophobia than of feminine identification—and even if it were compensation for a feminine identification, the thrust of the imagery is undeniably and powerfully male nevertheless. Within male-male Eros the masculine is contacted, lived, and embodied both in fantasy and in real relationships of flesh and blood. To assign this rich masculinity to the realm of the feminine is both logically fallacious and notoriously pathologizing. As we have seen, the phallos of "Revenge of the Captive" is hardly the dainty *puer* phallos of the Valentine Day's Cupid but a darker, primeval phallos, Eros in all his thrusting, maddening, passionate masculinity, the phallos of maturity, a *senex*-possessed organ under the domination of no woman. The result of the homosexual initiation in "Cop Brothers" is not a relationship to woman or to femininity, but rather a richer and more mature appropriation of masculinity, an entry into the community of men, brothers, lovers, and peers. The drive to know oneself as a man through an erotic bond to another man seems the real purpose inherent in the initiatory, *puer-senex* relationships undertaken by the men in these stories and by gay men in real life, men who have been robbed of their masculine self through social values and stereotypes which deny that they are men at all. Should we thus be surprised to find the collective imagery of phallic masculinity so much at the forefront of contemporary gay male culture and—more important—should we persist in denying the undeniable masculinity that gay men live and embody as they love and make love to other men? Only through accepting and honoring the collective masculinity that seeks acknowledgment through male-male erotic love can we help contemporary gay men toward a fuller and more deeply felt sense of their individual lives as men. To deny or distort the masculine nature of gay men is to perpetuate and invite exaggerated collective compensations.

8. The Androgyne and Gay Male Culture: The Recovery of a Native American Tradition for Contemporary Gay Men

WE HAVE SEEN how male homosexuality may function to relate gay men to not only their inner and outer femininity but also
their inner and outer masculinity. For this reason and in this
way, homosexuality may not be the major failure in a man's individuation process that some call it, but in fact may serve the very
same individuation function as heterosexuality: to bring one into
deeper contact with the Self in both its feminine and masculine
manifestations and consequently into deeper, more abiding relationship with the feminine and masculine Other. Psychological
wholeness and depth, therefore, are certainly not the exclusive
prerogative of heterosexuals but every bit as available to gay men
and women, if they go beyond the collective identities assigned to
them by convention and recover both their femininity and masculinity in their relationships with other gay men and lesbians.

Perhaps this intuition of gay wholeness, supported by gay liberation's removal of conventional masks and its confrontation of
external and internalized homophobia, has led the image of the
Androgyne to assume at least as prominent a place in postlibera-
tion culture as has the masculine symbol of the butch black-
leather stud. Here we recall that Jung suggested that homosexuality may be the result not simply of a feminine identification but
rather of an incomplete detachment from the archetype of the
Hermaphrodite, which would counteract any identification one
might have with oneself as a one-sided sexual being. However, it
has remained to gay men to develop this intuition. The popularity of June Singer's book *Androgyny* when it appeared in 1976
paralleled the feminist and gay liberationist challenges to rigid
patriarchal sex roles. The gay liberation culture of that era before
AIDS was one in which gay men went about avidly appropriating
the accoutrements not simply of masculinity—joining gyms,

wearing jeans and muscle shirts, sporting mustaches—but of androgyny as well—donning earrings while dressing as men or dressing as women for public occasions such as parades or Halloween in gay neighborhoods while making no attempt to hide their masculine physical attributes such as body hair or bulging biceps. The term current in the gay community for such militant androgyny expresses both its intention and the affect surrounding such behavior: gender fuck.

As times have quieted down and the heyday of liberation moves into the matters of life and death surrounding the AIDS epidemic, we see the gay male community's collective attention still riveted on the imagery of the Androgyne. Indeed, there is a movement afoot—reflecting, one assumes, yet another of the collective themes important to gay men—to recover the tradition of androgyny historically and archetypally enacted by homosexual men. Part of this movement is to pay greater attention to the figure of the berdache in Native American culture and to attempt to recover the myth and meaning of the berdache for contemporary gay male Americans.

A French term derived from an Arabic word for the passive male partner in sodomy, *berdache* (sometimes *berdeche*) was the word used by early French explorers to describe a certain figure who occupied a role in many of the Native American tribes they came across, a role unknown or persecuted in Western European societies: that of an anatomical male who dressed as a woman, who performed many of the social tasks of women, and who often assumed a position of great tribal importance. The response of European Christians, particularly the Spanish conquerors and French missionaries, was, as one can well imagine, a mixture of shock, repulsion, and disgust, which fueled their intention to wipe out such an "abomination" by means of the imposition of Christian rituals and European customs. For this reason, the tradition of the Native American crossdresser has over the past three hundred years been all but obliterated from the consciousness of Americans, though there is evidence to suggest that the European Christian suppression of the berdache was not totally effective.

For instance, there is a small group of anthropologists, many of whom are self-identified as gay or lesbian, whose fieldwork experiences with Native American tribes have attempted to go beneath Native American fears of revealing traditionalist religion to white people. These researchers have spent time piecing together various tribes' traditions surrounding the berdache, either from the recollections of traditionalist Native Americans or, at times, by being fortunate enough to meet living examples of the berdache tradition, kept discreetly away from the view of non-natives. An anthropological literature on the berdache exists, and it is growing larger through the efforts of gay men and lesbians whose sexual orientation affords them entrée into this less obvious layer of Native American practice and belief.[1] Certainly the most comprehensive and important work on the berdache to date is the anthropologist Walter L. Williams's *The Spirit and the Flesh: Sexual Diversity in American Indian Culture,* wherein the fullest and most thoughtful description of this tradition can be found and whose description of the berdache role in native cultures affords analytical psychology a number of interesting parallels to its own conception of the archetypal Androgyne and its psychological function and symbolism.[2]

The berdache tradition is widely distributed throughout North America and is not a singular aberration to be found in a single tribe or a group of related tribes. Moreover, the berdache tradition may appear in one tribe and not in a neighboring tribe. The role of the berdache varies from tribe to tribe, but the presence of the tradition in a tribe seems to remain constant, however much it may have been impeded or suppressed by Western settlers.[3]

Perhaps the most important insight of Williams and his fellow gay anthropologists concerning Native American crossdressers (a more neutral term, which I prefer to the slightly derogatory but by now accepted *berdache*) is that Native American societies seem not to share the Western European assumptions of two genders and two sets of sex roles. The berdache clearly forms a third sex in native societies, a gender–sex role status sometimes referred to as mixed-gender by anthropologists, which is quite distinct from what is considered male or female. The berdaches form a group separate from women in these cultures and are not seen as ersatz women, as gay men are often seen in Western culture.[4] The berdache seems psychologically to live out not an identification with the feminine, but, if anything, an identification with the Androgyne. In traditional native societies this identification was both supported and valued.

This distinctive social status and gender designation is reflected in the derivation of many of the Native American words for these crossdressers, which points to yet another important characteristic of the berdache: Spiritual transformation goes hand in hand with the adoption of—one might even say vocation to—the way of the berdache. For instance, as Williams reports and explains, the Navajo word for this figure is *nadle*, meaning "one who is transformed"; the Zuni word, *lhamana*, means "meditating spirit"; and the word in the Omaha language, *mexoga*, means "instructed by the moon." The clear mixed-gender status of the role is evident from other terms, such as the Lakota *winkte*, meaning simply "would become woman"; the Chukchee *yirka-la ul*, meaning "soft man"; and Yuki *i-wa-musp*, meaning "man-woman."[5]

As Williams makes very clear, the role of berdaches in native cultures is largely spiritual. They are seen as endowed with berdache status by the supreme deity of the tribe (sometimes the supreme female deity), a calling discerned by way of various rituals used with young boys who display berdache characteristics early on. Big dreams (that is, dreams with important sacred meaning)—for example, dreams of himself in women's clothing or doing women's work—are used to determine whether a boy is called to be a berdache. At times and in some tribes, certain tests are used to see whether the boy prefers the "female" role or the "male." In either case, the berdache status is seen in these tribes as an expression of the divinely endowed character of the man-woman who is, as some of Williams's informants made clear, simply "made that way."

These androgynes in Native American culture carry the function of the Self for the tribe and function as spiritual leaders: presiding at ritual events, granting spiritual power-names to children, healing, prophesying, and generally performing the role of shaman in the tribe. Because of this clearly understood connection to the divine, the berdaches are honored members of the tribes and tend to represent the best and the brightest of the society in terms of wealth, social prestige, and tribal power.[6]

Alongside the spiritual mana they carry for the tribe, berdaches also perform crucial caretaking functions for the tribe, using their male strength and concern for productivity in tasks generally assigned to women, such as craft work, cooking, and the rearing and instruction of children. For this reason, in addition to the spiritual esteem in which they are held, berdaches are also highly prized as spouses by men. Williams reports men with berdache "wives" being looked on as extremely fortunate.[7]

What is also clear from Williams's careful research is that the majority of the berdaches are homosexual, though the matter is not seen in the simple heterosexual-homosexual way white Americans might tend to see it. Behaviorally, the majority of berdaches marry other men and seem to enjoy sexual relations with their male spouses. The men berdaches marry, however, are never berdaches themselves and may not be understood as homosexuals either, but are simply regarded as normal men lucky to have a berdache "wife." Nevertheless, there are berdaches who may also have been or be involved intimately and sexually with women, though Williams makes clear this pattern is in the minority. If one were to use Western categories based on behavior, one would have to say that the great majority of berdaches indicate a homosexual orientation, though, for the reasons just mentioned, the matter is not so simple to classify.

Lest we be tempted to paint a picture of a rosy berdache paradise, we must recognize the effect of Western suppression of Native American sexual diversity. Among some contemporary Native Americans the words for berdache in their native language are often used with the derogatory edge reserved for our own slang terms for homosexuals, and the berdache is not accorded the respect and reverence given him by traditionalist Native Americans. Likewise, the repression of Native American religion has left the berdache role largely meaningless in contemporary native societies whose confinement to reservations has been so shot through with Western influences as to have alienated most Native Americans—including berdaches—from their own history and culture. Although certain aspects and memories of the berdache tradition still survive (indeed, Williams met a number of living berdaches in North America and Mexico), for the most part it is a tradition most alive in the past.

That the image of the berdache has exerted a powerful influence on the imagination and lives of gay people can be seen in the gay liberation classic *Gay American History*, in which historian Jonathan Katz assembled an overwhelming number of documents, some of which were published for the first time, concerning the history of homosexuals in the United States since North America's early exploration and settlement. Katz devoted an entire section of the book to the berdache, using anthropological reports by sympathetic observers from the late nineteenth century to bring forward the real stories of berdaches living in traditionalist cultures in a time before American expansionism in the West strained and even at times destroyed the fabric of Native American religion.[8]

In this collection, two berdache stories stand out as particularly affecting and poignant. The first is the story of We'Wha, a Zuni male transvestite; the second is the story of a Gros Ventre woman, captured by a Crow warrior, who adopted male habits and eventually went on to sit in the tribal council.[9]

We'Wha (of whom Katz includes a number of impressive pictures) is characterized by the anthropologist Mathilde Coxe Stevenson in her account as "the most remarkable member of the tribe."[10] An anatomical male (rumors of physical hermaphroditism to the contrary), We'Wha was referred to in the feminine gender, though her attributes showed exactly why the berdache is better understood as a gender-mixing status than as a cross-gender status. She was strong and physically impressive as a man, with masculine attributes including what Stevenson calls "an indomitable will and an insatiable thirst for knowledge,"[11] as well as a kind of emotional strong-headedness and severity that brooked no resistance. For these reason, We'Wha performed ceremonial duties for her clan, and Stevenson remarks that "in fact, she was the chief personage on many occasions."[12] Her female attributes, her women's dress, her excellence at household chores, and her concern with keeping the family running through the participation of all its members in the household work marked her as an exceptional individual much valued in the clan.

Stevenson's account of We'Wha's death takes up the greatest part of her report and makes clear the great affection and respect felt for her, as well as Stevenson's closeness to this remarkable figure. For example, Stevenson, a white woman, was included in the family's bedside death watch. We'Wha's dying words were spoken to Stevenson and consisted of a series of good-byes to the white people We'Wha had known, including President Grover Cleveland, and a promise to remember these people to the gods when she went to meet them. Thus We'Wha acknowledged even at the end of her life the mediating function between white and native that her acquaintanceship with Stevenson had served. Her funeral garb consisted of both female attire and trousers, "the first male attire she had worn since she had adopted women's dress years ago,"[13] and much care was given to her hair and jewelry. Stevenson"s account of the burial and the ritual destruction of the dead man-woman's possessions is moving and sad.

Similar themes and characteristics occur in Edwin T. Denig's "Biography of a Woman Chief," included in Katz's collection. Although this woman did not adopt male dress except for hunting gear, and, unlike the male berdaches, she was acknowledged throughout her life as a woman, she, like We'Wha, nonetheless incarnated a powerful combination of characteristics traditionally understood as both male and female. Tall and strong, endowed with "strength of nerve and muscle,"[14] she excelled at the male pursuits of hunting and all the hunting-related activities important to the tribe, such as the butchery and transportation of the kill. Yet when her protector-father died, she assumed the role of both father and mother to her sibling-children.

Denig reports a tale of her bravery in which she used her feminine appearance to fool attacking Blackfeet into thinking she was vulnerable, only to lure them close enough to the besieged fort where her own tribe was being held captive so she could turn fire on them and rout them. This incident served to enhance her reputation among the camp and the entire nation, as did a number of subsequent battles in which her fame as a warrior became so secure that she could no longer be denied a voice in the tribal council. Naturally such an unusual woman was regarded as divinely endowed and, like the male berdache, was called on to perform ceremonial functions. Denig makes clear that, for all her fame and fortune, she was intent on serving the greater good of the tribe and was generous with the spoils of war and the hunt.

Though acknowledged publicly as a woman, she went on to take for herself a wife, largely, writes Denig, because her social prominence and personal distaste for women's work made the acquisition of a wife necessary. Her biographer's exclamation on this point is germane to our purposes and humorous, too: "Strange country this, where males assume the dress and perform the duties of females, while women turn men and mate with their own sex!" [15]

As with We'Wha and berdaches in general, this woman chief served a mediatory function for the tribe, not only between the women and men in her own person, but through an important diplomatic mission to her own original tribe, the Gros Ventre, whom she visited in the name of establishing peace with the Crow. Unfortunately, despite her bravery, her attempt at mediation ended in her assassination by Gros Ventre warriors, assuring the continuation of warfare between the two tribes.

These stories would certainly be affecting on their own, given the remarkable character of the two people involved. However, for the purposes of our analysis we see a view of the Androgyne presented by the lives of these two Native American individuals and by berdaches in general that in every way corresponds to Jungian insights concerning this archetypal dominant of human experience: a symbol of the Self in its divine power and mediatory wholeness, a bridge between tribes at war, man and woman, white and native, homosexual and heterosexual. More important, however, the contact these Native American individuals had psychologically to the divine Androgyne is not understood in some abstract symbolic way but is enacted in a culture that reveres and honors this wholeness, regardless of—indeed, perhaps because of—its unusual nature. Rather than understanding this contact as an inner experience, to be kept private and hidden and to be revered in the careful confines of analysis or one's own inner world, these individuals and the societies they lived in were able to enact the Androgyne in ways that enriched the entire tribe spiritually, socially, and materially. Denig's biography of the woman chief shows that such androgyny was not always smoothly accepted, but despite social obstacles such as the inferior status of women, the richness of the Androgyne could be brought into the real life of the community.

Small wonder the sacred figure of the berdache holds such fascination and power for gay men, since the berdache tradition in Native American cultures represents precisely the solution to the oppressive, rigid, and inherently conflictual conceptions of man and woman that exclude gay experiences, especially the gay man's dual experience of both femininity and masculinity. The berdache seems to represent a pattern of gay male archetypal experience repressed and denied by Western culture. Even Jungians, such as Singer, acknowledge the Self-connection that the symbol of Androgyne represents but draw back from a full embracing of androgynous enactments in outer life. Nor do they see this kind of androgynous mixture of male and female characteristics as one of the most special characteristics of gay men in our culture. The figure and history of the berdache thus gives a social and psychological form to an essential and archetypal gay experience, that of bringing the opposites of male and female experience together *through living an acknowledged connection to one's homosexuality as a spiritual reality*—living the passion and excitement of erotic bonding with another man as spouse, working in areas of society traditionally defined as feminine, aware of a kind of differentness they cannot be denied. Indeed, at times this differentness may even be celebrated and honored ritually.

Understanding the berdache and its connection to both the Jungian Self and an archetypal pattern of homosexuality cross-culturally makes it necessary to reformulate certain Jungian views or interpretations of the appearance of the Androgyne in the inner and outer lives of gay men and women. For example, the dream reported in chapter 7, in which the young man concerned about control in his life found himself involved in passing a militant transvestite out of a back window of a Victorian house to save her from the onslaught of policemen, is fairly obvious as a manifestation of the Androgyne in the life of a gay man. But one can see how easily one might understand the dream symbolism literally—as a symbol of some sort of repressed urge to cross-dress—or if not that literally and crudely, perhaps without any of the sophistication gained from greater knowledge of the archetypal currents of the berdache tradition. By passing the transvestite out of the back window, my patient indeed saves the androgyne from the clutches of his murderous masculine authority complex, but in the process of doing so loses an important part of his archetypal experience as a gay man. We ought not to have been surprised, then, to find the next episode of the dream depicting a headlong rush in a car out of control ostensibly to end in the death of the dream ego: To deny the Androgyne its contemporary enacted life, which may be characterized by militancy and self-assertion after hundreds of years of repression and symbolization, is to cut oneself off from the *coniunctio* represented by the transvestite of the dream and to leave oneself vulnerable to rapacious, one-sided patriarchal ways of being.

The archetype of the Androgyne as a pattern of gay male identity certainly seems to stand behind the well-known presence of gay men in the clergy, particularly in Roman Catholic monastic and clerical orders, for whom the enactment of a "not-man" identity by way of celibacy enables a greater contact with the mystical and ceremonial presence of the divine in human life. While Roman Catholics priests and brothers certainly do not adopt female dress in any conventional sense of the term, since the priestly robes and monk's habit, however effeminate they may seem nowadays, are historically derived from male clothing of antiquity, their continued use despite the change in male fashion constitutes a kind of de facto unconscious transvestism. Undeniably, priests and monks of these orders find themselves involved in just those activities that were the domain of the berdache in Native American life: education, caretaking, and ceremonial and shamanistic duties.

A young gay male patient in seminary brought in the following big dream early on in his analysis:

> I'm at an American Indian rite in Utah in which two tables are put at right angles with heaps of clothes and objects spaced out at certain intervals with a cord run from the ends of the tables to form the hypotenuse of the triangle. When I step into the triangle, I am possessed by the spirit of a dead old woman whom the Indians wish to contact. At first I am not frightened but become terrified when I go in and feel the possession. I wake up scared [misspelled as "sacred"].

The patient, a theology student from a thoroughly Christian background, knew absolutely nothing about Native American rituals, though he had admitted to reading such accounts of the berdache crossdresser as appeared in the popular gay press without their having made much of an impression. At the time of the dream and coincident with the start of his therapy, he had become disappointed in the church, especially the amount of political machinations involved in becoming a member of the clergy in his Protestant denomination, and had decided to opt out of his seminary program and pursue another carer. Needless to say, his homosexuality, which he thoroughly accepted, and his political-social activism on gay liberation issues were closely related to his decision to leave seminary. So the time of this nightmare-dream was a time of transition from his old conceptions of spirituality to new forms of being in the world.

I use this dream precisely because it would be extremely easy to see the theme of feminine possession in it: the patient's terror at entering the triangle, the clothes and objects (later identified by the patient as bracelets and rings) ostensibly to be donned by him as part of the possession ritual. And yet I felt the proper amplificatory referent was not entry into the world of the Great Mother but rather entry into the world of the sacred berdache. Not only does the dream explicitly name a Native American rite in Utah, but it is a striking example of the action of the collective unconscious in its depiction of a berdache ritual in which the initiate is given choices of clothing and guided by the Great Female Spirit—the dead old woman of the patient's dream. The differences in these interpretations would be considerable, especially in the analysis of a gay man whose relationship to femininity, masculinity, and androgyny is not easily discerned by even the most sensitive of analysts: The feminine-possession interpretation leads one to see the dream as a warning of the dangers of such possession, especially considering the patient's dread; the Androgyne interpretation, on the other hand, accounts not only for the emergence of this powerful femininity in the gay man's psyche, as one half of the Androgyne, but also for the patient's holy terror (the slip of the pen in the patient's written account, confusing "scared" and "sacred," reveals the source of the patient's fear). The patient is being drawn out of his safe religious tradition toward a new and unknown spirituality, and the motivation for the transition had as much to do with his homosexuality as with his relationship to the church. The dream reveals him involved in an unconscious ritual adoption of androgyny, becoming a man-woman under the influence of a divine feminine presence, a sacralization that is at once terrifying and unifying. The nightmarish quality of the dream, as well as its character as a big dream, a dream with important spiritual meaning, haunting the patient for many years afterward, is, if anything, a sign of not being quite prepared psychically, not having the proper inner protection—hence the clothing offered to the naked patient—to behold and feel the insurgence of such contact with the transpersonal Self.

As Jung points out in his many discussions of the Androgyne, this figure indeed has a monstrous, nightmarish quality, a quality that sometimes emerges in the dreams of gay men I have seen. The horror that the aberration of hermaphroditism inspires may in fact undergird the general resistance to seeing it as an important archetypal pattern for gay men and the common misinterpretation of an androgynous epiphany as a feminine identification. We could easily focus on the striking imagery of the feminine in the following dreams of gay men without seeing that the feminine here is but one part of a movement toward the Androgyne, which appears initially sometimes in gruesome and troubling form. Bear in mind, the dreamers are all men:

> I have gotten pregnant, which is and should be miraculous but the unnaturalness of it requires that I be stripped of my baby through a speeding up of the pregnancy and birth, which entails lots of bloating and bloody discharge from my breasts and groin—the baby dies. Grisly.

> I am in a support group for religious people with my parents and my lover. My lover goes into another room but I stay in the first one. I vocalize some of my problems with the church because I am gay and another person behind me, who I assume is a lesbian, does the same: Gay people's spirituality is ignored and, indeed, considered nonexistent. She and I talk for a long time. Later, at an informal gathering, I go up to the "lesbian," who is a big blond man with close-cropped hair in a tight tank top—kind of sexy. He/she asks how old I am. I tell him 29. He says he/she is 65, but I think he looks about 35.

> I am giving my friend John [married man] a long massage to which he responds intimately, touching me. This is after an epi-

sode of the TV program "Brothers" which has a rather physical sequence in it, leaving John sore from my massage. He is lying down and I am at his head, massaging him upside-down. He reaches in my shirt and runs his hand over my chest lazily. He then becomes at the same time Karen [his wife], who is in the army and is telling me of her/his problems in getting glasses made.

I wear a crisp, neat skirt to work (made of the same material as my brown pants) and after shopping, I buy a beautiful multicolored sweater in rainbow stripes to go with the skirt. I am very stylish.

I am sleeping with a man but the bed begins to swing around in an arc, dividing into two, with me and the man on one of the beds and a man and a woman on the other. In the dream this happens because my mother feels morally uncomfortable with us all sleeping together in her house.

These androgynous images of miraculous male pregnancies, physical contact with acquaintances who are simultaneously male and female, crossdressing, and division into male-female couples all point out how Hermes, messenger of the gods, and Aphrodite, the goddess of love and physical connection, unite into the sometimes monstrous, sometimes unifying image of the gay male Hermaphrodite. The symbols of union here—the rainbow, the coupling and doubling, the matching male-female dress—ought not to be passed over in favor of exclusive focus on the feminine for these gay men.

The pattern of androgyny seen in the Native American berdache tradition has archetypal roots, and Jung's ideas on the nature and the function of the Hermaphrodite are an important theoretical tool in understanding many characteristics of these figures: their sacredness, their mediatory functions, their usefulness to the continuation of society and the family, their shamanistic endowment, and their ability to reconcile the opposites of male and female for themselves and for others. This pattern of androgyny is one archetypal pattern that, alongside the feminine and masculine patterns, appears in the lives of contemporary gay men.

One might, in our one-sidedly patriarchal culture, misperceive the emergence of the Androgyne as a symbol of the feminine, particularly in the lives of gay men, who are assigned the sociocultural status of inferior men. For gay men in particular, who live in a culture that denies the feminine and who may, like heterosexual men, need to find a more whole masculinity *and* femininity, contact with the Androgyne may, at first, consist of seeing her feminine face shine forth from the darkness to which she has too long been consigned. In our society and in psychological circles—where introversion and abstraction, rather than extraversion and bodily experience, rule the day—it is gay men and lesbians who must recover for themselves the value of androgyny, and not merely through symbolic integration. The berdache is most useful as a symbol of the Self, a fact that gay men have clearly perceived and are working to own. Perhaps those working in psychology who are most open to such archetypal themes and symbols can be helped to see the important presence of the living Androgyne in the lives of the gay men and women they know and love.

9. Conclusion: Looking Forward by Looking Back

THE IDEA THAT sexual orientation emerges from a complex interaction of the personal and archetypal masculine, feminine, and Androgyne gives one a deeper and clearer vision of the inner lives and loves of homosexual and heterosexual men and women in Western cultures, affording each individual the potential wholeness that lies symbolically and emotionally in a primary erotic relationship. Yet the simplicity of this theory is deceptive, for such an archetypal notion of sexual orientation has much wider ramifications.

To conceive of sexual orientation as a multifaceted archetypal phenomenon is to make room for sexual orientations and erotic attractions that do not fit into the strict Western categories of gay and straight. Such a theory permits one to approach bisexuality with as firm a theoretical footing as one has in looking at hetero-sexuality or homosexuality: If all sexual orientation is the result of a personal and archetypal confluence of the masculine, femi-nine, and Androgyne, then bisexual men and women are not strange creatures, sexual anomalies, outsiders, fence sitters, but individuals whose masculine, feminine and androgynous ener-gies merge and flow in a particular individual pattern in response to certain archetypal and personal experiences. Such a theory also permits one to understand how an individual's sexual orien-tation might change over the course of a lifetime, from adoles-cence to young adulthood to middle age and beyond, and pro-vide a way to look at who and what has shifted in the life of the individual. At the same time, this Jungian theory allows for the possibility that an individual's sexual orientation may indeed be constitutionally determined, a kind of sexual type analogous to Jung's idea of personality type, tied inextricably in certain cases to a predominance of certain archetypal configurations.

The simplicity of such a theory gives way to astonishing depth and breadth when one begins to examine the three archetypes in all their fullness. To state that a particular aspect of someone's personality or behavior is tied to the archetypal feminine is to say very little really, for the archetype of the feminine is extremely complex. Mother and daughter, Aphrodite and Artemis, the expulsive womb and the devouring cave, birth and death, wounding and healing, Gorgon and Kore, Marilyn Monroe and Bette Davis, Wise Old Woman and *puella aeterna*, Sophia and Eve, the domesticated feline and the roaring tigress, spiritual and chthonic, fierce and tender, high and low, earth and moon, water and fire—all are aspects of the archetypal feminine.

Likewise with the archetype of the masculine: father and son, Wotan and Loki, seed and spirit, priapic and impotent, Hermit and Emperor, Fool and Magician, animus and Logos, sun and sky, Neptune and Hades, Peter Pan and Charles Bronson, intellect and heedless sexuality, light and shadow, thrusting and withdrawing, wolfish beast and man's best friend—all these and countless more are aspects of the archetypal masculine.

Likewise with the Androgyne: original Anthropos and nonexistent being, divisible and indivisible, everything male and everything female, the unitary cosmic egg and multiplicity itself, spiritual perfection and monstrous aberration, incestuous coupling and highest union, berdache and eunuch, shaman and pervert, Boy George and Tootsie, Yentl and Gertrude Stein.

The seeming simplicity of this theory of sexual orientation demands that one look at the indescribable multiplicity inherent in each individual soul, the countless archetypal configurations that might lie beneath a person's attraction to women or to men. Is it the beneficent father that a gay man seeks out in his erotic attraction to older men? Or is this the result of his feeling identified with a beneficent mother figure, his all-giving personal grandmother, for whom a benevolent, strong, and wise older man would the most appropriate partner?

And what results when the young man embarks on a relationship with his long-sought older lover? Might he not derive a greater sense of self as both male and female, a strengthening of his phallic power, and a heightened sense of his ability to love and yield to and receive from a man? To call such a psychological situation masculine or feminine or androgynous, mature or immature, is to miss all the subtlety of this young gay man's relationship with his older lover. This theory of sexual orientation makes it vitally important to see not just *why and how* his sexual orientation knits together a wholeness for him, but also *who and what* this particular configuration of archetypal meaning is based on and striving toward. Such a theory may be called typically Jungian in its emphasis on where these aspects of the young man's personality seem to move, rather than staying exclusively focused on where his erotic longings come from.

And what of the older man who responds to his younger lover? Is it his integration of his idealized personal father that permits him to take joy in being with his younger boyfriend, his wish to nurture and initiate and encourage? Or is it the need to control and dominate from an unhealthy identification with his personal father's archetypal shadow? Or is it both of these aspects of father? And where is his femininity in this relationship? Is it projected on the androgynous *puer*-lover or can this older man use his emotional sensitivity to modify his need to control and manipulate? Could he not be searching for an inward femininity through this erotic relationship, finding it in the quiet domesticity and mutual give and take of everyday life? And might not the result of such a process be a flexible emotional and spiritual wholeness of both male and female elements, which come together as he grows toward and past midlife?

Such brief sketches clearly point to how the theory proposed here might be used to ensure that one not miss the subtlety or teleological thrust of the real erotic longings and relationships of actual individuals. By positing the coequal presence of masculine, feminine, and Androgyne in every expression of sexual orientation, the depth and breadth of an individual can be honored in its wholeness and yet analyzed and understood in all its conflictual, interactional parts. The theory moves one past a conception of sexual orientation as a static condition to see it rather as a fertile crossroads of various archetypal energies, a kind of dynamic configuration of deep passion and abiding senses of self and others.

Deceptively simple yet as all-encompassing as each of its archetypal components, this theory clearly allows room for conceptions of sexual orientation and gender categories that do not correspond to Western cultural ideas of man or woman, heterosexual or homosexual. If Jungian thought has strained at times to account for the variety of sexual orientation in Europe and North

American among Caucasians, our examination has also shown how little contribution it has made to understanding other sex-role and gender conceptions that exist in non-Western cultures or in other racial groups. This lack of cross-cultural understanding is ironic, since by definition the collective unconscious and its archetypal phenomenology is not geographically restricted to Europe or North America but is to be understood as a universal human phenomenon. Layard, for example, is constrained by Western heterosexism to explain male-male incest in terms of a sublimation of male-female incest, without noting that the culture he examines may indeed conceive of sex roles and gender in alternative ways, which anthropologists have discovered in other cultures, particularly Native American and Polynesian societies. The very terminology Jungians so frequently use when doing cross-cultural work, especially the description of non-Western cultures or practices as primitve, undifferentiated, or the result of unconscious participation mystique, belies a perhaps ineradicable European bias and a certain kind of benign though insidious racism.

To begin to regard all sexual orientations everywhere as a result of a particular combination of the archetypal masculine, feminine, and Androgyne leaves room for the various gender categories, sex roles, and definitions (or nondefinitions) of sexual orientation that exist throughout the world. The sexually aggressive women and submissive men of Kaulong of Papua New Guinea can be approached, theoretically at least, in the exact same way as one might approach the macho husbands and dutiful wives of Mexico, with the exact same tools and the exact same archetypal insights. One need not posit "primitiveness" or do theoretical contortions regarding contrasexuality to deepen one's awareness of the archetypal movements inherent in these two very different social structures and personal identities and relationships. Homosexual relationships, therefore, between these submissive males and their initiate sons, or between these ostensibly hypermasculine Latino men in certain social situations no longer remain a baffling mystery to be called immature, undifferentiated, or sublimated, but rather might at last be seen as expressions of the particular combination of masculinity, femininity, and androgyny that has been filtered through the society's sexual values and norms. Just as heterosexuality and homosexuality need not be understood as static and opposite conditions, so in other cultures the fluidity and boundlesssness of human sexual expression might be taken fully and completely seriously.

The point of theorizing, especially Jungian theorizing, is never really to solve something definitively. I am fully aware that the theory of sexual orientation I propose here tends, if anything, to open questions about human sexual interactions and their psychological meaning and purpose rather than to provide answers to long-standing questions about sexual orientation. In keeping with Jung's own attitude toward theory as a pragmatic tool rather than as fixed dogma, this theory is meant to be a provisional conception of sexual orientation. It may help those of us who must examine sexual orientation to think about this phenomenon in a way that is practical, all-encompassing, archetypally based, culturally neutral, and spiritually profound. For some people, especially gay men and women, who have long been branded different or perverse by society and consequently by psychologists (even those with good intentions), an archetypal theory of sexual orientation that is at once simple and complex, spiritual and empirical, archetypal and personal, analytical and synthetic is not a luxury but an urgent necessity.

The great wealth of Jung's insights and of Jungians' elaborations of those insights needs to be welded into a theoretical instrument that will shine a light on one of the more powerful experiences of human beings: our sexuality and its passions, its movements, its orientation, its meaning, and its purpose. This theory is one way of using Jungian thought to illuminate rather than to categorize, to foster rather than to solve, to celebrate diversity rather than to pathologize differences. Though at times I am critical of a failure of courage or a certain parochialism in Jungian thought, which has tended to focus on issues perhaps less thorny or controversial than sexuality, and particularly homosexuality, I nevertheless have found, time after time, that Jung's and Jungians' insights into the working of the human mind and heart provide deep transformation for individuals. This book and the theory proposed here are a starting point, a place to begin to bring some of analytical psychology's richness to the wide variation that exists within the lives and passions of individuals of all sexual orientations.

THE TITLE OF this chapter was chosen to emphasize the purpose of our walk through Jung, Jungians, and homosexuality and to serve as a fitting reminder of the way change occurs for human beings. In looking backward, as many have found through the process of therapy, we discern with greater and greater clarity what the way forward must be. In looking and then going forward with our lives, we inevitably bring with us that which has gone before, for better or for worse.

While there has certainly been much in this book that has been critical of past formulations concerning homosexuality in analytical psychology, the point of this review and this criticism has been to break open past formulations and to disclose how complex and varied a phenomenon homosexuality really is—individually, socially, and archetypally. In particular, I hope that the extensive review of Jung and Jungians as well as my own theory of the archetypal forces at play in sexual orientation serve to make clear certain key points.

First, all three of the archetypal patterns of human sexual identity we have examined, the feminine, the masculine, and the Androgyne, play a role in the lives of gay men and lesbians. There seems to be no one single archetype of homosexuality or a single type of homosexual but rather a kaleidoscope of patterns, urges, impulses, fantasies, and purposes to homosexuality, which reflect the infinitely varied interaction among these three archetypes, which are themselves extraordinarily multifaceted and full of conflictual polarities. The wide variety of views on homosexuality in Jung's own writings and among Jungian writers makes this point fairly obvious, if the extraordinary personal and collective variety of the gay and lesbian community were not sufficient to do so itself.

Second, developing a mature and individual relationship to any one of these archetypal patterns may not (indeed probably will not) result in heterosexuality for a homosexual man or woman, but such a process will definitely result in the kind of enlargement of personality and self-knowledge that Jung called individuation. Because homosexuality is in fact a vehicle for a multiplicity of archetypal forces in an individual life, every bit as much as heterosexuality can be, the individuation process of a gay man or lesbian may not, in certain respects, be all that dramatically different from that of nonhomosexual clients.

Third and most important, however, the individuation process of gay men and lesbians does not take place in a vacuum but rather in a particular psychosocial context, which in fact does affect and perhaps even distort the unfolding of Self for the gay or lesbian individual. The patriarchalism of traditional sexual mores, which values a one-sided type of masculinity—concerned mostly with control, dominance, power, effectiveness, and intellect— while denigrating femininity and all other kinds of masculine behavior, serves to oppress lesbians and gay men by robbing them of a positive self-identity as women or men. The homophobia of contemporary culture, an outgrowth of this patriarchalism, goes further in inflicting damage on the psyches of gay men and lesbians by consigning their sexual identity to invisibility and enforcing this invisibility through the threat of hatred or of very real social-political consequences. For gay men and women, patriarchalism and homophobia are not simply inner issues but at times very painful outer realities, and any process that aims at helping gay men and women toward individuation must take account of this relationship between outer oppression and inner individuality.

If I have been critical of Jung and Jungian writers, it has been either because of the rather extraordinary neglect of homosexuality in the literature of analytical psychology or because I feel few have availed themselves of the unique insights Jung had concerning the human psyche to illuminate in an unbiased and comprehensive way that particular pattern of relationship we call homosexuality. This book has been an attempt to go beyond simplistic or reductive formulations, to apply a self-examination for bias to the literature in analytical psychology on homosexuality, and to foster the kind of real contact with the real inner and outer lives of real gay individuals out of which a clearer and deeper vision of homosexuality can come. It is precisely because of my conviction that Jung and analytical psychology have much to offer to contemporary gay men and women that it pains me to see

Jung's concepts applied unthinkingly, to see potentially positive attitudes and theories left unused and undeveloped, to find analytical psychologists woefully (and sometimes blissfully) ignorant of their own literature on homosexuality, and to hear things concerning homosexuality that are dated or sometimes just baldly untrue. In looking back through what has been written, however, we have found points of light and growth, places here and there where a lack of bias, a true appreciation of the variety of sexual expression and a deeper awareness of that which makes us human shine through. It is with the insights of these writers, beginning with Jung's own positive attitudes and theoretical suggestions, that one might best begin.

Perhaps it is time for the gay men and women whose lives Jung has touched, directly or indirectly, to come forward and begin speaking for themselves about their individuation process as homosexuals. Perhaps it is time for gay and lesbian analysts to begin to confront more forcefully, publicly or personally, the neglect and misconceptions as well as the nourishment and power that lie in Jung's ideas on sexuality and human relationship. Perhaps it is time for heterosexual men and women, analysts and patients, to begin to come to terms with their own homosexuality and find a common ground with gay men and women so that greater understanding and common good may abound. My fondest hope is that this book is, indeed, only the beginning of a clearer vision of the meaning and purpose of homosexuality.

Notes

The following abbreviations are used in the notes:

CW: *The Collected Works of C. G. Jung* (Princeton: Princeton University Press). Number following CW indicates volume.

MDR: *Memories, Dreams, Reflections* (New York: Vintage Books, 1965).

Letters: *Letters*, vols. 1 and 2, ed. by Gerhard Adler (Princeton: Princeton University Press, 1975).

Freud/Jung: *The Freud/Jung Letters*, ed. William McGuire (Princeton: Princeton University Press, 1974).

Chapter 1. Why Jung, Jungians, and Homosexuality?

1. Alfred Kinsey, Wardell Pomeroy, and Clyde E. Martin, *Sexual Behavior in the Human Male* (Philadelphia: W. B. Saunders, 1948).
2. Kinsey, *Sexual Behavior*, p. 625.
3. The reader interested in the details of this fascinating story, which gives an excellent overview of the history of homosexuality in twentieth-century psychology, may wish to read Ronald Bayer's excellent historical account of the APA's decision in *Homosexuality and American Psychiatry: The Politics of Diagnosis* (New York: Basic Books, 1981).
4. American Psychiatric Association, *Diagnostic and Statistical Manual of Mental Disorders*, 3d ed., rev. (Washington, D.C.: American Psychiatric Association, 1987).
5. Robert H. Hopcke, *A Guided Tour of the Collected Works of C. G. Jung* (Boston: Shambhala Publications, 1989).

Chapter 2. C. G. Jung and Homosexuality

1. CW 10, p. 544 n. 5.
2. MDR, p. 150.
3. C. G. Jung, *Dream Analysis: Notes of the Seminar Given in 1928–1930*, ed. William McGuire (Princeton: Princeton University Press, 1984).
4. C. G. Jung, *C. G. Jung Speaking: Interviews and Encounters*, ed. William McGuire and R. F. C. Hull (Princeton: Princeton University Press, 1977).
5. CW 18, p. 382.
6. CW 4, p. 109.

7. CW 4, pp. 109–110.
8. CW 4, p. 110.
9. CW 4, p. 110.
10. CW 4, p. 86.
11. CW 7, p. v.
12. CW 7, p. 81.
13. CW 7, p. 82.
14. CW 7, p. 83.
15. CW 7, p. 83.
16. CW 7, pp. 86–87.
17. CW 7, pp. 102–103.
18. CW 7, p. 106.
19. CW 7, p. 106.
20. CW 7, pp. 106–107.
21. CW 7, pp. 107–108.
22. MDR, p. 207.
23. CW 6, pp. 471–472.
24. CW 10, p. 99.
25. CW 10, p. 105.
26. CW 10, p. 107.
27. CW 10, pp. 107–108.
28. CW 10, p. 100.
29. CW 10, p. 112.
30. CW 17, p. 127.
31. CW 17, p. 127.
32. CW 17, p. 191.
33. CW 10, p. 119.
34. CW 10, pp. 117–118.
35. CW 5, p. 388.
36. CW 9, part I, p. 71.
37. CW 9, part I, p. 85.
38. CW 9, part I, pp. 86–87.
39. Jolande Jacobi, *Complex/Archetype/Symbol in the Psychology of C. G. Jung* (Princeton: Princeton University Press, 1959, 1971), p. 6.
40. CW 9, part I, p. 199.
41. CW 16, p. 170.
42. CW 16, p. 218n.
43. CW 9, part II, p. ix.
44. CW 9, part II, p. 11.
45. CW 9, part II, p. 12.
46. Freud/Jung, pp. 297–298.
47. Letters, vol. 1, p. 69.
48. CW 11, pp. 311–315.

49. Letters, vol. 2, p. 16.
50. Letters, vol. 2, pp. 16–17.
51. MDR, p. 239.
52. MDR, pp. 263–264.

Chapter 3. Jung's Attitudes and Theories on Homosexuality

1. Ronald Bayer, *Homosexuality and American Psychiatry: The Politics of Diagnosis* (New York: Basic Books, 1981), p. 11.
2. Alfred Kinsey, Wardell Pomeroy, and Clyde E. Martin, *Sexual Behavior in the Human Male.* (Philadelphia: W. B. Saunders, 1948); Alan P. Bell and Martin S. Weinberg, *Homosexualities: A Study of Diversity Among Men and Women* (New York: Simon & Schuster, 1978); Alan P. Bell, Martin S. Weinberg, and Sue K. Hammersmith, *Sexual Preference: Its Development in Men and Women* (Bloomington, Ind.: Indiana University Press, 1981).
3. Cleland S. Ford and Frank A. Beach, *Patterns of Sexual Behavior* (New York: Harper & Row, 1951).
4. Evelyn Hooker, "Inverts Are Not a Distinct Personality Type," *Mattachine Review*, January 1955; Evelyn Hooker, "A Preliminary Analysis of Group Behavior of Homosexuals," *Journal of Psychology* 14 (1956); Evelyn Hooker, "The Adjustment of the Male Overt Homosexual," *Journal of Projective Techniques* 21 (1957); Evelyn Hooker, "Male Homosexuality in the Rorschach," *Journal of Projective Techniques*, 1958; Evelyn Hooker, "Homosexuality," *International Encyclopedia of the Social Sciences* (New York: Macmillan, Free Press, 1968).
5. Judd Marmor, ed., *Sexual Inversion* (New York: Basic Books, 1965); Judd Marmor, ed., *Homosexual Behavior: A Modern Reappraisal* (New York: Basic Books, 1980).

Chapter 4. Jungians and Homosexuality

1. Erich Neumann, *The Origins and History of Consciousness* (Princeton: Princeton University Press, 1954), p. 141.
2. Jolande Jacobi, *The Way of Individuation* (New York: Harcourt Brace Jovanovich, 1970), p. 28.
3. Jacobi, *Individuation*, pp. 38–39.
4. Jolande Jacobi, *Complex/Archetype/Symbol in the Psychology of C. G. Jung* (Princeton: Princeton University Press, 1959, 1971), pp. 92–93.
5. Jacobi, *Complex*, pp. 92–93.

6. Jolande Jacobi, "A Case of Homosexuality," *Journal of Analytical Psychology*, January 1969.
7. Jacobi, "Case," p. 48.
8. Jacobi, "Case," pp. 49–50.
9. Jacobi, "Case," p. 51.
10. Jacobi, "Case," p. 52.
11. Jacobi, "Case," p. 52.
12. Jacobi, "Case," pp. 52–53.
13. Jacobi, "Case," p. 56.
14. Jacobi, "Case," p. 59.
15. Jacobi, "Case," p. 62.
16. Jacobi, "Case," p. 63.
17. M. Esther Harding, *The Way of All Women* (New York: Harper & Row, 1970), pp. 93–94.
18. Harding, *Way*, pp. 94–95.
19. Harding, *Way*, pp. 102–103.
20. Harding, *Way*, pp. 118–119.
21. John Layard, "Homo-Eroticism in Primitive Society As a Function of the Self," *Journal of Analytical Psychology*, July 1959: 101.
22. Layard, "Homo-Eroticism," p. 102.
23. Layard, "Homo-Eroticism," p. 103.
24. Layard, "Homo-Eroticism," p. 105.
25. Layard, "Homo-Eroticism," p. 107.
26. Layard, "Homo-Eroticism," p. 108.
27. Layard, "Homo-Eroticism," p. 108.
28. Layard, "Homo-Eroticism," p. 110.
29. Layard, "Homo-Eroticism," p. 114.
30. We will examine in chapter 5 articles by Melvin Kettner and Jerome Bernstein in which Layard's work is used as reference.
31. One excellent collection of this kind of anthropological work is Evelyn Blackwood, ed., *The Many Faces of Homosexuality: Anthropological Approaches to Homosexual Behavior* (New York: Harrington Park Press, 1986); Gilbert Herdt's brief overview and bibliography, "Cross Cultural Forms of Homosexuality and the Concept 'Gay,'" *Psychiatric Annals*, January 1988: 37–39, is equally useful. We will examine in chapter 8 the work done by gay anthropologist Walter Williams among Native American tribes in more detail.
32. Louise Carus Mahdi, Stephen Foster, and Meredith Little, eds., *Betwixt and Between: Patterns of Masculine and Feminine Initiation* (La Salle, Ill.: Open Court, 1987).
33. G. S. Prince, "The Therapeutic Function of the Homosexual Transference," *Journal of Analytical Psychology*, July 1959: 117.

34. Anthony Storr, "The Psychopathology of Fetishism and Trans-
    vestitism," *Journal of Analytical Psychology*, July 1957.
35. Storr, "Psychopathology," p. 157.
36. Storr, "Psychopathology," p. 158.
37. Marie-Louise von Franz, *Puer Aeternus* (Santa Monica, Calif.: Sigo
    Press, 1981).
38. Von Franz, *Puer Aeternus*, p. 1.
39. Von Franz, *Puer Aeternus*, pp. 4–5.
40. Von Franz, *Puer Aeternus*, p. 9.
41. Von Franz, *Puer Aeternus*, p. 9.

Chapter 5. Contemporary Views of Homosexuality

1. One concise collection of articles concerning current thought is a
   special issue of *Psychiatric Annals*, "Sexuality and Homosexuality,"
   January 1988.
2. Andrew Samuels, Bani Shorter, and Alfred Plaut, *The Critical Dictionary of Jungian Analysis*. (New York: Routledge & Kegan Paul,
   1986), p. 69.
3. L. Zinkin, "'Death in Venice': A Jungian View," *Journal of Analytical Psychology*, October 1977.
4. Jerome S. Bernstein, "The Decline of Masculine Rites of Passage in
   Our Culture: The Impact on Masculine Individuation," in *Betwixt
   and Between: Patterns of Masculine and Feminine Initiation*, ed.
   Louise Carus Mahdi, Stephen Foster, and Meredith Little (La
   Salle, Ill.: Open Court, 1987), p. 147.
5. Melvin Kettner, "Some Archetypal Themes in Male Homosexuality," *Professional Reports* (San Francisco: C. G. Jung Institute of
   San Francisco, 1967; privately distributed).
6. Melvin Kettner, "Patterns of Masculine Identity," in *The Reality of
   the Psyche*, ed. Joseph B. Wheelwright (Proceedings of the Third
   International Congress for Analytical Psychology, 1968), p. 177.
7. Steven R. Centola, "Individuation in E. M. Forster's 'Maurice,'"
   Journal of Analytical Psychology 26 (1981): 49–63; K. Marriott,
   "Comment on S. R. Centola's 'Psychic Confrontation and Integration: The Theme of Individuation in E. M. Forster's "Maurice"': A
   Clinical View," *Journal of Analytical Psychology* 26 (1981): 65–68.
   (While the title of Marriott's article refers to a title different from
   that given for Centola's article, this seems a small editorial error,
   and Marriott's article *does* comment on the article by Centola,
   which precedes it in the journal, and not any other article by
   Centola.)
8. Centola, "Individuation," p. 51.

9. Centola, "Individuation," p. 56.
10. Centola, "Individuation," p. 58, quoting Forster.
11. Centola, "Individuation," p. 61.
12. Centola, "Individuation," p. 62.
13. Marriott, "Comment," p. 65. Emphasis in original.
14. Marriott, "Comment," p. 68.
15. David Walsh. "Homosexuality, Rationality and Western Culture," *Harvest* 24 (1978).
16. Walsh, "Homosexuality," p. 74.
17. Sylvia Brinton-Perera, *The Scapegoat Complex: Toward a Mythology of Shadow and Guilt* (Toronto: Inner City Books, 1986).
18. John Boswell, *Christianity, Social Tolerance, and Homosexuality: Gay People in Western Europe from the Beginning of the Christian Era to the 14th Century* (Chicago: University of Chicago Press, 1980).
19. Walsh, "Homosexuality," p. 79.
20. Walsh, "Homosexuality," pp. 79–81.
21. Walsh, "Homosexuality," p. 97.
22. J. Michael Steele and David Stockford, review of *Homosexual Behavior: A Modern Reappraisal*, by Judd Marmor, *San Francisco Jung Institute Library Journal* 1, no. 4 (1980): 47.
23. James Hillman, "Senex and Puer," in *Puer Papers*, ed. James Hillman (Dallas: Spring Publications, 1979), p. 12.
24. Hillman, "Senex and Puer," p. 28.
25. Hillman, "Senex and Puer," p. 29.
26. Hillman, "Senex and Puer," p. 34.
27. Rafael Lopez-Pedraza, "The Tale of Dryops and the Birth of Pan: An Archetypal and Psychotherapeutic Approach to Eros between Men," *Spring*, 1976. This article was revised and included in Lopez-Pedraza's *Hermes and His Children* (Dallas: Spring Publications).
28. Lopez-Pedraza, "Tale of Dryops," p. 178.
29. Lopez-Pedraza, "Tale of Dryops," p. 189.
30. Mitchell Walker, "The Double: An Archetypal Configuration," *Spring*, 1976: 165.
31. Walker, "Double," p. 169.
32. Walker, "Double," p. 170.
33. Walker, "Double," p. 172.
34. James Hillman, *Anima: An Anatomy of a Personified Notion* (Dallas: Spring Publications, 1985), p. 65.
35. Edward C. Whitmont, "Reassessing Femininity and Masculinity," *Anima* 7, no. 2: 138.

36. John Beebe, "On Male Partnership," lecture at the Nexus Conference, Los Angeles, California, 1987.
37. For a concise and similarly re-visionary discussion of the animus concept and its adequacy in describing women's experience, see Mary Ann Mattoon and Jeanette Jones, "Is the Animus Obsolete?" *Quadrant* 20, no. 1 (1987): 5–21, and Demaris S. Wehr, *Jung and Feminism: Liberating Archetypes* (Boston: Beacon Press, 1987), esp. pp. 117–126.
38. Eugene Monick, *Phallos: Sacred Image of the Masculine* (Toronto: Inner City Books, 1987), p. 36.
39. Monick, *Phallos*, pp. 115–116.
40. June Singer, *Androgyny: Toward a New Theory of Sexuality* (Garden City, N.Y.: Anchor Books, 1979), p. 289.
41. Singer, *Androgyny*, p. 291.
42. Singer, *Androgyny*, p. 291.
43. Singer, *Androgyny*, p. 292.
44. Singer, *Androgyny*, p. 294.
45. John Sanford, *Invisible Partners* (New York: The Paulist Press, 1980), pp. 94–102.
46. Mattoon and Jones, "Is the Animus Obsolete?"
47. Betty De Shong Meador, "Transference/Countertransference between Woman Analyst and Wounded Girl Child," *Chiron*, 1984: 163–174; Marion Woodman, *The Pregnant Virgin: A Process of Psychological Transformation* (Toronto: Inner City Books, 1985).
48. Karin Lofthus Carrington, review of *The Book of Lilith*, by Barbara Black Koltuv, *Quadrant* 20, no. 2 (1987): 101.

Chapter 6. Toward a Jungian Theory of Sexual Orientation

1. Ann Belford Ulanov, *The Feminine in Jungian Psychology and Christian Theology* (Evanston, Ill.: Northwestern University Press, 1971).
2. Carol Tavris and Carole Offir, *The Longest War: Sex Differences in Perspective* (New York: Harcourt Brace Jovanovich, 1977).
3. John Boswell, *Christianity, Social Tolerance, and Homosexuality: Gay People in Western Europe from the Beginning of the Christian Era to the 14th Century* (Chicago: University of Chicago Press, 1980); Ronald Bayer, *Homosexuality and American Psychiatry: The Politics of Diagnosis* (New York: Basic Books, 1981).
4. Evelyn Blackwood, ed., *The Many Faces of Homosexuality: Anthropological Approaches to Homosexual Behavior* (New York: Harrington Park Press, 1986).

5. Robert H. Hopcke, "Eros in All His Masculinity: Men As Lovers, Men As Friends," *The San Francisco Jung Institute Library Journal* 7, no. 4 (1987): 27–41.
6. Dennis Altman, *Homosexual Oppression and Liberation* (New York: Discus Books, 1971); George Weinberg, *Society and the Healthy Homosexual* (Garden City, N.Y.: Anchor Books, 1972).
7. Jung, CW 8, p. 100.
8. Jung, CW 7, pp. 157–158.
9. Jung, CW 7, pp. 192–193.
10. Jolande Jacobi, *The Way of Individuation* (New York: New American Library, 1983), p. 37.
11. Malcolm Boyd, *Take Off the Masks* (Garden City, N.Y.: Doubleday, 1978).

Chapter 7. Imagery of the Archetypal Masculine

1. David P. McWhirter and Andrew M. Mattison, *The Male Couple: How Relationships Develop* (Englewood Cliffs, N.J.: Prentice Hall, 1984), p. 286.

Chapter 8. The Androgyne and Gay Male Culture

1. Evelyn Blackwood, ed., *The Many Faces of Homosexuality: Anthropological Approaches to Homosexual Behavior* (New York: Harrington Park Press, 1986).
2. Walter L. Williams, *The Spirit and the Flesh: Sexual Diversity in American Indian Culture* (Boston: Beacon Press, 1986).
3. Williams, *Spirit*, p. 4.
4. Charles Callender and Lee M. Kochens, "Men and Not-Men: Male Gender-Mixing Statuses and Homosexuality," in Blackwood, ed., *Many Faces*, pp. 165–177; Williams, *Spirit*, pp. 21–22, 65–86.
5. Williams, *Spirit*, pp. 18–30.
6. Williams, *Spirit*, pp. 22–38, 41–43.
7. Williams, *Spirit*, pp. 44–64.
8. Jonathan Katz, ed., *Gay American History: Lesbians and Gay Men in the U.S.A.* (New York: Thomas Y. Crowell Company, 1976).
9. Katz, *History*, pp. 313–317; 308–311.
10. Katz, *History*, p. 315.
11. Katz, *History*, p. 315.
12. Katz, *History*, p. 315.
13. Katz, *History*, p. 317.
14. Katz, *History*, p. 309.
15. Katz, *History*, p. 310.

Index

Index

Mann, Thomas, 105, 117
Marmor, Judd, 5, 57, 111–112
Marriott, K., 107, 109
Masculine (archetype), 35, 71, 114, 132–135, 188; in gay individuation, 143–146, 166–172
Masculinity, 62–64, 66, 111, 119, 143, 156–172; lunar, 120, 167
Matriarchal psychology, 71
Mattison, Andrew, 160
Mattoon, Mary Ann, 126
Maurice (E. M. Forster), 107–109, 114, 118
Meador, Betty De Shong, 126
Mercurius, 114
Misogyny, 110–111
Monick, Eugene, 120–121, 128
Mother (archetype), 36, 38, 71, 92, 97, 106, 120–121, 123, 124, 155, 156, 168, 183; Phallic Mother, 97, 144–145, 166
Mother complex, 38, 97, 104
Movies: as archetypal symbols, 138; and movie stars, 119, 138, 145, 188
Munchkins, 141

Native American culture, 124, 174–186
Nature, 110–111
Nekyia, 144
Neptune, 188
Neumann, Erich, 70–72, 92, 120

Oedipal complex, 23, 32, 105
Original Man, 37

Pan, 115–116
Patriarchy, 114, 120, 139–140, 143, 165, 193
Paul, Saint, 89
Pedophilia (pederasty), 105, 114
Persephone, 114, 144
Persona, 24, 25, 72; in gay male individuation, 141, 146–151
Phallos, 120–121, 164–165, 167

Plato, 38, 47
Pocahontas, 151
Policemen, as symbols of masculinity, 161–163, 164–166, 168–169, 181
Prince, G. Stewart, 94–95, 128
Psyche, 8, 119
Psychoanalysis, 8, 15, 16, 18, 50, 111, 112, 121; sexual theory in, 16
Puella aeterna, 39, 188
Puer aeternus (Divine Child), 72, 94, 97–101, 105, 113–115, 116–118, 160, 162, 172; homosexuality as identification with, 72, 97–101; positive aspects of, 100–101

Qualls-Corbett, Nancy, 126

Rainbow, as gay/lesbian symbol, 137
Rationality, 109–111
Read, Herbert, 18
Romans (St. Paul's Letter), 89
Ruby slippers, 142

Sado-masochism, 157, 163–166, 168–171
Sanford, John, 121, 124
Saturn, 113–114
Scapegoat, 110
Scarecrow, 143, 144, 147
Self (archetype), 37, 41, 64, 85, 91, 93, 116–117, 120, 180–186, 193
Senex, 113–115, 116–118, 160, 162, 166, 172
Sex roles, 35, 62–64, 110, 119, 123, 134; in various cultures, 93, 175–177, 190
Sexual orientation: archetypal theory of, 10–11, 128–129, 130–135, 187–192; as culturally determined, 57, 62–64, 92–93; as range of behavior, 4, 54, 57; fluidity of, 27–28, 31, 109

Index

Credits

Thanks are extended to the following publishers, institutions, and individuals for permission to reprint material copyrighted or controlled by them:

Princeton University Press and Routledge and Kegan Paul Ltd. for *The Collected Works of C. G. Jung*, trans. R. F. C. Hull, Bollingen Series XX, vol. 4; *Freud and Psychoanalysis*, copyright © 1961, vol. 5; *Symbols of Transformation*, copyright © 1956, vol. 6; *Psychological Types*, copyright © 1971, vol. 7; *Two Essays on Analytical Psychology*, copyright © 1953, 1966, vol. 9; I, *The Archetypes and the Collective Unconscious*, copyright © 1959, 1969, vol. 9; II, *Aion: Researches into the Phenomenology of the Self*, copyright © 1959, vol. 10; *Civilization in Transition*, copyright © 1964, 1970, vol. 16; *The Practice of Psychotherapy*, copyright © 1954, © 1966, vol. 17; *The Development of Personality*, copyright © 1954, vol. 18; *The Symbolic Life*, copyright © 1950, 1953, 1955, 1958, 1959, 1963, 1968, 1970, 1973, 1976; *Letters* by C. G. Jung, ed. Gerhard Adler and Aniela Jaffé, trans. R. F. C. Hull, Bollingen Series 95, vol. 1, *1906–1950*, copyright © 1971, 1973, vol. 2, *1951–1961*, copyright © 1953, 1975; *The Freud/Jung Letters: The Correspondence between Sigmund Freud and C. G. Jung*, ed. William McGuire, trans. Ralph Mannheim and R. F. C. Hull, Bollingen Series 94, copyright © 1974 by Sigmund Freud Copyrights Ltd. and Erbengemeinschaft Prof. C. G. Jung; *The Origins and History of Consciousness* by Erich Neumann, trans. R. F. C. Hull, Bollingen Series 42, copyright © 1954, 1982; *Complex/Archetype/Symbol in the Psychology of C. G. Jung* by Jolande Jacobi, trans. Ralph Mannheim, Bollingen Series 57, copyright © 1959.

Pantheon Books, a division of Random House, Inc., and William Collins, Sons & Company, Limited, for *Memories, Dreams, Reflections* by C. G. Jung, recorded and edited by Aniela Jaffé, translated by Richard & Clara Winston, translation copyright © 1961, 1962, 1963 by Random House, Inc.

Harcourt Brace Jovanovich, Inc., Hodder & Stoughton Ltd., and Niedieck Linder AG for *The Way of Individuation* by Jolande Jacobi, copyright © 1967 by Harcourt Brace Jovanovich.

The C. G. Jung Foundation for Analytical Psychology, Inc., of New York for *The Way of All Women* by M. Esther Harding and "Review of *The Book of Lillith* by Barbara Black Koltuv" by Karin Carrington, in *Quadrant*, vol. 20, no. 2, copyright © 1987.

June Singer for *Androgyny: Toward a New Theory of Sexuality* by June Singer.

The *San Francisco Jung Institute Library Journal*, David Stockford, M.D., and J. Michael Steele, M.D., for "Review of *Homosexual Behavior: A Modern Reappraisal* by Judd Marmor," vol. 1, no. 4, copyright © 1980.

Spring Publications, Inc., for "Senex and Puer: An Aspect of the Historical and Psychological Present" by James Hillman in *Puer Papers* (Dallas: Spring Publications, 1979), copyright © 1979; "The Tale of Dryops and the Birth of Pan: An Archetypal and Psychotherapeutic Approach to Eros between Men" by Rafael Lopez-Pedraza in *Spring 1976*, copyright © 1976; "The Double: An Archetypal Configuration" by Mitchell Walker in *Spring 1976*, copyright © 1976.

Inner City Books for *Phallos, Sacred Image of the Masculine* by Eugene Monick.

Sigo Press for *Puer Aeternus* by Marie-Louise von Franz.

Journal of Analytical Psychology for "The Psychopathology of Fetishism and Transvestitism" by Anthony Storr, vol. 2, no. 2, July 1957; "Homo-Eroticism in Primitive Societies as a Function of the Self" by John Layard, vol. 4, no. 2, July 1959; "A Case of Homosexuality" by Jolande Jacobi, vol. 14, no. 1, January 1969; "Individuation in E. M. Forster's *Maurice*" by Steven R. Centola, vol. 26, no. 1, January 1981; "Comment on S. R. Centola's 'Psychic Confrontation and Integration: The Theme of Individuation in E. M. Forster's *Maurice*" by K. Marriott, vol. 26, no. 1, January 1981.

Harvest/Analytical Psychology Club, London, and David Walsh for "Homosexuality, Rationality and Western Culture" by David Walsh.